Progress into Silence

PROGRESS INTO
SILENCE

A Study of Melville's Heroes

Alan Lebowitz

Indiana University Press

BLOOMINGTON / LONDON

For My Parents

Contents

Preface

IN A PROFESSIONAL WORKING CAREER of some twelve
years, Melville wrote and published nine novels, eight
variously flawed and one a ranking work of American literature. Not surprisingly, considering the short intervals between
works, one novel significantly illuminates another, and all
bear notably on *Moby-Dick*. Because Melville was a repetitive,
even obsessed, writer whose every work reveals deep private
involvements, the nine novels also reflect a continuing personal development, one that culminates, finally, in a denial of
his art, a lengthy, willful silence. My concern in these pages
is with the novelist's progress, as seen through the recurrent
patterns in his fiction, and also with certain elements of the
psychic biography implicit in that progress. The latter aim
sounds perhaps somewhat more ominous—and pretentious—
than it should. Nonetheless, overtly or dimly, all of Melville's
fiction mirrors his own turmoiled efforts to comprehend
himself and structure his world in the creative act of writing.
And while it may be said that every serious writer does something of the same, for Melville the personal investment is
more direct, more self-conscious, and more passionate. I have
confined my study exclusively to the nine novels and, further-
more, to what seems to me their central, dominant concern,
the complex relation between the Promethean hero and the

young aspiring neophyte who gains important education from him. Essentially, Melville had only the two characters, Ishmael and Ahab, and only the one story. When that story gives out and the characters disappear—the younger into disillusionment, the older into an oblivion of history and dream —the fiction-writing stops.

There are, needless to say, other studies of the Melvillian hero. Given the repetitive nature of Melville's thematic and narrative concerns, it could not be otherwise. The quester-hero, called variously Promethean, Enceladan, Christian, and anti-Christian, has been the subject of interpretive studies by, among others, Merlin Bowen, Richard Chase, Milton R. Stern, and Lawrance Thompson. My own approach is distinct from such writers in that my concern is with the dynamic process rather than the collective result, with Melville's hard struggle to write what he called and conceived of as great, enduring literary works, and not with his thought and art as such. I have tried to treat Melville as a working novelist who wrote his books one by one in certain circumstances, under certain pressures, in response to certain needs and drives. It may be argued—and indeed it has been—that Melville was no novelist at all. To such contentions, I can only plead the obvious difficulties involved in finding likelier labels for his long prose fictions. Whether or not the genre is properly that of Sterne as well as Trollope, surely in this age of *Finnegans Wake* and anti-novel novels, one may for simplicity's sake at least term novels even those odd books *Mardi* and *The Confidence-Man*.

It will be noted that I have written at greater length of the earlier novels, especially *Mardi*. I have done so in part because these works have not received the close attention they warrant, but primarily because by the time he finished *Mardi*, Melville had raised virtually every question that appears in *Moby-Dick*. To see in detail how closely *Moby-Dick* is prefigured by *Mardi* is to see as well how quickly and how capably Melville progressed, transforming the materials of what is at best an interesting book into what is unquestionably a great one. There are also certain omissions, justified with less reason, perhaps, but with some. I have not discussed Melville's poetry, the long stories published in 1856 as *The Piazza Tales,* the magazine stories and sketches published between 1853 and 1855, or even *Billy Budd,* that remarkable instance of his brief awakening as a fiction writer at the end of his long life. My concern throughout, as noted, is with the nine novels and what seems to me the essential coherence of their development from one to another. My aim is not to confront Melville's work as a whole, but rather, by tracking the progressive changes in his treatment of the one lofty theme, to measure the dimension of his ambitions and to convey something of the drama of both his achievements and his failures. To the latter end I have appended what for want of a better term I have called an Epilogue, a brief survey of his life in the years between 1856 when the fiction stops and his death in 1891. The facts will surely be familiar to Melvillians, but they may prove useful and interesting to those readers of Melville—a surprisingly large number—who are unaware of the forty years after *Moby-Dick* and who may find in their sketchy history some general significance as well as a very poignant and moving story.

Literary criticism is, in a sense at least, the public expression of a private homage, and to some extent one can judge a writer by the kind of people who have chosen to write about him. No American, I think, has inspired more humane, perceptive criticism than Melville has. According to their various interests and disciplines, such men as Newton Arvin, Leon Howard, Harry Levin, Jay Leyda, F. O. Matthiessen, Henry Murray, Charles Olson, William Ellery Sedgwick, and Raymond Weaver have created a literature that does honor to Melville and his craft, as well as to their own. From the works of all these men I have learned so much that, as with good teachers, it is not always possible to say where their thought ends and mine begins.

From other, closer sources, I have profited more directly. From Monroe Engel I have over many years learned much of what I know about novel-writing, novelists, and novels. To Harry Levin I owe special debts. Without his knowledge and his insights, my book would have been much poorer. Without his constant interest and encouragement, I suspect that it would not have been at all. To both these men I am most deeply grateful.

Progress into Silence

Prologue: Ahab

HAD THERE BEEN NO *Moby-Dick,* Herman Melville surely would have belonged to literary history, not to literature, and as a minor curiosity at that, remembered if at all for several stunning tales written near the end of an odd, unsuccessful career. Eventually someone might have dug up even so slight a figure as the self-educated, seagoing author of *Mardi* and *Pierre,* but the result could only have been the studied rehabilitation of an interesting, overambitious minor writer and no undiscovered genius. Or else, more likely, Melville might have gained a small niche for himself as Hawthorne's friend, a lesser novelist pictured through history at the feet of a greater one. The thought, at any rate, is both suggestive and relevant, for the author of America's greatest single novel is also a great American prototype. His story embodies important national themes—those of hard, un-rewarded effort, of great aspiration and small fame, of terrible futility, deep despair, foredoomed failure, and, eventually, of enduring recognition. The full drama of the creative life has often been obscured by the amount of at-tention paid to *Moby-Dick.* However reasonable, this is re-grettable, for Melville's literary career illuminates and typifies that distinctly romantic state of being—the profession of novel-writing in America. No American novelist has had a sharper sense of his trade as a comprehensive way of life; no one has had more of the familiar angst, the demon-driven exultations spaced with pain. And though some have had as hard a time getting work done, no one had a longer or a more imponderable silence. Beginning, in 1846, with great élan and high expectation of success, Melville published six novels in six years, capping this remarkably prolific phase of his career with *Moby-Dick* in 1851. Three novels follow: *Pierre* in 1852, *Israel Potter* in 1854,[1] and *The Confidence-Man* in 1857. And then, as everyone concerned with American literature knows, until *Billy Budd,* written sporadically in 1888–1891 at the very end of his long life, there is a drama not of effort but of silence. Melville the aspiring novelist took a modest job at the Custom House in New York City and for thirty years wrote only poetry. From the scant facts on hand, one can do no more than guess at the reasons for this long farewell to his profession. It is possible, however, to see at least one aspect of the drama in the fiction itself. Melville's nine novels, viewed in sequence, proceed with an awesome logic to that abrupt and premature conclusion.

There is an obvious unity to the first six novels. They have essentially the same subject—the young American coming of age by adventuring at sea—and the same basic theme—that young man's quest for an ultimate, transfiguring knowledge and experience. In the first three works, the neophyte confronts life directly, on his own. With *Redburn,* Melville initiates a twofold scheme, exploring the relationship between an Ishmael, the innocent who pursues dark knowledge, and an Ahab, the hero who possesses it. Redburn gains his profoundest perceptions from the diabolical Jackson, White Jacket from Jack Chase, Ishmael from Ahab. The last, of course, is decisive, fulfilling and defining all the earlier adumbrations. That the terms lack accuracy save as characters' names—the Ishmaels and the Ahabs—need not, I think, be very troubling. Melville himself expressly tags almost all of his young neophytes as Ishmaels. And Ahab, as Melville's prototypical hero, embodies a cohesive syndrome of char-

4

acteristics that are clearly recognizable in fragmentary form throughout the other novels, albeit difficult to label precisely save as Ahab. What is important is that, whether we term him Promethean or Enceladan, the God-defying, blasphemous redeemer is, for Melville, not only a recurrent literary theme but a continuing personal obsession. The fictional search for such a hero, with all its implications for the searcher, consistently reflects Melville's own attempts to write an ultimate novel. As the questers in Mardi pursue the shadowy, ideal Yillah, Melville himself, as author, provides a running commentary on his own efforts to write in *Mardi* a perfect, lasting fiction.

Insofar as the first five novels build steadily to *Moby-Dick,* they constitute an interesting apprenticeship, notable in strictly literary terms for what they tell us about the quick development of Melville's art. With *Moby-Dick,* however, Melville rounds a period and achieves a goal, and as the remarkable, exuberant letters to the Hawthornes at the time make clear, he well understood the dimensions of his success. What follows is a darker, stranger, sadder story, that of a novelist peaked too early and of a man increasingly unconfident of his subjects and either unwilling to relinquish them or incapable of doing so. In *Pierre,* and then *Israel Potter,* we see the Ishmaels of the previous novels in premature decline. And in *The Confidence-Man,* there is neither youth nor age but only a deep despairing after-dinner sleep, dreaming now and then on both.

The last three novels, then, reveal an almost methodical retreat from Melville's basic conception of his hero, as well as from the format that had embodied the lofty drama. Although Melville describes Pierre in all the terms previously used to denote the hero, the context is significantly changed. A landlocked Ahab who must function within society, Pierre is appreciably diminished in stature. He is less a questing than a driven man, doomed first to poverty and then to a small, dark, noisy act of self-destruction, the purpose of which is to escape legal execution for a shabby, unheroic murder. In

Israel Potter there is a further and more obvious dilution of the original hero, fragmented now into three specific historical figures, each of whom embodies something of Ahab, but without the force and substance. A movement in *Israel Potter* toward realistic appraisal of the contemporary American scene —only tangential to *Mardi* and incidental to *Pierre*—becomes more pronounced in *The Confidence-Man,* which is, among other things, a firm, bitter judgment on an America where there are few remaining Ahabs and where no man can be effective against an opponent more insidious and cunning than any whale. It is also, because of persistent analogies throughout all the work between the author and his central character, Melville's implicit statement of his own dead end as a novelist.

From *Mardi* through *Israel Potter,* then, Melville's story is that of the young neophyte's quest for a distinctive hero in his own image and of that hero's pursuit of an ultimate knowledge and authority. The controlling theme, basic to American literature, is that of the necessary fall, the innocent's emergence into manhood by means of a literal ordeal that offers, in all its pain and difficulty, important perceptions into the nature of the world. The first, and decisive, discovery is of mortality. Only by confronting the hard fact that he will die, recognizing, as Melville often put it, the universal sentence of annihilation, does a boy become a man. Testing that perception, probing ever deeper into the mystery of things, asking questions of the meaning of annihilation as well as of its agent, man becomes a potential hero. The fullest understanding causes, inevitably, the greatest pain. Few penetrate the deepest mystery of things, and those who do are Melville's heroes. The greatest, of course, is Ahab.

"I love all men who dive," Melville wrote in 1849 to his close friend Evert Duyckinck. "Any fish can swim near the surface, but it takes a great whale to go down stairs five miles or more; and if he don't attain the bottom, why, all the lead in Galena can't fashion the plummet that will. I'm not talking of Mr. Emerson now—but of the whole corps of thought-divers, that have been diving and coming up again with bloodshot eyes since the world began."[2] Ahab, we know, touches bottom, and thus raises significant problems of novelistic craft as well as metaphysics. The Melvillian hero is *Mardi*'s Taji, the "unreturning wanderer" who cannot, by definition, tell his own story, having passed irrevocably into what Melville expressly terms the "deep beyond . . . from which no voyager e'er puts back." Melville's subsequent efforts to give substance and relevance to this inaccessible hero comprise at once his theme and his basic fictional format. The method derives from a series of correspondences between author and work, author and reader, as well as between the major characters within a single work. Just as the novelist himself necessarily returns from his literary wanderings, so must Ishmael and his like—the neophyte-narrators —return from voyaging to play a storyteller's role as intermediary between the ideal heroics of an Ahab and the commonplace realities of an ordinary landlocked reader. With Melville, then, as with Emerson, Thoreau, and Hawthorne, there are always crucial links between an ideal fiction and an ultimate truth, between the fiction writer and the hero of his work, between the imagined reader and the fictional neophyte emerging into manhood. The innocent reader, safe at home, falls into hard knowledge by his reading of that book wherein hard knowledge lurks. He is scarred and transfigured by vicarious communion with an Ishmael, even as Ishmael is by his much closer contact with an Ahab.

The scheme is most notably set forth in the great opening chapter of *Moby-Dick*. The daily life of ordinary man is safe, secure, tedious, and inadequate. The vague dissatisfaction of "landsmen . . . tied to counters, nailed to benches, clinched to desks," is reflected in the "thousands upon thousands of mortal men" who spend their Sundays "fixed in ocean reveries." They approach the water "seemingly bound for a dive," but they stop, the great majority, at the "extremest limit of the land," content merely to gaze out. "They must get just as nigh the water as they possibly can without falling in." The lure is universal, reflecting a basic urge to escape landlocked monotony. It is that of "almost every robust healthy boy with a robust healthy soul in him, at some time or other crazy to go to sea." Those who do embark, if but "falling in," achieve at once "a mystical vibration, when first . . . out of sight of land." Melville's divers are those who respond to this vibration, as to the first, by continuing further, leaving the relative safety of the ship. The exemplary diver is Narcissus, "who because he could not grasp the tormenting, mild image he saw in the fountain, plunged into it and was drowned. But that same image, we ourselves see in all rivers and oceans. It is the image of the ungraspable phantom of life; and this is the key to it all" (I.2-4).[3]

Melville makes no overt plea to these countless countrymen standing at the water's edge to plunge in and be drowned. His immediate concern is with those Ishmaels who react to the "damp drizzley November in the soul" by setting out beyond the land's "extremest limit." Such men provide a standard by which the mass of men can measure their lives of quiet desperation against their Sunday longings, and also by which the ultimate fate of Narcissus may be measured against the lesser pains and griefs of those who manage to come up again "with bloodshot eyes." The conception is essentially scalar, and the image most frequently used is of a kind of ladder to the godhead. "In all the universe," Melville writes in *Mardi*, "is but one original; and the very suns must to their source for their fire; and we Prometheuses must to them for ours; which, when had, only perpetual vestal tending will keep alive" (I.267). Just as the deepest descent drowns, so the highest upward striving necessarily burns. The sun, to Melville, is fire, not light; its energy is at once cleansing and destructive. The requisite "perpetual vestal tending" necessarily estranges even as it enlarges; it is both dehumanizing and ennobling. In Ahab, associated repeatedly with Prometheus, heroic dedication becomes a self-destructive monomania, allowing him no thought and no life apart from his relentless pursuit of the White Whale. He is "gnawed

within and scorched without, with the unfixed, unrelenting
fangs of some incurable idea" (I.232). The mysterious scar
that brands one side of his "tawney scorched face and neck"
(I.152) is the result of some long-past encounter with an
oriental fire god. The ivory leg he brings back from his first
encounter with the whale is lost.in his second, before he dies.
It is a hard life and an awful end, but "Ahab is forever
Ahab, man. This whole act's immutably decreed . . . I am the
Fates' lieutenant; I act under orders." And as if to fulfill the
image of the Promethean ladder entirely, he adds to Starbuck, who for the last time has tried to stop him, "Look thou,
underling! that thou obeyest mine" (II.352).

"The search after the great man is the dream of youth and
the most serious occupation of manhood," Emerson wrote in
"Uses of Great Men." Melville's constant subject is the great
man's search for something greater, a pursuit literally en-
acted, involving both physical and psychic struggle. His concept of human greatness is not radically different from
Emerson's: "I count him a great man who inhabits a higher
sphere of thought, into which other men rise with labor and
difficulty; he has but to open his eyes to see things in a true
light and in large relations, whilst they must make painful
corrections and keep a vigilant eye on many sources of error.
His service to us is of like sort. It costs a beautiful person no
exertion to paint her image on our eyes. . . . It costs no more
for a wise soul to convey his quality to other men." This
vision, though similarly hierarchic, assumes an ultimate
benignity. Emerson's great man, opening his eyes, sees light
and not the transcendent fire that blinds and scorches. Melville's heroes see things in "large relations," but the meanings
are informed by less benign assumptions. His lesser figures
do, however, receive from the hero's grim drama benefits
similar to those that Emerson goes on to posit. "But he must
be related to us, and our life receive from him some promise of
explanation. I cannot tell what I would know; but I have
observed there are persons who, in their character and actions,
answer questions which I have not skill to put. One man

answers some questions which none of his contemporaries put, and is isolated."[4] It is precisely the promise of explanation that Narcissus offers merely by the fact of his pursuit of it. Ahab answers questions about man, his character and fate, that Ishmael cannot frame. He raises questions about whales and gods that Ishmael cannot, or dare not, ask. And so he is isolated.

Ahab is at once the loneliest and the grandest of American literary heroes. Like Whitman's epic Self, he is large and he contains symbolic multitudes as contradictory as Christ and Satan. In conception, the character fulfills Melville's subsequent definition of original literary character in *The Confidence-Man:* "The original character . . . is like a revolving Drummond light, raying away from itself all round it—everything is lit by it, everything starts up to it . . . so that, in certain minds, there follows upon the adequate conception of such a character, an effect, in its way, akin to that which in Genesis attends upon the beginning of things" (318). It is this circular conception, revealing now one facet, now another, which makes interpretation at once so alluring and so complicated. Just as Melville provides no fixed moral standard by which Ahab's course and fate may be precisely judged, so he gives him so many varying faces that finally all commentary must fall back upon the basic paradox of the "grand, ungodly, god-like man" which informs the character throughout.

The scale is epic. Ahab is introduced as the largest of large men, the foremost of whaling men who are themselves preeminent among sailors, who in turn, according to the opening chapter, are the chief thought-divers of humanity. "How it is, there is no telling, but Islanders seem to make the best whalemen. They were nearly all Islanders in the *Pequod, Isolatoes* too, I call such, not acknowledging the common continent of men, but each *Isolato* living on a separate continent of his own" (I.149). Though briefly and voluntarily "federated along one keel," the whaler reflects in his isolation, self-containment, and sufficiency the basic conditions of the western frontier, and repeatedly Melville draws the specific analogy. Of the islands that furnish the best whalemen, Nantucket is singularly isolated, "away off shore, more lonely than the Eddystone lighthouse," bound to as well as by the sea, "all beach without a background" (I.77). Melville pays a loud, lusty tribute to these "naked Nantucketers" who have "overrun and conquered the watery world like so many Alexanders; parcelling out among them the Atlantic, Pacific, and Indian oceans, as the three pirate powers did Poland" (I.78). Still higher in the scheme of things, foremost among Nantucketers, are the "fighting Quakers," who are "Quakers with a vengeance." And it is even among these that Ahab stands out:

> there are instances among them of men, who, named with Scripture names . . . and in childhood naturally imbibing the stately dramatic thee and thou of the Quaker idiom; still, from the audacious, daring, and boundless adventure of their subsequent lives, strangely blend with these unoutgrown peculiarities, a thousand bold dashes of character, not unworthy a Scandinavian sea-king, or a poetical pagan Roman. And when these things unite in a man of greatly superior natural force, with a globular brain and a ponderous heart; who has also by the stillness and seclusion of many long night-watches in the remotest waters, and beneath constellations never seen here at the north, been led to think untraditionally and independently; receiving all nature's sweet or savage impressions fresh from her own virgin voluntary and confiding breast, and thereby chiefly, but with some help from accidental advantages, to learn a bold and nervous lofty language—that man makes one in a whole nation's census—a mighty pageant creature, formed for noble tragedies.   (I.91–92)

Thus Ahab, greatest of great whalemen, "one in a whole nation's census," wages by right of "vengeance" and by some transcendent logic, if not justice, his "everlasting war" against the mightiest of mighty whales.

This general view of Ahab as "a mighty pageant creature" comes in the chapter called "The Ship," where Ishmael first visits the *Pequod.* Just previously he has learned that

"Captain Ahab," echoed repeatedly, "is the captain of this ship," and not "Captain Peleg" or "Captain Bildad," fighting Quakers both, who are entirely in awe of their contemporary. It is shortly after Ishmael has conjured up his portentous if slightly premature view of his new captain's character and the impending tragedy that Peleg describes Ahab by means of the paradoxical "grand, ungodly, god-like man." Immediately, the basic terms are elaborated. "Ahab's above the common; Ahab's been in colleges, as well as 'mong the cannibals; been used to deeper wonders than the waves; fixed his fiery lance in mightier, stranger foes than whales. His lance! ay, the keenest and the surest that out of all our isle! Oh! he ain't Captain Bildad; no, and he ain't Captain Peleg; *he's Ahab,* boy; and Ahab of old, thou knowest, was a crowned king!" To this Peleg adds vague rumor of an ancient Indian squaw's belief that Ahab's evil name "would somehow prove prophetic." And though "a kind of moody—desperate moody and savage sometimes" because of his recent ordeal, Ahab is "a good man—not a pious, good man, like Bildad, but a swearing good man." Peleg concludes by revealing that Ahab "has a wife—not three voyages wedded—a sweet, resigned girl. Think of that; by that sweet girl that old man has a child: hold ye then there can be any utter, hopeless harm in Ahab? No, no, my lad; stricken, blasted, if he be, Ahab has his humanities!" (I.99–100).

The whole character is here at the outset. Ahab's "humanities," which recur throughout to threaten his implacable determination, provide a special poignance and a continuing drama. Otherwise the character is essentially fixed, static and unchanging. Like the "revolving Drummond light," Ahab moves on his own axis and not progressively through time. Melville does not develop Ahab by means of the sudden pressures of a narrative upon a character capable of growth. Ahab, from the first, is Ahab. The sense of Ahab's increasing power and vitality derives rather from a steady accumulation of details amplifying the basic qualities described in "The Ship," and by a simple process of continuing repetition. He

is "an enraged and mighty man" (I.143), "this gray-headed
ungodly old man" (I.233), a "wonderful old man" (I.289),
"the wondrous old man" (II.242), and so on. Narrative
events only enforce the initial assumptions. Fedallah embodies
Ahab's mysterious pagan involvement. When Starbuck stands
ready to kill his captain, it is Ahab's image, both literal and
figurative, which informs and determines his decision.

The process is much the same as that employed to compel
complete belief in the whale's transcendent force and meaning. One might in fact extract from *Moby-Dick* a list of
testimonials to Ahab comparable in scope, if not in variety,
to the Extracts on the whale that begin the novel. There are,
for instance, many allusions, some specific, some not very
subtly implied, and most of them repeated. Ahab is variously
identified with Hamlet, Lear, and Macbeth, with Prometheus
and Faust, with Manfred and kindred Romantic heroes, and
even, it would seem, in a startling irony of the third day's
chase, with Don Quixote "run tilting at [the wind]" (II.
355). He is Milton's Satan—"In his fiery eyes of scorn and
triumph, you then saw Ahab in all his fatal pride" (II.298)—
"the mad fiend himself" (II.345), and he baptizes his
harpoon "in nomine diaboli" (II.261). Yet when he appears
before his assembled crew for the first time, it is as Christ,
standing above them on the quarter-deck "with a crucifixion
in his face, in all the nameless regal overbearing dignity of
some mighty woe" (I.154). No emperor or king, Ahab is a
tragic hero of democratic America: "I must not conceal that
I have only to do with a poor old whale-hunter like him; and,
therefore, all outward majestical trappings and housings are
denied me. Oh, Ahab! what shall be grand in thee, it must
needs be plucked at from the skies, and dived for in the deep,
and featured in the unbodied air!" (I.183). Yet Melville
repeatedly presents him as a king, an oriental sultan, "his
old Mogulship" (II.237), a "Grand-Lama" (II.230), "a
khan of the plank, and a king of the sea, and a great lord of
Leviathans" (I.160). Still more to the point perhaps, besides
Christ and Prometheus, he is associated with other epic saviors

of humanity, "heroes, saints, demigods, and prophets," legendary dragon slayers whose symbolic battles had redemptive purpose: Perseus, Saint George, and Hercules, and, in a typically Melvillian twist, with "that antique Crockett and Kit Carson" (II.103). A social as well as a mythic savior, he is the revolutionary Anacharsis Clootz leading his "deputation from all the isles of the sea, and all the ends of the earth . . . to lay the world's grievances before that bar from which not very many of them ever come back" (I.149–50).

This savior of his people, of course, ends by destroying them, all but one, either because of some crucial flaw, or because his fated course must by its nature corrupt. Whatever the interpretation, Ahab earns a terrible destruction, and the why of it seems finally unimportant. It is in the earning that he ultimately moves us. At the end he is neither godlike nor ungodly, but only man, all mutilated, powerless, and puny. Throughout the novel whenever Ahab is viewed without the heroic machinery, there is reference to his age: a "monomaniac old man," an "insane old man," a "frantic old man." When his ivory leg is snapped off in the battle of the second day, Ahab returns cursing fate "that the unconquerable captain in the soul should have such a craven mate," and when Starbuck, pointing this extraordinarily timed pun, takes exception, Ahab answers, "My body, man, not thee" (II.350). The authority remains, no longer epic but grandly human. To his men he has been "a grand old cove" (I.219), and it is this view, finally, which prevails. Near the end Stubb, no philosopher, attests to it with a strange, comradely admiration: "Damn me, Ahab, but thou actest right; live in the game, and die it" (II.275). The same view is more impressively advanced, and the pun elucidated, shortly before Stubb's comment, when Queequeg, calmly preparing to die according to his portents, is eulogized as if already dead by Pip: "Queequeg dies game!—mind ye that; Queequeg dies game!—take ye good heed of that; Queequeg dies game! I say; game, game, game! but base little Pip, he died a coward; died all a'shiver;—out upon Pip" (II.250). "Old Thunder" he may have been, as Elijah first called him and Ahab himself later echoed (II.278), but it is in a radical weakness that Ahab dies. Yet he does die game, raging and battling to the last:. "To the last I grapple with thee; from hell's heart I stab at thee; for hate's sake I spit my last breath at thee" (II.366). Though like Macbeth he has been hoodwinked by trick prophecies, he does not try to run but goes alone to his last battle, as to his first, "an Arkansas duellist at his foe, blindly seeking with a six-inch blade to reach the fathom-deep life of the whale" (I.229).

Ahab's leg, his "craven mate," is instance of his mortality. However lofty, whether godlike or ungodly, he is finally powerless and ultimately nothing. Unlike Captain Boomer of the *Samuel Enderby,* who is content to lose one arm to the White Whale and return no more, Ahab, Old Thunder himself and no mere boomer, returns a second time to lose his leg and then returns once more to lose his life. In opposition to the White Whale, he is dwarflike, to use a figure developed at length in *Mardi,* and the difference between Ahab and the others is that Ahab knows he is mortal, small and powerless, and in this knowledge—because of it, in fact—he enacts his grand defiance. Stubb, to the end "brave as fearless fire (and as mechanical)" (II.341; II.352), is a dwarf who does not know he is a dwarf. Starbuck, on the other hand, knows too well that he is radically weak and so shuns the final test. After the first encounter, Stubb laughs at the omen of the shattered boat and Starbuck fears it. Ahab knows them both, even as he knows himself: "Begone! Ye two are the opposite poles of one thing; Starbuck is Stubb reversed, and Stubb is Starbuck; and ye two are all mankind; and Ahab stands alone among the millions of the peopled earth, nor gods nor men his neighbors!" (II.341).

The source of Ahab's special isolating knowledge and its power is symbolized by his other physical mutilation, the mysterious scar that brands the Promethean hero, scorched from having dared too near the sun. It is the scar that Ishmael notices first when Ahab makes his grand appearance on the quarter-deck, looking "like a man cut away from the stake, when the fire has overrunningly wasted all the limbs without consuming them. . . . Threading its way out from among his gray hairs, and continuing right down one side of his tawney scorched face and neck, till it disappeared in his clothing, you saw a slender rod-like mark, lividly whitish. It resembled that perpendicular seam sometimes made in the straight, lofty trunk of a great tree, when the upper lightning tearingly darts down it, and without wrenching a single twig, peels and grooves out the bark from top to bottom, ere running off into the soil, leaving the tree still greenly alive, but branded" (I.152–53). The origin of the scar is not immediately made known, though two rumored explanations are provided. "Tashtego's senior, an old Gay-Head Indian among the crew, superstitiously asserted that not till he was full forty years old did Ahab become that way branded, and then it came upon him, not in the fury of any mortal fray, but in an elemental strife at sea." His Christian counterpart, "a gray Manxman . . . an old sepulchral man," has other views. Though he has never previously "laid eye upon wild Ahab," he is "popularly invested . . . with preternatural powers of discernment," and so "no white sailor seriously contradicted him when he said that if ever Captain Ahab should be tranquilly laid out—which might hardly come to pass, so he muttered—then, whoever should do that last office for the dead would find a birthmark on him from crown to sole"· (I.153). The Indian, it develops, is more right, though the punster prophet is aptly suggestive. Some "elemental strife at sea" has branded Ahab's soul (and perhaps given him thereby his crown, that "regal over-bearing dignity of some mighty woe"), but it is a birthmark only symbolically, stemming from some sort of initiation by fire in savage rites to the pagan fire god of Fedallah.

In his magnificent address to the corposants in "The Candles," Ahab finally reveals the origin of his brand as well as its crucial meanings.

> Oh! thou clear spirit of clear fire, whom on these seas I as
> Persian once did worship, till in the sacramental act so burned
> by thee, that to this hour I bear the scar; I now know thee, thou
> clear spirit, and I now know that thy right worship is defiance.
> To neither love nor reverence wilt thou be kind; and e'en for
> hate thou canst but kill; and all are killed. No fearless fool
> now fronts thee. I own thy speechless, placeless power; but to
> the last gasp of my earthquake life will dispute its uncondi-
> tional, unintegral mastery in me. In the midst of the personified
> impersonal, a personality stands here.   (II.281)

The posture of heroic defiance is not the final, furious activity
of self-destructive combat, but rather this stance rooted in
an awareness of ultimate inadequacy. In *Mardi,* the image of
a motionless upright stance is consistently a touchstone to
heroic opposition, instancing a refusal both to crawl and to
run. Ahab, "no fearless fool" like Stubb, stands here a
personality though only on one real leg, because in under-
going his ordeal of fire he has taken on something of its
essential character. The "upper lightning" has branded the
trunk in its own image.

The origin of Ahab's diabolist dark side is the mystic East,
embodied in the persistent ghostly specter of Fedallah. The
actual sources, however, are the South Sea islands where the
young Herman Melville himself adventured among cannibals,
gaining one knows not what important knowledge in the
process. Throughout *Moby-Dick* the pagan, the primitive,
and the diabolical are interlinked and the moral implications
deliberately ambiguous.[5] Though Ahab baptizes his harpoon
"in nomine diaboli," and tempers its barb with blood from
Queequeg, Tashtego, and Dagoo, the three squires themselves are noble savages and Ahab, metaphorically, the cannibal. Queequeg's coffin, signifying love as well as death, is
the means of Ishmael's salvation. The final image of the
sinking *Pequod* is of the upraised arm of the aboriginal
American, Tashtego. White Stubb eating the whale he kills
is likened to a predatory shark by black Fleece. The source

of all such references, however, is the transcendent, omni-present barbarism symbolized by Ahab's scar and stemming, ultimately, from Heaven itself. In the chapter entitled "Midnight, Forecastle," when a storm comes up to mirror the human storm raised by Ahab's revelation of his mission and the crew's wild dedication to his quest, the old prophetic Manxman likens a flash of lightning to Ahab's "birth-mark," calling it "another in the sky—lurid-like . . . all else pitch black." A battle immediately follows between Dagoo and a nameless Spanish sailor who insults his race, calling it "the undeniable dark side of mankind—devilish dark at that," and likens the lightning to "Dagoo showing his teeth." Here the proliferating ambiguities of black and white throughout *Moby-Dick* infuse the meanings of Ahab's symbolic scar. Again there are two comments, one pagan and one Christian, and again, though opposite, they are interdependent. Voicing the anthropomorphic position is Tashtego: "A row alow, and a row aloft—Gods and men—both brawlers!" As the sailors, black and white, begin to form a ring around the combatants, the old Manxman tells them the ring is "ready formed. There! the ringed horizon. In that ring Cain struck Abel. Sweet work, right work! No? Why then, God, mad'st thou the ring?" Pip caps the ambiguity, praying futilely to a God neither brawler nor willer of brawls: "Oh, thou big white God aloft there somewhere in yon darkness, have mercy on this small black boy down here; preserve him from all men that have no bowels to feel fear" (I.219–21).

Beyond the immediate symbolic and metaphysical implica-tions of darkness and light,[6] the interfusion of civilized man and savage is broadly relevant to all the novels as both cause and emblem of the heroic quester's necessary abdication from his humanities. The half-civilized savage, though of minor interest to Melville, serves generally as a definitive gloss on his counterpart, the half-savage white man. Thus Queequeg is "George Washington cannibalistically developed" (I.61); and "dark Ahab" is captain of "a cannibal of a craft, tricking herself forth in the chased bones of her enemies," though like her captain, "a noble craft, but somehow a most melancholy! All noble things are touched with that" (I.86). The shadowed nobility is that of Melville's quester; the shadow itself, the brand of savagery he wears. The commitment to barbarism is sometimes literal, as with Ahab's fire ordeal, and sometimes symbolic, as when the nameless narrator of *Mardi* commits murder to assume his quest and the new identity of Taji, oriental demigod. It is always, however, a major facet of the character. And for the aspiring neophyte—Ishmael moving from boredom into great, near-fatal danger—it is always a grim possibility. One can only guess at the ultimate importance of Melville's own experience in the South Seas. But whether or not the experience inspired the metaphysics, there was clearly a fortunate coincidence of actual happening and intellectual need. The first two novels, which chronicle Melville's youthful adventuring, also establish the theme, and they mark its limits and its meanings.

PART ONE

SOUNDINGS

$\star$ **1** $\star$

THOUGH NATURALLY TENTATIVE, Melville's initial assay at deep-diving—encompassing *Typee, Omoo,* and *Mardi* —is remarkably true. The young, self-educated sailor with an appetite for language and naïve notions of literary fame and fortune turns instinctively in his first books to the basic situation and the issues that will concern him as long as he writes fiction. His subject, at the outset, is the neophyte Ishmael, linked to ordinary landsmen, who may in time become an Ahab, ineradicably maimed, immensely lofty. It is equally striking, if less immediately relevant, that these first books also commence a process of composition that will recur significantly throughout the career. Driven by peculiar and conflicting needs as well as by his deeply personal subjects, Melville wrote his novels in groups of three, each separate triad developed, no doubt unconsciously, with an almost dialectical formality. The scheme evolves as follows: A first novel thrusts the basic story outward as if Melville himself were embarking freshly with his young hero for those dark and distant regions wherein lie both supreme dangers and possible ennoblement. In the sequel, not so much purged as deeply frustrated, he returns his hero, not notably changed, to a context that is lighter in spirit and far less serious in substance. The pattern is repeated in the first two novels of each triad. The youthful heroes of *Typee, Redburn,* and *Pierre* are all voyagers in search of some dark ultimate experience; those of *Omoo, White Jacket,* and *Israel Potter* are variously in quest of home. The first seek important knowledge; the second, respite and security. And as might be predicted, the third work in each sequence represents a major effort of synthesis, a deliberate striving for a decisive, comprehensive statement. Related to this process, whether as cause or as effect, is the land-sea antinomy most forcefully articulated at the start of *Moby-Dick.* The seaward effort is self-consciously heroic; the landward reaction is sometimes contemptuously and sometimes wistfully nonheroic. The first attempts a grand and lofty prose, resonantly romantic in conception. The second, in sharp contrast, is essentially realistic, and its language, like its subject, is often that of satire. Where the first posits heroic possibility in terms of psychic journeying, the second reacts by considering the limited alternatives of a landlocked society anatomized intellectually. And, as noted, the major work of each triad combines the contraries, simultaneously involving both psychic and social exploration, incipient tragedy and satire, darkness and dark angry humor.

Clearly such a formulaic view sheds more light on Melville than on the novels themselves. Only *Pierre* is meaningfully illuminated by considering it as the beginning of a new phase, rather than as a sequel to *Moby-Dick.* Yet it is the recurrence of these patterns, coupled with his obsessive repetition of theme and his steady progress toward *Moby-Dick* and then silence, that makes Melville a representative and a deeply moving novelist as well as the creator of Ahab and the White Whale. One cannot read the early works with pleasure, but one should not read them strictly as a gloss on *Moby-Dick.* If *Typee* and *Omoo* are slight and *Mardi* impossibly tedious, they nonetheless represent the initial phase of a drama that has continuing interest and significance. And so they merit full and serious study.

Typee is a curious mixture of conventional travelogue and highly unconventional story, of benign pastoral and nightmare. The sparseness of the narrative, as well as its content, is typically Melvillian. In it, a youthful seaman deserts his ship out of boredom to go exploring among South Sea savages. He descends into a characteristic heart of darkness, filled with dark omens of unspeakable horrors, and finally—after a few thin adventures—he emerges from it ostensibly, if not actually, transfigured by his contact with primal barbarism. The point of view throughout is oddly ill-defined. Always afraid, yet never really threatened, the hero—renamed Tommo by the natives—never seems to know what to make of his experience. Repeatedly Melville takes him to the brink of a definitive terror only to pull him back abruptly into situations that are almost comic in conception. For instance, in the Taboo groves where the natives apparently practice ritual sacrifice, Tommo and his companion Toby eat a pleasant supper with their hosts, then fall asleep. They awaken about midnight, suddenly "apprehensive of some evil," and their fears mount as they watch some strange ceremony in the "depths of the grove," where "shoots of flame . . . illuminated the surrounding trees, casting, by contrast, into still deeper gloom the darkness around us." Then "dark figures" appear, "moving to and fro before the flames; while others, dancing and capering about, looked like so many demons." Toby expects that they are shortly to be boiled and eaten. Tommo, his heart "beating like a trip-hammer," is forced to agree that they are "indeed at the mercy of a tribe of cannibals, and that the dreadful contingency to which Toby had alluded was by no means removed beyond the bounds of possibility." Their terror soars as the natives abruptly start toward them, "noiselessly, nay stealthily, and glided along through the gloom that surrounded us as if about to spring upon some object they were fearful of disturbing before they should make sure of it." Their first view of the gloomy Taboo groves, "scene of many a prolonged feast, of many a horrid rite," seems imminently to be realized. It is all a joke, of course. They are summoned to eat, not to be eaten. "Suddenly the silence was broken by the well-remembered tone of Mehevi, and at the kindly accents of his voice, my fears were immediately dissipated. 'Tommo, Toby, ki ki!' (eat). He had waited to address us until he had assured himself that we were both awake, at which he seemed somewhat surprised" (127).

Yet the vaguely ominous note remains. Throughout his sojourn in Typee, the crux of Tommo's problem is that he is never entirely certain that things are as benign as they seem, that the imagined terrors are not in fact an integral part of things, hovering just beyond his powers of perception. The elaborate melodramatic hoax at the groves is similar to an earlier moment when he and Toby have finally descended into the valley, not knowing whether it is the place of the dread Typees or of the gentle Happars with whom they have hoped to make contact. With their apprehensions at a peak, they suddenly come upon the gentlest and loveliest of Typee's pastoral scenes: "a boy and girl, slender and graceful, and completely naked, with the exception of a slight girdle of bark. . . . An arm of the boy, half screened from sight by her wild tresses, was thrown about the neck of the girl, while with the other he held one of her hands in his; and thus they stood together, their heads inclined forward, catching the faint noise we made in our progress, and with one foot in advance, as if half inclined to fly from our presence" (90). Yet it is Typee, not Happar. Underlining the obvious irony, the Happars brutally attack Toby on first sight, when, making his first attempt to leave Typee, he goes up to them expecting a greeting in keeping with their benign reputation.

The welcoming scene is with few and momentary exceptions typical of life there. Yet by the end, driven half insane with fear, Tommo runs frantically out to the boat carrying men sent to barter for his release. The natives' "fixed determination of purpose" to keep him intensifies his desire to escape, and he does so in a sudden, extraordinary act of self-assertion: "in despair, and reckless of consequences, I exerted all my strength, and shaking myself free from the grasp of those who held me, I sprung upon my feet and rushed towards Karakoee" (336). Tommo is obviously no Ahab, hurling his battered body at the whale. He is, in fact, leaping in the opposite direction. But in the passion of his frenzied, desperate recklessness, and the outburst of physical strength born of a will to escape that is as determined and purposeful as theirs to keep him captive, there is a momentary energy indicative of the possible values of dark journeying.

Tommo's regeneration, such as it is, culminates a consciously structured drama of initiation and rebirth. Bored with "gliding along" on the *Dolly* through a "delightful, lazy, languid" period with nothing to be done so that "every one seemed to be under the influence of some narcotic" (9), Tommo resolves to escape, as does the narrator of *Mardi* under similar conditions. The relation of this do-nothing boredom to the safe life of what Melville contemptuously terms "state-room sailors" should be noted. Though cannibals may await him, Tommo is "willing to encounter some risks in order to accomplish [his] object" (39). The alternative to the potential dangers of the unknown is the continued boredom of a lengthy whaling voyage that might last "four or five years" or even more: "Some long-haired, bare-necked youths, who, forced by the united influences of Captain Marryat and hard times, embark at Nantucket for a pleasure excursion to the Pacific, and whose anxious mothers provide them with bottled milk for the occasion, oftentimes return very respectable middle-aged gentlemen" (25–26).

In rejecting boredom now and a settled, worldly smugness later, Tommo is like the nameless narrator of *Mardi* who becomes the demigod Taji, wandering in endless quest of white Yillah, an image of some transcendent absolute. Tommo, who begins his journey as Tom, has no such specified goal. But the directions, for a time at least, are similar. As in the later novels, it is a movement from civilization into "unknown regions" which are wild, primeval, and suggestively mythic. The journey begins with a long, difficult climb to the peak of a high mountain, and their efforts are at times suggestive of a kind of preliminary ritual testing. Encountering a thicket of dense reeds, Tommo first tries cautious means of getting through. Then, "half wild with meeting an obstacle we had so little anticipated, I threw myself desperately against it, crushing to the ground the canes with which I came in contact; and, rising to my feet again, repeated the action with like effect" (49). Finally, they achieve the summit and begin the steep and dangerous descent which marks Melville's first effort at deep-diving and his first fictional diver.

D. H. Lawrence aptly described the descent into the valley as a mythic rebirth. "Down this narrow, steep, horrible dark gorge he slides and struggles as we struggle in a dream, or in the act of birth, to emerge in the green Eden of the Golden Age, the valley of the cannibal savages."[1] What is important is the energy of the struggle. In their constant, arduous effort and their sufferings, the deserters are like castaways at sea, like Owen Chase, whose account of the sinking of the *Essex* was already familiar to Melville.[2] They must ration their small store of food. They spend a first "horrid night" in a chasm which, like the barren island where Chase's group found a brief refuge from the sea, they decide to abandon because it "presented no inducement for us to remain, except the promise of security" (62). Despite their hardships, they are resolved not to turn back: "There is scarcely anything when a man is in difficulties that he is more disposed to look upon with abhorrence than a right-about retrograde movement—a systematic going over of the already trodden ground; and especially if he has a love of adventure, such a course appears indescribably repulsive, so long as there remains the least hope to be derived from braving untried difficulties" (72). And so they slip and slide and crawl and leap toward a place increasingly terrible to them: "The very name of Typee struck a panic into my heart which I did not attempt to disguise. The thought of voluntarily throwing ourselves into the hands of these cruel savages, seemed to me an act of mere madness" (67).

If the descent into the valley is, as Lawrence calls it, "a bit of birth-myth, or rebirth myth," it is no mechanical return to nature. The necessary struggle is toward hard manhood; with the achievement comes a corresponding loss of innocence, instanced by a physical malady. Tommo descends into Green Eden limping. The journey has hardly begun when his leg becomes mysteriously infected. "Cold shiverings and a burning fever succeeded one another at intervals, while one of my legs was swelled to such a degree, and pained me so acutely, that I half suspected I had been bitten by some venomous reptile" (63–64). He goes on to note that he subsequently learned that there were no such reptiles on the island. It is tempting to make much of this, perhaps overmuch. In this vaguely mythic context, the possible implications of snakebite are obvious, and the specific link with Ahab's similar disability is intriguing. However, though the facts of Tommo's experience accord only sketchily with those of Melville's own life among the cannibals—much license was taken in the interests of a longer as well as a better fiction—there is no question that Melville's own leg was seriously infected during his stay there, and this literal fact may well be the sole concern. Yet in addition to Melville's insistence on the mysterious aspects of this physical disorder, repeated connections are made between the condition of Tommo's leg and his state of mind.

Immediately on arriving in Typee, Tommo is treated by a native doctor and the leg improves somewhat. As his mind, despite the evidence of his eyes, is increasingly "consumed by the most dismal forebodings," his physical agony grows: "I was almost a cripple, and the pain I endured at intervals was agonising. The unaccountable malady showed no signs of amendment; on the contrary, its violence increased day by day, and threatened the most fatal results, unless some powerful means were employed to counteract it" (157). Immediately there follows the festive visit to the Taboo groves, where Tommo's dread of being eaten is dispelled with offerings of food. With no other "powerful means" of treatment than this, his leg abruptly improves and remains so throughout the long middle period of his adjustment to native life. When his terrors resurge toward the end of the novel, under the specific threat of imminent tattooing, his leg goes bad again (311). Soon, with his discovery that his kindly hosts possess three shrunken heads, one a white man's, he is "reduced to such a state, that it was with extreme difficulty I could walk, even with the assistance of a spear, and Kory-Kory, as formerly, was obliged to carry me daily to the stream" (326). But Tommo is not entirely "unmanned"; when news arrives that a boat has appeared to rescue him, he rouses himself to the same sort of supreme physical effort that originally enabled him to descend into the valley. Kory-Kory, "that hitherto faithful servitor," has disappeared. He asks help of one "muscular fellow," then another and a third. Finally he realizes that Mehevi has given him "liberty to continue my progress toward the sea because he supposed that I was deprived of the means of reaching it." At this point he becomes "desperate," and using a spear as a crutch, "almost insensible to the pain which I suffered," he starts off alone to the beach, where an even larger physical effort becomes necessary before he can get away (333). Ultimately, then, it hardly matters whether or not Melville deliberately intended Tommo's injured leg to indicate a primal flawed humanity, some radical mutilation deriving from heroic willingness to undergo the crippling ordeal of the terrible valley. The Tommo who suffers through the descent to Typee and who, once there, glimpses something of its terrors, however nameless, is no longer quite the affable young whaling man who deserted the *Dolly* in a high-spirited search for adventure. Still, he is not a quester.

In *Mardi,* where the spiritual journey is at once more pointed and more elaborate, the philosopher Babbalanja, himself a precursor of Ahab, formulates the question of deep-diving more specifically: "He knows himself, and all that's in him, who knows adversity. To scale great heights, we must come out of lowermost depths. The way to heaven is through hell. We need fiery baptisms in the fiercest flames of our own bosoms. We must feel our hearts hot—hissing in us. And ere their fire is revealed, it must burn its way out of us; though it consume us and itself" (II.324). Melville's concept of this descent into a fiery hell as a necessary affirmation of high manhood and heroic aspiration is premised on the conviction that a "state-room sailor's" life is far more intolerable. And, like Thoreau, Melville conceives the journey as a stripping away of all the artifacts of a decadent civilization, as a kind of westward movement of the soul. Thoreau at Walden trains down to bare necessities—"Simplify, simplify. Instead of three meals a day, if it be necessary, eat but one; instead of a hundred dishes, five; and reduce other things in proportion." To Melville, even as early as *Typee,* this same purgative act involves an ultimate commitment to even an ultimate savagery. Thoreau urges that we "wedge our feet downward through the mud and slush of opinion, and prejudice, and tradition, and delusion, and appearance, that alluvion which covers the globe . . . till we come to a hard bottom and rocks in place, which we can call reality." Thoreau's bedrock reality is predicated on a transcendent harmony. The light of the sun concerns him, not its fire, and he goes "to the woods . . . to front only the essential facts of life," to try to live with "no path to the civilized world."[3] Melville posits fiercer "lowermost depths." His heroic questers go to the South Seas, and from savages acquire a hard and bitter knowledge that provides both energy and burden for a course continually run between the savage and the civilized worlds.

In *Typee* the embryonic hero refuses such knowledge and commitment. Throughout his stay, he has been alternately intrigued and disgusted by the practice of tattooing: "Most remarkable in the appearance of this splendid islander [Mehevi] was the elaborate tattooing displayed on every noble limb. All imaginable lines and curves and figures were delineated over his whole body, and in their grotesque variety and infinite profusion, I could only compare them to the crowded groupings of quaint patterns we sometimes see in costly pieces of lace-work" (104).[4] Shortly after meeting Mehevi, Tommo is appalled by the tattooed bodies of the old men of the Taboo groves, "four or five hideous old wretches, on whose decrepit forms time and tattooing seemed to have obliterated every trace of humanity" (124). The function and status of these ancients are never revealed, but since they seem at home in the Taboo groves while others of nearly comparable age, like old Marheyo, live happily in their own homes, they are probably involved in some way with the tribe's religious practices. However, it is not their age or role in life which troubles Tommo, but rather the special quality of their repulsive, dehumanizing tattooing. Tommo's initial setting out is marked, like Ishmael's, by a prophecy of sorts, which specifically warns that ultimate disfigurement awaits him on the island. Fearing just such a desertion as Tommo and Toby have in mind, the captain of the *Dolly* cautions his men against taking shore liberty by telling the terrible tale of the *Dido*'s crew, which went off on liberty and "never were heard of again for a week . . . and only three of them ever got back to the ship again, and one with his face damaged for life, for the cursed heathens tattooed a broad patch clean across his figure-head" (44). The tone, of course, is comic, yet this offhand, probably exaggerated account proves a genuine forecast.

The tattoo artist of Typee, seeing in Tommo's white skin an ideal canvas, is filled with "a painter's enthusiasm." Tommo is instantly "horrified at the bare thought of being rendered hideous for life if the wretch were to execute his purpose." Briefly they struggle and dispute. Finally, "not knowing to what extremities he might proceed, and shuddering at the ruin he might inflict upon my figure-head," Tommo offers to "compromise" by allowing him an arm to be tattooed (294). The compromise is rejected, and "half wild with terror and indignation," Tommo finally runs away "pursued by the indomitable artist, who ran after me, implements in hand." Again an essentially comic situation grows quickly serious. King Mehevi and others shortly begin to insist that he be tattooed, and he realizes that "the whole system of tattooing was . . . connected with their religion; and . . . that they were resolved to make a convert of me" (296). It is at this point that his serious physical decline begins. Their constant importunities drive him "half wild"; his leg is suddenly worse than ever; and his life becomes one "of absolute wretchedness." Finally, filled "with forebodings of evil, and with an uncontrollable desire to penetrate the secret" (312) of the mysterious packages hanging from the ridgepole of Marheyo's house, he forces his way into a family conclave where the packages are being considered and discovers the three heads. It is to the point that the heads are possessions of the family that has literally adopted him and treated him with such extraordinary and unvarying kindness. Whatever Tommo's fears, the issue is not that he will one day be served up to his faithful Kory-Kory on a platter, but that, being made a convert, he will himself some day be forced into an act of cannibalism.

As I have said, there is a shadow, if not the actual substance, of Ahab in Tommo's final raging determination to escape—but his great leap is from the whale, not toward it. Repeatedly, Tommo is "half wild," an ordinary adjective that would warrant no attention were it not for the fact that, in *Mardi* and the later novels, "wild" becomes a crucial word, consistently overused to indicate a Byronic passion, stature, and isolation, the roots of which are manifestly primitive. Tommo is a spectator, not a participant, only a guest and foster son of Typee. The nameless young whaling man of *Mardi* puts on the "free, flowing, and Eastern" clothing of an Oriental emir, becoming first captain of his ship and ultimately of his soul. When it begins to look as though his stay will be a long one, Tommo also changes into native dress, but only to preserve his own clothes "in a suitable condition for wear, should I again appear among civilised beings"

(161). Taji commits an act of murder to win Yillah and becomes the fated "unreturning wanderer." Just as his escape
has almost been effected and his return to civilization assured,
Tommo commits a near murder of one of the natives swim-
ming toward the boat in a last effort to stop him. "Even at
the moment I felt horror at the act I was about to commit;
but it was no time for pity or compunction, and with a true
aim, and exerting all my strength, I dashed the boat-hook at
him. It struck him just below the throat, and forced him
downward. I had no time to repeat my blow, but I saw him
rise to the surface in the wake of the boat, and never shall I
forget the ferocious expression of his countenance" (339).[5]

Although Tommo's situation is of major interest, he is
essentially without character and is defined strictly by the
experience he undergoes. His friend Toby, in sharp contrast,
is the first in a series of extraordinary portraits that culmi-
nate in Ahab. The presentation is sketchy and confined to
a static introductory study (40–41) which is completely unrealized in the actual narrative. Darkness is the dominant fact
of Toby's appearance: "His naturally dark complexion had
been deepened by exposure to the tropical sun, and a mass
of jetty locks clustered about his temples, and threw a darker
shade into his large black eyes." His character corresponds
to Melville's subsequent notions of connection between dark
looks and dark spirit: "He was a strange wayward being,
moody, fitful, and melancholy—at times almost morose. He
had a quick and fiery temper too, which, when thoroughly
roused, transported him into a state bordering on delirium."
Like his most immediate counterpart, the malign Jackson in
Redburn, Toby, though physically small, has a strange power
over others: "It is strange the power that a mind of deep
passion has over feebler natures. I have seen a brawny fellow, with no lack of ordinary courage, fairly quail before
this slender stripling, when in one of his furious fits." Finally, Toby is the first of several vagabonds whose way of life
gradually becomes for Melville symbolic of the condition of
the *"Isolato,"* the solitary self-contained wanderer who has

plunged beyond the land's limit to test himself against an overwhelming destiny. "He was one of that class of rovers you sometimes meet at sea, who never reveal their origin, never allude to home, and go rambling over the world as if pursued by some mysterious fate they cannot possibly elude."[6]

The early disappearance of this potentially dynamic hero is one relevant oddity of *Typee*. Another is Melville's peculiar use of Tommo as a first-person narrator. The returned romancer who has clearly spent much recent time researching the literature of the South Seas bears little resemblance to the Tommo who experienced all the imagined horrors of life among the cannibals. The radical uncertainties that Tommo himself felt while resident in Typee are reflected in a curious ambivalence in the narrative voice. The story plays out in two distinct styles. The first is essentially journalistic, proper to a detached traveloguer and amateur anthropologist. The second, more clearly novelistic, recounts the immediate dramatic experience. The characteristic pose of the first is that of an objective, scholarly reformer, righting a sorry record of Western treacheries and atrocities in the lands of the noble savage. The moral tone throughout is high-minded, enlightened, and outraged. For even that most terrible of savage acts, the eating of human flesh, there is some justification on the grounds of a just vengeance for "unprovoked injuries":

> But it will be urged that these shocking unprincipled wretches are cannibals. Very true; and a rather bad trait in their character, it must be allowed. But they are such only when they seek to gratify the passion of revenge upon their enemies; and I ask whether the mere eating of human flesh so very far exceeds in barbarity that custom which only a few years since was practised in enlightened England:—a convicted traitor, perhaps a man found guilty of honesty, patriotism, and suchlike heinous crimes, had his head lopped off with a huge axe, his bowels dragged out and thrown into a fire; while his body, carved into four quarters, was with his head exposed upon pikes, and permitted to rot and fester among the public haunts of men.
> (166)

And yet, in that other part of *Typee* which tells the story of Tommo, cannibalism arouses the most horrendous and shattering fears.

Melville's spirited defense of the savage is predictably twofold. Not only is the civilized white at fault, but also the native is inherently benign and noble. Again the basic assumption is commonplace. The noble savage, happily pastoral, is entirely sheltered from all of civilization's various woes. The terms and allusions are literary, as in the first sight of the valley of Typee. "Had a glimpse of the gardens of Paradise been revealed to me I could scarcely have been more ravished with the sight. . . . Over all the landscape there reigned the most hushed repose, which I almost feared to break, lest, like the enchanted gardens in the fairy tale, a single syllable might dissolve the spell" (64–65). A hundred pages later, the general position remains the same, though the literary allusion is updated: "When I looked around the verdant recess in which I was buried, and gazed up to the summits of the lofty eminence that hemmed me in, I was well disposed to think that I was in the 'Happy Valley,' and that beyond those heights there was naught but a world of care and anxiety" (165). Individually, too, the natives are fit residents of Paradise. Mehevi, chief of the tribe, presents on first sight the traditional image of the noble savage, scrutinizing his visitors with calm intelligence, quietly but scornfully rejecting their conciliatory offering of tobacco. This "splendid islander . . . one of nature's noblemen" (104) is only the foremost of Tommo's gracious hosts. Kory-Kory, "my tried servitor and faithful valet," is "the most devoted and best-natured serving-man in the world" (110), his old father, Marheyo, "a most paternal and warm-hearted old fellow" (113), and his mother "had the kindliest heart in the world, and acted toward me in particular in a truly maternal manner" (114). Finally, perfect complement to this new foster family, there is Fayaway, whose "general loveliness of appearance" cannot be described save in terms of a primal Paradise: "The easy unstudied graces of a child of nature like this, breathing from infancy an atmosphere of perpetual summer, and nurtured by the simple fruits of the earth; enjoying a perfect freedom from care and anxiety, and removed effectually from all injurious tendencies" (115).

The traveloguer and the novelist are, of course, one and the same, and my distinction between them has to do with the tone and general area of interest of each, not with two wholly separate lines of development. At times they merge, most notably when Fayaway is on the scene and the story proper naturally accords with the assumptions of pastoral romance. Nonetheless, I think the distinction a valid one. Virtually all that the journalistic eye perceives is benign, and every general attitude is favorable to the natives; at the same time, the central character's inner life is one of almost continual fear and torment. Roughly midway through the stay in Typee, there is specific comment on this curious situation.

> In looking back to this period, and calling to remembrance the numberless proofs of kindness and respect which I received from the natives of the valley, I can scarcely understand how it was that, in the midst of so many consolatory circumstances, my mind should still have been consumed by the most dismal forebodings, and have remained a prey to the profoundest melancholy. It is true that the suspicious circumstances which had attended the disappearance of Toby were enough of themselves to excite distrust with regard to the savages, in whose power I felt myself to be entirely placed, especially when it was combined with the knowledge that these very men, kind and respectful as they were to me, were, after all, nothing better than a set of cannibals. (157)

This is clearly not the voice which at the outset cautioned that, if these are savages, it is because the whites have made as well as named them so. Yet it is in the chapter immediately following this one that their cannibalism, "a rather bad trait," is justified on the grounds that they eat only enemies, and only for revenge, and that the English not too long ago were still holding legal executions of an equally barbarous character. Repeatedly through *Typee* there are moments like this when the narrative goes one way and a succeeding voice from its distant vantage point in time and space calmly and objectively contradicts. Near the end, for instance, where the narrative, after a long descriptive lull, is finally driving toward Tommo's escape, Melville pauses to insert yet another account of general customs, Typean singing, and such (Chapter 31). Tommo has by now been driven almost mad with vague fears and with the specific threat of being tattooed and having to remain there permanently or else roam the world indelibly branded as a savage. But here again the romantic tone and mood reappear, and also the functional contrast between the noble savage and a decadent civilization. "No wonder that the South Sea islanders are so amphibious a race, when they are thus launched into the water as soon as they see the light. I am convinced that it is as natural for a human being to swim as it is for a duck. And yet, in civilised communities, how many able-bodied individuals die, like so many drowning kittens, from the occurrence of the most trivial accidents!" (308). It is not merely that vague terrors lurk beneath the benign surfaces. Two distinct voices are consistently presenting two almost entirely distinct views of the same experience, one immediate and one far removed.

I say almost entirely distinct because, although the narrative proper frequently corroborates the commentary, there are several instances where the general view suggests something of the latent fearfulness of Tommo's immediate situation. Significantly these have to do with religion or with tattooing, the measure of religious or social status. The visit to the Taboo groves elicits a description notably different in character from the usual view of the Happy Valley.

> Here were situated the Taboo groves of the valley—the scene of many a prolonged feast, of many a horrid rite. Beneath the dark shadows of the consecrated bread-fruit trees there reigned a solemn twilight—a cathedral-like gloom. The frightful genius of pagan worship seemed to brood in silence over the place, breathing its spell upon every object around. Here and there, in the depths of these awful shades, half screened from sight by

masses of overhanging foliage, rose the idolatrous altars of the savages, built of enormous blocks of black and polished stone, placed one upon another, without cement, to the height of twelve or fifteen feet, and surmounted by a rustic open temple, enclosed with a low picket of canes, within which might be seen, in various stages of decay, offerings of bread-fruit and cocoa-nuts, and the putrefying relics of some recent sacrifice.

(122)

For a moment Tommo's drama is seen in a context relevant to his situation. The world about him briefly tallies with the inner, psychic conflagration, justifying it objectively. Yet later, according to the method of *Typee,* Melville seems to deny entirely this memorable spectacle. Answering published accounts of human sacrifice and other savage rites in the Marquesas, Melville matter-of-factly asserts that "all I can say is, that in all my excursions through the valley of Typee, I never saw any of these alleged enormities. If any of them are practised upon the Marquesas Islands, they must certainly have come to my knowledge while living for months with a tribe of savages, wholly unchanged from their original primitive condition, and reputed the most ferocious in the South Seas" (228).

Whatever the immediate causes, the ambivalent voice and uncertain identity of *Typee*'s narrator foreshadow a recurrent dilemma in Melville's mind and art, a problem at once technical and thematic. In terms of the novelist's craft, the question is simply how to control a first-person narrator who is also the story's hero and thus, by Melville's definition, significantly isolated from the society that constitutes his audience. How, in other words, can a transfigured hero be returned from hell to tell his awful story meaningfully to bland, untraveling countrymen? Not until *Redburn* does Melville hit upon a workable scheme by the simple device of distinguishing his neophyte-narrator from the Promethean hero he encounters. But the larger thematic implications are never really resolved at all, as the peculiar disappearance of Ishmael's voice from *Moby-Dick* would seem to indicate.

It is clear enough that once he has confronted the White Whale with full awareness of its meanings, Ahab is permanently isolated from human society. But even Ishmael's possibilities for meaningful accommodation—and hence for fully coherent storytelling—are obscure. He disappears as a narrative presence in part at least because Melville can give us no real sense of what his later life will be. He is saved from the holocaust because of his humanity and because someone must be saved to tell the awful story. But how he lives with that hard knowledge—and where he wanders carrying it—are the great unanswered questions of *Moby-Dick.* Pierre, similarly exposed to radical evil, becomes a murderer. Israel Potter, educated by worldly misfortune only, is destroyed. And Melville, by his own account purged spotless pure by writing *Moby-Dick,* if not immediately consumed by a descent like that described by Babbalanja in *Mardi,* grew first darker, then misanthropic, and was finally silent.

★ 2 ★

THERE IS NO AMBIVALENCE in the narrative voice in *Omoo*, and very little mystery in the story. Like its counterparts, *White Jacket* and *Israel Potter*, its context is the familiar social life of the landsman, its mood and subject is one of homecoming, and its structure and language are those of conventional fiction. It is a more coherent piece of work than *Typee* but a less interesting one. Yet insofar as it concerns the further adventures of Tommo, it necessarily extends the psychic implications of his journey into the primal valley.[1] In certain set portraits (Bembo, Lem Hardy), like that initial one of Toby in *Typee*, there is a little more specific prefiguration of Ahab. But Tommo himself, unlike Conrad's Marlow, seems entirely unaffected by his brief, inadequate glimpse into the savage heart of darkness. There is in fact no development of any basic action in *Omoo*, but only wayward ramblings, picaresque in character. Still the world through which Tommo wanders with his new friend Long Ghost is, by reason of its very formlessness and pointlessness, a comment on the continuing process of dark journeying. The terms are here negatively defined; the atmosphere is of the land, not the sea, and the land itself is no valley of savages but a decayed half-civilized world where vitality and meaning are diminished and heroic action an impossibility.

The frenzied daring that precipitated near-murder at the end of *Typee* quickly disappears with Tommo's first sight of the *Julia*, "a small, slatternly-looking craft, her hull and spars a dingy black, rigging all slack and bleached nearly white, and everything denoting an ill state of affairs aboard" (1). The crew is similarly bedraggled. Nearly half have already deserted, including the three junior mates and three of the four harpooners. And of the rest, "more than half . . . were more or less unwell from a long sojourn in a dissipated port; some of them wholly unfit for duty, one or two dangerously ill, and the rest managing to stand their watch, though they could do but little" (11). Having sojourned in a harder port, Tommo is on first sight disappointed with his rescuers and fondly, though with qualification, recalls his recent hosts: "But how far short of our expectations is oftentimes the fulfillment of the most ardent hopes. Safe aboard of a ship— so long my earnest prayer—with home and friends once more in prospect, I nevertheless felt weighed down by a melancholy that could not be shaken off. It was the thought of never more seeing those who, notwithstanding their desire to retain me a captive, had, upon the whole, treated me so kindly" (7). Throughout *Omoo* he is indeed to be safe, whether on ship or as a wholly different sort of captive imprisoned with his fellow sailors or in his wanderings through the island with Long Ghost. But with the safety comes a kind of intellectual and spiritual sloth that reflects a general state of illness and disease in his surroundings. The mysterious infection in his leg disappears virtually without comment and with no indication of medical treatment. When he arrives on the *Julia* there is talk of amputation (9). Almost immediately he begins to recover, and by the time of the nonviolent mutiny his leg is only an excuse to join the others in claiming illness.

The *Julia's* captain, Lady Guy, is "a young man, pale and slender, more like a sickly counting-house clerk than a bluff sea-captain" (6). "Miss Guy," or "The Cabin Boy," as the men sometimes call him, altering the terms of their contempt, is "essentially a landsman, and though a man of education, no more meant for the sea than a hair-dresser" (11). Moreover, he is ostensibly the sickest of them all, reportedly "fast declining" and even "dying." The characterization is in every respect one of weakness and effeminacy. Even carefully dipped into a warm bath, his cries are "most painful to hear." It is no wonder then that Tommo is uneasy at the thought of "a ship like ours penetrating into these regions" which remain still "wholly unexplored" (42), or that such a whaling ship cannot even spot sperm whales, let alone go after them (59).

Some contrast to Captain Guy is provided by the *Julia's* mate, who oversees the actual running of the ship. "So far as courage, seamanship, and a natural aptitude for keeping riotous spirits in subjection were concerned, no man was better qualified for his vocation than John Jermin . . . the very beau-ideal of the efficient race of short, thick-set men" (12). Though a standout on the *Julia,* "stout little Jermin" is actually a kind of forerunner of Stubb, a tough pugnacious battler with "a heart as big as a bullock's" (13). He has suffered the terrible hardships of shipwreck at sea, like Owen Chase, "the most preposessing-looking whale-hunter" that Melville had ever seen,[2] but he is only a would-be captain. His talent for subjecting "riotous spirits" does not extend to the rebellious members of the crew, who refuse his proffered leadership. The thought that "our fate was absolutely in the hand of the reckless Jermin" (57) merely makes Tommo want to change that fate as soon as possible. Jermin's recklessness is not heroic, nor is his power absolute. His boldness, however, is admirable. He descends into the dark forecastle, where "no prudent officer ever dreams of entering . . . on a hostile visit," to do battle with an insolent seaman named Beauty, but he is shamefully defeated, beaten down, and then sat upon. Still this defeat is more manly than the behavior of Captain Guy who, looking down from above, refuses to heed his fallen mate's raging admonitions to "jump down . . .

and show yourself a man" (21). It is not irrelevant, then, that Jermin's noblest action is in bringing the *Julia* safely through a dangerous channel into port.

The Maori harpooner Bembo, in sharp contrast, is Melville's first strikingly recognizable version of an Ahab, both in the figure he presents and in the brief single action he performs. A solitary man who "held little intercourse with anybody but the mate," Bembo, having no work aboard the *Julia,* spends his time "out on the bowsprit, fishing for albicores with a bone hook; and occasionally he waked all hands up of a dark night dancing some cannibal fandango all by himself on the forecastle. But, on the whole, he was remarkably quiet, though something in his eye showed he was far from being harmless" (16). This is all we hear of Bembo until he becomes the acting captain of the ship when Jermin escorts the invalided Captain Guy to shore for medical treatment. The portrait quickly fills out, as if in testimony to the justice of the promotion. An excellent seaman ("in truth, a better seaman never swore"), Bembo is "far from being liked. A dark, moody savage, everybody but the mate more or less distrusted or feared him. Nor were these feelings unreciprocated. . . . Hard stories, too, were told about him; something, in particular, concerning an hereditary propensity to kill men and eat them." Physically he is impressive, dark-skinned, muscular, and tattooed, with "small, intense eyes, always on the glare. In short, he was none of your effeminate barbarians." Unlike the Polynesians soon to be encountered, Bembo has apparently been unaffected by the ways of civilized life: "A man among us who had sailed with the Mowree on his first voyage . . . told me that he had not changed a particle since then." Among "some queer things this fellow told" is a legendary exploit attesting to the fact that "Bembo was a wild one after a fish" (83). Encountering "a large lone whale," and missing with his harpoons, Bembo performs in a manner worthy of an Ahab, leaping onto the whale's back to kill it.

If this act seems somewhat more professional than titanic,

something of the psychic force that underlies it is soon suggested. A white sailor insults Bembo, a blow is struck, and the two come "together like magnets" in a furious struggle. Though the white "was a practiced bruiser and the savage knew nothing of the art pugilistic," the battle ends with Bembo's teeth at the white man's throat. The others, rushing to save their friend, "hauled the savage off, but not until repeatedly struck on the head would he let go." Bembo is left "glaring and writhing on the deck, without attempting to rise," in a rage that is "absolutely demonic," while the men, "rejoiced at seeing him thus humbled," taunt him "for a cannibal and a coward," presumably because he has not fought according to the "art pugilistic" (102–3). Later that night with the rest of the crew asleep, Bembo attempts a grim revenge. Alone at the helm, "his dark figure slowly rising and falling with the ship's motion against the spangled heavens behind," he deliberately heads the *Julia* toward a coral reef that will destroy it. Tommo, a solitary witness, summons help just in time, and Bembo's "fell purpose" is thwarted. The maddened whale-killer is also, thus, a would-be murderer, and in terms that foreshadow Melville's subsequent avengers. As in the later works, however, the moral implications are ambiguous. Bembo's savagery is matched immediately by the crew's howling for his life, and only the brave and timely intervention of Jermin saves him. He is immediately locked up and never seen again.[3]

In the flabby, decadent world of *Omoo,* Bembo's stay is necessarily brief and incidental, providing at most an image against which the "effeminate barbarians" of Polynesia may be measured and found wanting. Lem Hardy, a renegade Englishman, plays an even smaller role, but his function is more clearly illustrative. Like the introductory portrait of Toby, though not the Richard Tobias Greene who leaves Typee as quickly as he can, Hardy is of a type of vagabond "uncared for by a single soul, without ties, reckless, and impatient of the restraints of civilisation, who are occasionally found quite at home upon the savage islands of the Pacific."

He appears in a canoe filled with natives come to visit the *Julia:* "a stranger, a renegado from Christendom and humanity—a white man in South Sea girdle, and tattooed in the face. A broad blue band stretched across his face from ear to ear, and on his forehead was the taper figure of a blue shark." Tommo, sorely besieged and thinking to compromise, finally had offered up his arm to his Typee hosts for tattooing. His horror at the prospect of a tattoo on the face, a brand that would irrevocably separate him from civilization, is renewed at the sight of Hardy, especially on discovering that he had voluntarily submitted. Moreover, the tattoo itself is now specifically symbolic: "What an impress! Far worse than Cain's—*his* was, perhaps, a wrinkle, or a freckle, which some of our modern cosmetics might have effaced; but the blue shark was a mark indelible, which all the waters of Abana and Pharpar, rivers of Damascus, could never wash out." Hardy's legendary feats fully accord with those of Melville's other branded heroes. Like Tommo, he deserted his ship, but "he had gone ashore as a sovereign power armed with a musket and a bag of ammunition, and ready, if need were, to prosecute war on his own account." And in sharp contrast to Tommo and Long Ghost, who later go to court seeking minor employment but are not even allowed close enough to make their plea, Hardy became "the military leader of the tribe, and war-god of the entire island." Further, like all successful adventurers, he won "three days after landing, the exquisitely tattooed hand of a princess," a huge dowry, "and the sacred protection of an express edict of the Taboo, declaring his person inviolable forever" (32–34).

This heroic, branded demigod provides sharp contrast to both Captain Guy and Jermin. Just before meeting Hardy, Captain Guy and several men go ashore on one of the islands to look for English sailors rumored to be in the vicinity. They are well armed with cutlasses, and Guy, "on this occasion . . . determined to signalize himself," is also carrying pistols. To Tommo and Long Ghost, watching the operation through a spyglass, they seem "diminished to pygmies" once on shore and, lest the irony be missed, it is repeated more pointedly. Cautiously they poke around in a nearby grove, then quickly return to their boat and start back. Suddenly a crowd of natives appears on the shore. Guy turns the boat toward them, gesturing them to come closer, and when they do he fires his pistol into the crowd, missing from that distance but wounding "one poor little fellow" who limps away "in a manner which almost made me itch to get a shot at his assailant" (30).

This inherently comic anecdote is typical of *Omoo,* and the cumulative effect of many such moments is cloying and ultimately disturbing. Virtually all the whites are wildly ineffectual, greedy, drunken, physically and morally weak. And the natives, for their part, frighten too easily or else reveal through both character and action their dependence on the whites and the extent to which they have been corrupted by that dependence. It is not so much that the comedy fails as that it is too precisely emblematic of an explicitly serious, sociological concern: "The depravity among the Polynesians . . . was in a measure unknown before their intercourse with the whites" (223). Where the immediate experience of Tommo in Typee repeatedly contradicts the judgments of the armchair anthropologist and social historian, in *Omoo* the two are compatible throughout, and the underside of the comedy is therefore Tommo's own complete absorption in a soft and purposeless world.

Wilson, the English consul and supreme authority, is not merely "an unprincipled and dissipated man" (83), but a weak one, small and effeminate like his good friend Captain Guy. A thorough landsman and nontraveler who has never been to Europe or America, he begins to strut and act his office only after the *Julia* has entered the harbor: "The truth was, he felt safer *now,* than when outside the reef" (119). A petulant, womanish sort, his ineffectuality, though ridiculous, is in large part responsible for the miserable conditions on the island, as is his counterpart's for the sorry state of affairs aboard the *Julia.*[4] And though the crew is vaudevillian

(Ropey, Chips and Bungs, Beauty, Black Dan, and Jingling Joe), and the captain's own illness a comic sham, two actual shipboard deaths do occur, to no one's special concern except for the disposition of their belongings.[5] The natives are in a similar state. Jim the pilot shirks his duties, as does fat jovial Captain Bob, their jailer, who "bustled about, like an old woman seeing the children to bed" (136). Much of the humor, in fact, specifically derives from the incongruities of natives imitating whites, much as Shakespeare's clowns and rustics imitate their masters. Thus Arheetoo, a local launderer, "wished to have manufactured a set of certificates, purporting to come from certain man-of-war and merchant captains, known to have visited the island; recommending him as one of the best getters-up of fine linen in all Polynesia" (195). And Kooloo, a "blade" befriended by Tommo, is seen "standing up in the congregation in all the bravery of a striped calico shirt, with the skirts rakishly adjusted over a pair of white sailor trousers, and hair well anointed with cocoa-nut oil," ogling the girls "with an air of supreme satisfaction" (209). One such girl is Miss Ideea, who explains to Tommo that she is a " 'Mickonaree ena' (church member here) . . . laying her hand upon her mouth, and a strong emphasis on the adverb. In the same way, and with similar exclamations, she touched her eyes and hands. This done, her whole air changed in an instant; and she gave me to understand, by unmistakable gestures, that in certain other respects she was not exactly a 'mickonaree' " (210–11). White or native, the world through which Tommo now moves, taking pleasure but no clear knowledge, is both corrupt and diminished. Entirely absorbed in it, he loses the identity acquired in *Typee* and, renamed, he becomes the Paul half of the team of Peter and Paul, one of several such acts in *Omoo*.

From the mutiny that is not a mutiny and the prison that is not a prison, he and Long Ghost (Peter) proceed to a journey which, though comparable to Tommo's in *Typee,* is neither dark nor difficult. The valley of Martair, their first stop, resembles Typee only in physical background. Its steep cliffs are "gay with flowering shrubs, or hung with pendulous vines, swinging blossoms in the air." Though a wilderness, it is "a wilderness of woodland; with links of streams flashing through, and narrow pathways, fairly tunnelled through masses of foliage" (239). Their new employers, Zeke and Shorty, a Mutt and Jeff team, live "all alone in this wild place," but comfortably, as farmers "raising supplies for whaling-vessels" (241). Like Melville's other vagabonds, they are sailors who deserted, but for "embarking in the business" and not solely for adventure. The place chosen for a happy, industrious, bachelor life together (they reject the offer of native wives, unlike Lem Hardy) is "the quietest place imaginable," except for the mosquitoes (242). One burlesque routine follows another in the valley of Martair; Melville makes full use of his two pairs of comics, presenting Peter and Paul as inept farmers, incompetent hunters, clever shirkers whose cleverness consistently boomerangs. One noteworthy moment is their mock-heroic battle against the valley's single danger, the mosquitoes. Driven from the house "after a valiant defence," they take refuge in "an old war-canoe, crumbling to dust," but which still bears on its stern a "heraldic" looking device that Long Ghost "maintained to be the arms of the royal House of Pomaree . . . two sharks with the talons of hawks clawing a knot left projecting from the wood" (258). Even in this relic of once-glorious times they are not entirely safe. First the mosquitoes return and then, when they escape by paddling out a way and anchoring, they awaken in the morning to discover that they are adrift and almost floated onto the reef. This "narrow escape," so unlike the similar moment when Tommo woke from an uneasy sleep to find mad Bembo working his revenge, is characteristic of the dangers undergone in these surroundings.

The high point of their journey is Tamai, an isolated inland village, attainable only "by a lonely pathway, leading through the wildest scenery in the world" (278). There they expect to find delicious fish, fruit, and "the most beautiful and un-

sophisticated women in the entire Society Group" (278). In
Typee the expectations were quite different: "Naked houris—
cannibal banquets—groves of cocoa-nut—coral reefs—tatooed
chiefs . . . *heathenish rites and human sacrifices*" (4). To put
themselves "in travelling trim" for so difficult a journey,
Long Ghost changes into "the ancient costume of Tahiti,"
and Tommo assumes "an Eastern turban" (280), which he
later embellishes "with a band of flame-coloured ribbon; the
two long ends of which streaming behind, sailor-fashion,
still preserved for me the Eastern title bestowed by Long
Ghost" (335). Unlike Taji, whose Eastern dress heralds a
transfiguration by which his journey into unknown worlds
is made possible, Tommo's sole expectation is to create "no
small sensation" in the "green saloons" of Tamai. The trip
itself is predictably pleasant. The wildest scenery in the
world turns out to be "a green cool hollow" easily "descended
with a bound" (281). Midway through their climb up the
other side of the valley, they stop for a hearty hot lunch and
a nap. Resuming, they gain the mountain top, and "there,
to our surprise, lay the lake and village of Tamái. We had
thought it a good league off." The descent is made "with
whoop and halloo," and Tamai proves pleasant if not wondrous.

In the decayed world of Tahiti, the tension central to *Typee*
between civilized man and savage, white man and dark,
slackens completely, and the result is a soft, compromise
world, false and cheapening to both. Like Miss Ideea, it is
all "mickonaree" from the neck up, a compromise less serious
even than Tommo's willingness to have his arm tattooed.
The natives of Tamai, "being so remote from ecclesiastical
jurisdiction," retain something of their former ways. According to report, "many heathenish games and dances still
secretly lingered in their valley" (283). Like tourists determined to get a look at the real Tamai, Tommo and Long
Ghost induce their hosts to present "an old-fashioned
'hevar'," a "genuine pagan fandango," which of course
proves to be entirely different from the "cannibal fandango"

Bembo danced on dark nights alone on the *Julia*. Though the hevar takes place late at night to avoid detection and there is "a great deal of mystery about getting up the dance" (284), it is danced entirely by girls. Its rhythm is languid, and its spirit theatrically sensuous ("Ahloo! Ahloo! again cry the dance queens"). There is surely an ironic pun in its title: "the dance of the backsliding girls of Tamai."

The implicit contrast to Typee is furthered by the presence of a genuine mystery in Tamai. In a chapter aptly titled "Mysterious," a "little old man of a most hideous aspect" follows them around, and "when unobserved by others, plucked at our garments, making frightful signs for us to go along with him somewhere, and see something" (288). Finally, after several days Tommo decides to follow the "beckoning" old man to a filthy hut where the great mystery of Tamai is revealed. "Looking round fearfully, as if dreading a surprise, he commenced turning over and over the rubbish in one corner. At last, he clutched a calabash, stained black, and with the neck broken off; on one side of it was a large hold. Something seemed to be stuffed away in the vessel; and after a deal of poking at the aperture, a musty old pair of sailor trousers was drawn forth; and, holding them up eagerly, he inquired how many pieces of tobacco I would give for them" (289). As in Typee with the tattooist, Tommo immediately runs away, chased by the screaming old man. But if distinctly minor, it is clearly a happier mystery than the three shrunken heads; and shortly after this "inglorious" adventure, Tommo proposes that they settle down in Tamai because it is a thriving place. Long Ghost agrees, but soon after they are forced to flee before the missionaries.

Another resemblance to *Typee*, whether intentional or not, is that the penultimate action raises the question of Tommo's remaining more or less permanently among the natives. (The final episode is of course concerned with his leave-taking.) In *Omoo*, however, Tommo seems genuinely to want to remain. When the plan to settle in Tamai is foiled, they decide to seek positions in Pomaree's court at Taloo, an expectation not "altogether Quixotic. In the train of many Polynesian princes, roving whites are frequently found; gentlemen pensioners of state, basking in the tropical sunshine of the court, and leading the pleasantest lives in the world. Upon islands little visited by foreigners, the first seaman that settles down is generally domesticated in the family of the head chief or king. . . . These men generally marry well; often—like Hardy of Hannamanoo—into the blood royal" (292). But Tommo is no Hardy, whose legendary name reverberates so majestically through the islands. And he is not the first seaman to settle in Tahiti, though he had such an opportunity in Typee and rejected it.

In the world of Polynesia the opportunities for pioneering on a grand scale are limited, except for the few like Hardy whose nature is especially suited to it. Specific instances of the "roving whites" who serve as Tommo's examples are "a vagabond Welshman [who] bends his knee as cupbearer to his cannibal majesty," and "an old man-of-war's-man [who] fills the post of barber to the king." Still more menial are the court entertainers, "idle rascals [who] receive no fixed salary, being altogether dependent upon the casual bounty of their master." Such men are in fact fit counterparts of Long Ghost and his straight man. "Billy Loon, a jolly little negro, tricked out in a soiled blue jacket, studded all over with rusty bell-buttons, and garnished with shabby gold lace, is the royal drummer and pounder of the tambourine. Joe, a wooden-legged Portuguese, who lost his leg by a whale, is violinist; and Mordecai, as he is called, a villainous-looking scamp, going about with his cups and balls in a side pocket, diverts the court with his jugglery" (293). Though Tommo insists that "it was not as strolling players, nor as footmen out of employ," that they expect employment, he is willing to be practical about it: "But in our most lofty aspirations, we by no means lost sight of any minor matters which might help us to promotion. The doctor had informed me, that he excelled in playing the fiddle. I now suggested, that as soon as we arrived in Partoowye, we should endeavour to borrow a violin for him; or if this could not be done, that he should manufacture some kind of a substitute, and, thus equipped, apply for an audience of the queen" (294). The lengthy preparations, as in many similar instances throughout *Omoo,* come to nothing; they do not get close enough even to voice their small requests before being thrown out.

Rumors were previously heard of "a solitary whaler . . . lying in the harbour, wooding and watering, and said to be in want of men" (292). On arriving in Taloo, they find the *Leviathan,* and Tommo is impressed by its appearance. After their abortive foray into Pomaree's court, a place peopled by women and expressly not "in want of men," the turn is to the sea. "Disappointed in going to court, we determined upon going to sea . . . weary somewhat of life in Imeeo, like all sailors ashore, I at last pined for the billows" (370). This abrupt wish is enhanced by the general excellence of the *Leviathan* and its captain, "an uncommonly tall, robust, fine-looking man, in the prime of life." Everything is suddenly on the upsurge. They meet the third mate, "a right jolly fellow," who tells them that "a cosier old craft never floated; and the captain was the finest man in the world." It develops that he is also perceptive. Though he will ship Tommo, he refuses to have anything to do with Long Ghost, taking him for "an exceedingly problematical character" (372). The doctor, it turns out, is in complete agreement. He "laughingly declared, that the Vineyarder must be a penetrating fellow. He then insisted upon my going to sea in the ship, since he well knew how anxious I was to leave. As for himself, on second thoughts, he was no sailor; and although 'landsmen' very often compose part of a whaler's crew, he did not quite relish the idea of occupying a position so humble. In short, he had made up his mind to tarry awhile in Imeeo" (373).

The ending, though convenient and perfunctory, is none-theless curiously bracing. The amusement has long since ceased; like Tommo himself, we are "weary somewhat" of this impossibly repetitive life—from Martair to Tamai, back to Martair and finally to Taloo, "a place from which we were not far off when at Tamai; but wishing to see as much of the island as we could, we preferred returning to Martair, and then going round by way of the beach" (291). Yet everywhere, what they see they have already seen. The natives are the same and interchangeable, as is the scenery. Once Tommo says a last goodbye to Long Ghost and boards the *Leviathan,* there is a new vigorous tone and mood, a quickening, like a fresh wind after a calm. "Crowding all sail, we braced the yards square; and, the breeze freshening, bowled straight away from the land. Once more the sailor's cradle rocked under me, and I found myself rolling in my gait. By noon, the island had gone down in the horizon; and all before us was the wide Pacific" (375).

The final sentence, echoed in specifically Miltonic circumstances at the outset of *Mardi,* is more than allusive. From the first sight of the *Julia* at the opening of the novel, there has been no appreciable movement either of action or of developing character. The initial images of sickness, softness, and decay overspread the book, but there is no corresponding reaction from Tommo that might provide dramatic energy or any kind of moral stance. Except for Bembo's brief outburst, nothing of moment takes place through the entire work, though "hard stories" are occasionally told to provide a tangential gloss on the static happenings. As in *Typee* the process is one of coverings stripped away, but the core beneath is neither hard nor true, terrible nor ugly, but merely small and predictable. Repeatedly Melville overplays the approach to a situation and then ridiculously underplays its realization, as in the visits to Tamai and to Pomaree's court. The back door to the prison stockade opens almost as soon as the front door closes on them. Virtually the instant they decide to settle in Tamai, missionaries appear and they are sent running. Once all the jokes about inept hunters have been exhausted, they suddenly shoot and kill a small calf and its mother. Jermin, brandishing his cutlass, chases frightened natives who abruptly stop, disarm him, and take him off to Wilson's, where he proceeds to drink the night away with Guy and Wilson. For every action there is a negating counteraction. As in the story of the clothing salesman of Tamai, at the core of every mystery is a musty old pair of trousers. And then suddenly, at the very end as Tommo once again faces the sea, there is for the first time a genuine sense of possibility.

Although the continual presence of an overwhelming corruption (disease, drunkenness, avarice, envy, gluttony, lechery, sloth)[6] tends always toward dark satire, *Omoo* never realizes such aims. The instances of corruption are themselves too petty, diminished to a point where any serious moral standards are inapplicable. The final effect is one of tedium. Even Tommo, the readiest audience for Long Ghost's jokes, is ultimately bored with them. Instead of the hard descent into the valley of savages, the movement in *Omoo* is lateral to a land-oriented world where sailors go expressly to avoid the sea. On this journey Long Ghost is a guide, a teacher, and an index to the world through which they move.[7] Long Ghost is called a landsman—"among the sailors, he looked like a land-crane blown off the sea, and consorting with petrels" (91). He is not only knowledgeable but actually at home there in a way that Tommo is not. The men on the *Julia* enjoy his company because he makes them laugh. They defer to him, and Tommo with him, already basking in his light, but only as "distinguished guests" (44). The natives love him because, like the sailors, they "delight in a wag" (266). Though miserably hoodwinked by him, Zeke and Shorty admire him all the more for it and try to find easy work for him to do, such as cooking, the woman's work usually done by Shorty. Slowly Tommo realizes with some pique that Long Ghost is, against all logic, "rated far above myself" (275).

The dominant energy of *Omoo*, then, derives not from a Promethean hero but from this amiable wag whose course throughout is a kind of progress in foolishness until he becomes expressly an actor "assuming the part of a Merry Andrew" (318). The example he offers his young cohort is simply one of accommodation—of getting along and making do in an effete, corrupt society. Tommo, in *Omoo,* is neither unmanned by terror nor brutalized, but is literally depersonalized. He becomes Paul, the shorter one, the straight man, the nondescript. In its way, however, it has been a useful and an educational experience for him. If the terms of his involvement are small, it is a small, constricted world and he is learning to reject it. His final impulse is to the sea. And Melville, in his next work, hazards the boldest undertaking yet of his young career.

★ 3 ★

MARDI IS MELVILLE'S COMING OF AGE. It is his first major effort and also the first novel in which he assumes the character and essential postures of his major questing heroes. Where his first two novels attempt to fictionalize a personal experience, his third is a bold and studied attempt to erect a wholly imaginative analogue to his rapidly complicating state of mind. Important links between the author and his work are insistently reiterated throughout the novel. The hero's flight into the unknown is Melville's own; his discoveries in the allegorical world of Mardi, those of *Mardi* itself.

In a letter to John Murray dated March 25, 1848, Melville described the writing of *Mardi* as a kind of personal catharsis: "Proceeding in my narrative of *facts* I began to feel an incurable distaste for the same; & a longing to plume my pinions for a flight, & felt irked, cramped & fettered by plodding along with dull common places,—So suddenly standing [abandoning?] the thing alltogether, I went to work heart & soul at a romance which is now in fair progress, since I had worked at it under an earnest ardor. . . . My romance . . . is something new I assure you, & original if nothing more." He then goes on to explain something of the strategy: "it opens like a true narrative—like *Omoo* for example, on ship board—& the romance & poetry of the thing thence grow continually, till it becomes a story wild enough I assure you & with a meaning too."[1] Though the wildness—as Melville meant it—is at best no virtue and the singular meaning, such as it is, is of dubious educational value, there is in *Mardi* a private involvement so deep, pervasive, and above all so lasting that the work may be considered virtually as a touchstone to the man. Characters, concepts, even phrases from *Mardi* recur throughout all his subsequent work. More significant—if less immediately accessible—it represents Melville's first comprehensive exploration of his own distinctive heart of darkness.

The harried young novice Pierre, working at his wildly overambitious first novel, is surely Melville's retrospective view of his own experience in writing *Mardi*. Although Pierre becomes a murderer while Melville himself had gone on to *Moby-Dick,* the connection between black deeds and black perceptions is never far below the surface throughout the novels. Melville's psychic involvement in all his fiction after *Mardi* is everywhere attested to. "I have written a wicked book," he wrote of *Moby-Dick* to Hawthorne, "and feel spotless as the lamb."[2] More is involved here than the general purgation that ideally results from writing as a private act of exploration whereby the writer undergoes transubstantially an ordeal which could not otherwise be endured. Like Emerson on the one side and Poe on the other, Melville increasingly viewed himself as the possessed poet, beset by visionary angels and demons. And the role, as might be expected, tallies almost precisely with the character and situation of his questing heroes. The difference, as indicated in another letter to Hawthorne, dated June 29, 1851, is that, unlike his heroes, Melville is consistently returning to the civilized world. "This most persuasive season has now for weeks recalled me from certain crotchetty and over-doleful chimaeras, the like of which men like you and me and some others, forming a chain of God's posts round the world, must be content to encounter now and then, and fight them the best way we can. But come they will,—for, in the boundless, trackless, but still glorious wild wilderness through which these outposts run, the Indians do sorely abound, as well as the insignificant but still stinging mosquitoes."[3]

The concept of the artist as a sometime sojourner in the primeval wilderness, buttressed by the specific reference to Indian-fighting, foreshadows the distinction made in *The Confidence-Man* between the "Indian-hater *par excellence*" and the "diluted Indian-hater." The Indian-hater par excellence is an Ahab figure. From infancy he is trained to oppose Indians, as Ahab, raised in Nantucket, was trained to hunt whales. After "some signal outrage" at their hands, he goes through a preliminary stage in which he ponders his injury, and slowly swells to heroic proportions. Finally, "he makes a vow, the hate of which is a vortex from whose suction scarce the remotest chip of the guilty race may reasonably feel secure." Renouncing all human bonds, he "commits himself to the forest primeval; there, so long as life shall be his, to act upon a calm, cloistered scheme of strategical, implacable, and lonesome vengeance." Thus the Indian-hater par excellence can by definition never really be known: "There can be no biography of an Indian-hater *par excellence,* any more than one of a sword-fish, or other deep-sea denizen. . . . The career of the Indian-hater *par excellence* has the impenetrability of the fate of a lost steamer. Doubtless, events, terrible ones, have happened, must have happened; but the powers that be in nature have taken order that they shall never become news." Saved from the "closing vortex" of the sinking *Pequod,* Ishmael fulfills the predestined newspaper headline imagined in the first chapter, "Whaling voyage by one Ishmael." As such he performs the basic function of the diluted Indian-hater, a man "whose heart proves not so steely as his brain. Soft enticements of domestic life too often draw him from the ascetic trail; a monk who apostatizes to the world at times. Like a mariner, too, though much abroad, he may have a wife and family in some green harbor which he does not forget." An Indian-hater par excellence is an ideal of heroic perfection, "peeping out but once an age," and known only because "the diluted Indian-hater, although the vacations he permits himself impair the keeping of the character . . . by his very infirmity, enables us to form surmises, however inadequate, of what Indian-hating in its perfection is" (*CM,* 200–2).

The distinction is specifically anticipated in *Mardi,* as well as dramatically embodied there. Shortly after the voyagers begin the quest for the lost Yillah, Babbalanja, discoursing on the vanity of human aspiration, insists that the only way man may truly perpetuate his name is to "carve it . . . deep into a ponderous stone, and sink it, face downward, into the sea; for the unseen foundations of the deep are more enduring than the palpable tops of the mountains" (I.246). Some indication of the process by which this may be accomplished is provided in an accompanying fable of the origin of the great rock of Pella, an image that Melville reverts to in *Pierre* and *Israel Potter* in contexts directly suggestive of the White Whale. Even in *Mardi,* in fact, the analogy is peculiarly pointed: "Passing under this cliff was like finding yourself, as some sea-hunters unexpectedly have, beneath the open, upper jaw of a whale; which, descending, infallibly entombs you" (I.243). The legend itself prefigures Ahab in still other ways. In mythic times "a band of evil-minded, envious goblins, furlongs in stature and with immeasurable arms" attempted to steal one of the Mardian islands. Daylight interrupted their "audacious thieving" and, leaving the island upside down with "its foundations in air, they precipitately fled; in their great haste, deserting a comrade, vainly struggling to liberate his foot caught beneath the overturned land." The cries of this lamed and ineffectual Enceladan awaken the angry god Upi, who promptly destroys him, thus assuring him the immortality described by Babbalanja. Upi's first arrow, which misses its mark, alters the landscape eternally; his second sinks the "slain giant . . . prone to the bottom" of the sea, where the remains are "petrified into white ribs of coral," eternally visible to man. To pass on this legend of ultimate aspiration and defiance is the responsibility of Mohi the historian. Babbalanja the philosopher marks its meanings. The narrator who has somehow mysteriously returned to write their story fulfills, like Ishmael, the function of the diluted Indian-hater. The narrator who remains to become Taji, the "unreturning wanderer," the "hunter that never rests," seems destined to become an Indian-hater par excellence.

The "incurable distaste" Melville described to Murray has its fictional counterpart in Ishmael's aversion to the commonplace lives of landsmen "tied to counters, nailed to benches, clinched to desks." More immediately, Melville's state of mind as he began to write *Mardi* is precisely and deliberately figured in his initially nameless narrator's "bitter impatience of our monotonous craft" (I.3). The *Arcturion* is "exceedingly dull" in all respects. Like Tommo, the narrator is as a "prisoner in Newgate," but it is a secure, normal, civilized world ("like *Omoo* for example") which now binds him. In the second chapter, entitled "A Calm," this condition is more sharply objectified as an existential state of living death, "a state of existence where existence itself seems suspended." Supreme authority is specifically questioned as "horrible thoughts overtake him as to the captain's competency to navigate his ship," and "he begins to feel anxious concerning his soul" (I.9). To this limbo of unbeing, so like something out of Poe, Thoreau's reaction is sharp and direct: "If we are really dying, let us hear the rattle in our throats and feel cold in the extremities; if we are alive, let us go about our business."[4] Melville's response, though comparable, involves a quite different sort of business: "He wills to go; to get away from the calm; as ashore he would avoid the plague. But he can not; and how foolish to revolve expedients. It is more hopeless than a bad marriage in a land where there is no Doctors' Commons. He has taken the ship to wife, for better or for worse, for calm or for gale; and she is not to be shuffled off. With yards akimbo, she says unto him scornfully, as the old beldam said to the little dwarf: 'Help yourself' " (I.9). The will to go is no death wish, but rather, like

Thoreau's, a wish to be reborn. Melville's isolatos shuffle off this mortal coil in order to begin a lonely, terrible descent into an ultimate darkness wherein lies Babbalanja's anonymous immortality.

Committed to "sea in an open boat, and a thousand miles from land" (I.35), the narrator and his comrade Jarl are embarked on a new life. In the black night they have made their escape by means of a mock drowning. The following chapter, which opens at dawn, is titled "The Watery World Is All Before Them." From the first, there is no question where they are heading. Addressing the *Arcturion*'s captain just before the calm dissipates belief in him, the narrator speaks with a portentous omniscience: "It's very hard to carry me off this way to purgatory. I shipped to go elsewhere" (I.5). Once embarked in their frail boat, they are truly little dwarfs, "a mere toy . . . to the billows, that jeeringly shouldered us from crest to crest, as from hand to hand lost souls may be tossed along by the chain of shades which enfilade the route to Tartarus" (I.35–36). But the theology is not Christian, though the terms would seem Dantean. The purgative journey through hell demands complete participation in its rites. If it is bold, heretical defiance of an ultimate authority to abandon the world of "Doctors' Commons," faith has already been seriously sapped by the fact of the calm. The question is whether to comply like a dwarf or desperately to defy in full knowledge of inevitable destruction, like Ahab pitting himself "all mutilated" against the transcendent White Whale. The ultimate heroic posture demands full awareness of the terrible irony of the old beldam's mocking advice to the little dwarf. Ahab's apotheosis comes in his address to his "fiery father": "No fearless fool now fronts thee. I own thy speechless, placeless power; but to the last gasp of my earthquake life will dispute its unconditional, unintegral mastery in me" (II.281). It is only through defiance that "a personality stands here," that the living dead breathe, the voiceless speak, and the becalmed stir and finally find their place.

Taji is manifestly no Ahab. His course only takes him with a tortuous slowness to the point where he sets out to become Melville's archetypal Indian-hater. The conceptual development from *Typee* has already been suggested. *Mardi*'s narrator deserts ship in the middle of the sea; Tommo does so in port. Tommo's most heroic moment is at the very end, when he nearly kills a tattooed savage who rises to the surface after the abortive blow, glaring with unforgettable ferocity. His counterpart in *Mardi*, at the virtual start of his career, actually does kill an old native priest, and one whose tattoos, moreover, would seem to indicate a transcendent authority (I.151). His progress, however, is steadily upward to the role of the Promethean quester. With the discovery of the *Parki*, he becomes the captain of his own ship, his crew two savages and the aboriginal Jarl. He takes on corresponding vigor and authority as well as appropriate new clothes. Dressed in the "free, flowing, and Eastern" robes of an emir (I.147), he is more in tune with both his increasing status and his savage surroundings. The rescue of Yillah makes him at once a savior and a murderer. Landing in Mardi fully transformed, he immediately acquires an identity as a "superior being . . . White Taji, a sort of half-and-half deity . . . ranking among their inferior ex-officio demi-gods" (I.191). After a brief idyllic interlude, Yillah mysteriously disappears, and Taji becomes a quester.

The psychosexual implications of Yillah, though intriguing, ing, are not pertinent here. It is enough merely that she represents some ultimate ideal and that Taji pursues her. Initially the conception seems Christian: a pure white maiden saved from pagan immolation by the wandering Christian hero, as the narrator initially sees himself. She is, for instance, strangely drawn to Jarl's tattoo of the crucifixion. Later Taji images her in the same transcendent role, swearing "upon her white arms crossed" that Yillah is "the earthly semblance of that sweet vision, that haunted my earliest thoughts" (I.184). But as in the subsequent novels, whiteness is ambiguous. Like Moby-Dick, Yillah is an albino, an unnatural

white in a brown-skinned community. The sweet vision has
its darker side, instanced in the murder and a persistent
guilt that leads Taji almost immediately to question the purity
of his motives. His guilt is embodied in the three pursuing
avengers; the three emissaries of dark Hautia who regularly
appear in conjunction with the three avengers seem to represent a sexual guilt, deriving from Taji's originally impure
motives. Hautia, an exotic, sexual counterpoise to ethereal
Yillah, plays the conventional role of the seductive en-
chantress, a Queen of the Night, the Circe who keeps Odys-
seus from his faithful Penelope. But Melville uses the
traditional morality for other purposes. Hautia's emissaries
appear almost as soon as Taji and Yillah reach Mardi, but
Taji pays no attention to them and they leave. Only after
Yillah disappears do they return to dog him through his
travels. Although continually unsuccessful as seducers, they
nonetheless achieve their goal. The schematic association of
seducers and avengers connects Hautia with Taji's initial
crime and hence with Yillah, cause of the murder. As the
search continues, and Taji grows more and more Byronically
deranged, the early moral concerns blur entirely. His guilt is
subjugated: "Nor does the ghost, that these pale spectres
would avenge, at all disquiet me. The priest I slew, but to
gain her, now lost; and I would slay again to bring her back"
(II.118). He would follow Yillah even into absolute darkness: "I am the hunter that never rests! the hunter without a
home! She I seek still flies before; and I will follow, though
she lead me beyond the reef; through sunless seas; and into
night and death" (II.382). Finally, having searched everywhere else, he goes to Hautia's kingdom, "called Flozella-a-
Nina, or The-Last-Verse-of-the-Song," recognizing that light
and dark are in some way connected: "In some mysterious
way seemed Hautia and Yillah connected. But Yillah was
all beauty, and innocence; my crown of felicity; my heaven
below;—and Hautia, my whole heart abhorred. Yillah I
sought; Hautia sought me. One openly beckoned me here; the

other dimly allured me there. Yet now was I wildly dreaming to find them together" (II.386).

The surrender to Hautia is brief and only dimly sexual. Hautia and Taji "dive in deep waters" for pearls, but for Taji it is "bootless deep diving." "Down, down! down, down," he goes to no avail while "to Hautia, one shallow plunge reveals many Golcondas" (II.396). Taji rejects her offer to dive together and see "strange things," but only because she cannot help him. "Show me that which I seek, and I will dive with thee, straight through the world, till we come up in oceans unknown." Finally she tells him of "another cavern," where he finds a lake with channels leading to the sea, and in it, "round and round, a gleaming form slow circled in the deepest eddies;—white, and vaguely Yillah" (II.398). Again he plunges in, but is driven back by the currents. In a wild frenzy, he leaps into his boat to follow. This time, however, he goes alone. Accepting his hopeless fate, he turns completely from the world. "Let *me*, then, be the unreturning wanderer. The helm! By Oro, I will steer my own fate, old man. —Mardi, farewell!" This absolute assertion of self is "the last, last crime." He seizes the helm, his friends leap frantically from the ship, and Taji cries out, in Ahab's pride but not in his language, "Now, I am my own soul's emperor; and my first act is abdication! Hail! realm of shades." The three avengers fall in line, and the book ends. "And thus, pursuers and pursued flew on, over an endless sea" (II.400).

It is easy to ridicule all this. The final scenes, especially those in Hautia's bower, are so grotesque as to seem parodic. "Come! let us sin, and be merry," she calls, summoning "wine, wine, wine! and lapfuls of flowers," before coyly asking "did'st ever dive in deep waters, Taji?" (II.395). But however absurd the result, Melville is in deadly earnest. It is merely ironic that the letter to Evert Duyckinck in praise of "the whole corps of thought-divers, that have been diving and coming up again with blood shot eyes since the world began,"[5] was written on the same day that Richard Bentley agreed to publish *Mardi* in England. It is no less than astonishing that little more than a year later Melville would be writing *Moby-Dick*.

The allegory of the quest for Yillah, though central, actually occupies only a small portion of *Mardi*. Of the 195 chapters only 31 are taken up with Taji's quest, and of these 14 represent the initial encounter and 6 the final movement. The remainder deal with their brief, idyllic life together and with the recurrence of the temptresses and avengers over the course of the journey. Moreover, Taji is so unconvincing a hero in part because Melville has chosen to define him strictly in terms of his function as quester. Once he meets and loses Yillah, his entire role consists of the literal performance of his quest. His companions, however, to some extent fill out the character who will eventually become Ahab. Through Jarl (the "aboriginal tar"), the half-civilized Samoa, King Media, and above all Babbalanja, who carries the intellectual burdens of the quest, Melville provides a kind of composite identity which accords in several key respects with the essential character of the questing hero.

An islander from the isle of Skye—and so nicknamed "the Skyeman"—Jarl is "an old Norseman to behold." But where Ahab is like the ancient Viking kings, Jarl is only a debased descendant. Like Toby, Bulkington, and others, he is of that class of sea rovers Melville calls *"Isolatoes."* Like Queequeg and Ishmael, Jarl and the narrator are "chummies," a shipboard state defined as "a Fides-Achates-ship, a league of offence and defence, a co-partnership of chests and toilets, a bond of love and good feeling, and a mutual championship of the absent one" (I.17). They do not, however, remain so very long. In *Typee* and *Omoo*, where the chummies are equals, they are as interchangeable as their names: Tommo and Toby, Paul and Peter. The isolation requisite to heroic stature is incompatible with the practice of chummying, and as the narrator begins his slow ascent from his role as common seaman to that of Taji, abdicating emperor of his own soul, Jarl is necessarily dropped out. Whereas the primitive Samoa reacts to Yillah with a kind of superstitious reverence, Jarl considers her "as a sort of intruder . . . who might lead me astray" (I.171). Though he begins the quest with them, he finds his proper place as chummy to "that jolly old lord Borabolla," a king too jolly, fat, and undignified to be rated a demigod, with whom he remains until killed by the avengers.

The primitive element in the Promethean syndrome is provided in *Mardi* by Samoa, whose "style of tattooing . . . seemed rather incomplete; his marks embracing but a vertical half of his person, from crown to sole; the other side being free from the slightest stain" (I.112).[6] This colorful, half-civilized savage is also the first of Melville's mutilated heroes. Badly wounded in his defense of the *Parki,* he has been forced to amputate his own arm, an act which earns him kinship with "great Nelson himself" and other famous, similarly battle-scarred heroes who "like anvils, will stand a deal of hammering" (I.89–90).

Babbalanja, the philosopher of the group, is the novel's most resonant character and the clearest adumbration yet of Captain Ahab. He carries all the intellectual burdens of the quest that Taji merely exemplifies. It is Babbalanja who articulates the controlling ideas of anonymous immortality and of the necessary descent into baptismal fires in order to achieve great heights. In both tone and content, his words continually anticipate Ahab: "I am intent upon the essence of things; the mystery that lieth beyond; the elements of the tear which much laughter provoketh; that which is beneath the seeming; the precious pearl within the shaggy oyster. I probe the circle's center; I seek to evolve the inscrutable" (II.36). The process, as with Ahab, is expressly conceived in terms of battle: "I but fight against the armed and crested Lies of Mardi, that like a host assail me. I am stuck full of darts; but, tearing them from out me, gasping, I discharge them whence they come." And the battle itself is both destructive and dehumanizing. The arrows returned, he "slowly dropped, and fell reclining; then lay motionless as the marble Gladiator, that for centuries has been dying" (II.128). The trance, as with Ahab, is characteristic. Babbalanja is also possessed by a demonic incubus called Azzageddi, who plays a role similar to Fedallah's in *Moby-Dick*.

Babbalanja's inquiry into the essential mystery of things has a dramatic movement which from the outset parallels Taji's allegorical quest. Having "often expressed the most ardent desire to visit every one of the isles, in quest of some object, mysteriously hinted," Babbalanja responds to the idea of the journey with special interest and even, it would seem, a veiled awareness of its meanings. "Your pursuit is mine," he tells Taji. "Where'er you search, I follow" (I.230). Though the strategy falters as Taji fades into the background, the two are clearly intended as analogous deep-divers. Babbalanja's need to "probe the circle's center," akin to Ahab's compulsion toward the final vortex, begins with an intellectual "dive into the deeps of things" (II.75). Gradually the descent takes on a familiar character: just outside the palace of fierce King Bello, they pause momentarily afraid, then proceed at Babbalanja's urging that the center of peril is safer than the circumference (II.178). By the journey's end, Babbalanja has gained his goal, and though all he finds there is what he knew at the beginning—the inescapable fact of mortality— the very process of journeying has taught him to accept the hard conditions of his dwarfdom. A "death-cloud" suddenly sweeps past them, "one vast water-spout" hurrying before it "a thousand prows" filled with people desperate to escape. But only Babbalanja and his friends avoid the ensuing maelstrom because, at his urging, they merely up oars and wait, making no attempt to flee. "All things come of Oro; if we must drown, let Oro drown us" (II.314). The danger, once past, is conclusively examined: "We die by land, and die by sea; we die by earthquakes, famines, plagues, and wars; by fevers, agues; woe, or mirth excessive. This mortal air is one wide pestilence, that kills us all at last. Whom the

Death-cloud spares, sleeping, dies in silent watches of the night. He whom the spears of many battles could not slay, dies of a grape-stone, beneath the vine-clad bower he built to shade declining years. We die, because we live. But none the less does Babbalanja quake. And if he flies not, 'tis because he stands the centre of a circle; its every point a levelled dart; and every bow bent back:—a twang, and Babbalanja dies" (II.315). As with Ahab, the stature is heroic because the perception of mortality does not wholly temper the fears that are inseparable from it. Babbalanja is "no fearless fool," and therefore, as in *Moby-Dick,* "a personality stands here."

Yet no matter how maddened and bedeviled by his demonic Azzageddi, Babbalanja is never thrust beyond the farthest limit of psychic endurance. "You are on the verge," Media tells him repeatedly in one wild fit, "take not the leap" (II.157). A balance is consistently maintained between sanity and madness, though the weights are gradually shifted. As Babbalanja nears Serenia, the verge is not of ultimate madness but of total acceptance. Just prior to the advent of the death-cloud, he suddenly begins to preach a lengthy Christian sermon which seemingly contradicts everything heretofore believed. "The soul needs no mentor, but Oro; and Oro, without proxy. . . . Fellow-men! the ocean we would sound is unfathomable; and however much we add to our line, when it is out, we feel not the bottom. Let us be truly lowly, then; not lifted up with a Pharisaic humility. We crawl not like worms; nor wear we the liveries of angels" (II.301–2). Then abruptly he goes mad again, raving the gibberish language of Azzageddi. This outburst of madness following an extensive period of composure and conviction almost precisely reverses earlier instances. "Are you content?" Media had asked after Babbalanja discovered an ancient book by his favorite author, the pagan philosopher Bardianna. The answer seems to touch on every issue crucial to *Mardi.*

"I am not content. The mystery of mysteries is still a mystery. How this author came to be so wise, perplexes me. How he led the life he did, confounds me. Oh, my lord, I am in dark-

69

ness, and no broad blaze comes down to flood me. The rays
that come to me are but faint cross lights, mazing the obscurity
wherein I live. And after all, excellent as it is, I can be no
gainer by this book. For the more we learn, the more we un-
learn; we accumulate not, but substitute; and take away more
than we add. We dwindle while we grow; we sally out for
wisdom, and retreat beyond the point whence we started; we
essay the Frondize, and get but the Phe. Of all simpletons, the
simplest! Oh! that I were another sort of fool than I am, that I
might restore my good opinion of myself. Continually I stand in
the pillory, am broken on the wheel, and dragged asunder by
wild horses. Yes, yes, Bardianna, all is in a nut, as thou sayest;
but all my back teeth can not crack it; I but crack my own jaws.
All round me, my fellow men are new-grafting their vines,
and dwelling in flourishing arbours; while I am forever pruning mine, till it is become but a stump. Yet in this pruning will
I persist; I will not add, I will diminish; I will train myself
down to the standard of what is unchangeably true. Day by
day I drop off my redundancies; ere long I shall have stripped
my ribs; when I die, they will but bury my spine. Ah! where,
where, where, my lord, is the everlasting Tekana? Tell me,
Mohi, where the Ephina? I may have come to the Penultimate,
but where, sweet Yoomy, is the Ultimate? Ah, companions! I
faint, I am wordless:—something,—nothing,—riddles,—does
Mardi hold her?"

"He swoons!" cried Yoomy.

"Water! water!" cried Media.

"Away!" said Babbalanja serenely, "I revive." (II.80–81)

If Thoreau's resounding admonition to "simplify, simplify"
is recalled here, the essential differences between Melville and
the transcendentalists are of greater note. The process of
stripping down, as in *Typee,* involves a separation from one's
fellow men and a way of life that is not merely self-destructive ("I but crack my own jaws") but actually criminal.
"What is unchangeably true" is death, perhaps only the
"Penultimate." But the process of deep questioning itself
allows Babbalanja repeatedly to revive serenely, until he
achieves his final serenity.

As Babbalanja anticipates Ahab, so he also continually

reflects Melville himself, the young author aspiring presumptuously to literary immortality. Babbalanja's discontent with the Shakespearean Bardianna's work and especially his perplexity at the author's having lived "A Happy Life," the title of the discovered work, raises questions about the ultimate worth of literature and about the actual practice of writing which recur repeatedly in one form or another throughout *Mardi*. Babbalanja comes upon "A Happy Life" by accident in the catacombs of an ancient Mardian antiquarian named Oh-Oh. Considering the treasured collection of Bardianna's manuscripts, Babbalanja addresses them in the manner of Hamlet to Yorick's skull. "And is all this wisdom lost? Cannot the divine cunning in thee, Bardianna, transmute to brightness these sullied pages? Here, perhaps, thou didst dive into the deeps of things, treating of the normal forms of matter and of mind . . . these pages were offspring of thee, thought of thy thought, soul of thy soul. Instinct with mind, they once spoke out like living voices; now, they're dust; and would not prick a fool to action. Whence then is this? If the fogs of some few years can make soul linked to matter naught; how can the unhoused spirit hope to live when mildewed with the damps of death?" (II.75). Still he proceeds to ask old Oh-Oh for one of the precious pages. Oh-Oh refuses, echoing Babbalanja's image of the grave: "Philosopher, ask me for my limbs, my life, my heart, but ask me not for these. Steeped in wax, these shall be my cerements." Turning away in despair, Babbalanja discovers "A Happy Life" amidst "a heap of worm-eaten parchment covers, and many clippings and parings," all smelling like the rinds of old cheese, and this Oh-Oh freely gives him as rubbish.

The undiscovered work, it develops, is quite different from the catalogued works that concern "the normal forms of matter and of mind." Oh-Oh, valuing his cerements over his life, has also rejected Bardianna's living voice in favor of his dead works. In both style and substance, "A Happy Life" anticipates the divine utterances of Alma, *Mardi*'s Christ, whose teachings are realized in their purest form in Serenia. Unlike the dead works, this one literally does "prick a fool to action," a point heavily underlined immediately afterwards when Babbalanja in his discontent angrily wishes that he were "another sort of fool than I am, that I might restore my good opinion of myself." Even the specific philosophic terms of Babbalanja's acceptance of Serenia are anticipated in Bardianna's work: "And is it not more divine in this philosopher, to love righteousness for its own sake, and in view of annihilation, than for pious sages to extol it as the means of everlasting felicity?" (II.79). Finally, "A Happy Life" is discovered buried in rubble in a dark vault, the descent to which is described as "like going down to posterity" (II.72). It thus exemplifies the truly immortal literary work in its physical presence as well as in its substance. Later, in another discussion of the lasting fame of poets, Babbalanja makes the point still more emphatically: "This were to be truly immortal; —to be perpetuated in our works, and not in our names. Let me, oh Oro! be anonymously known!" (II.153).

Though some organic relationship between Babbalanja and *Mardi*'s author is apparent here, the identification itself is neither clear-cut nor complete. As already pointed out, in the area of human action the notion of anonymous immortality prefigures Taji and Ahab, Melville's Indian-haters, just as it characterizes the divine, enduring work of Bardianna. In the land of King Abrazza, where Babbalanja finds his nadir and articulates its central meaning to his journey, another literary figure is considered, a dark counterpart to Bardianna named Lombardo, who is unquestionably Melville himself and whose greatest work clearly resembles *Mardi*. Lombardo is introduced with reference to still another, far older poet, and the relationship between Lombardo and his archetype, Vavona, seems yet another curious foreshadowing of the distinction made in *The Confidence-Man* between the Indian-hater par excellence and the diluted Indian-hater. Vavona is one of the "old Homeric bards:—those who, ages back, harped, and begged, and groped their blinded way through all this charitable Mardi; receiving coppers then, and immortal glory now"

(II.320). The immortality of Lombardo, who flourished long ago, is still in doubt. Appropriate to Melville's notion of the hero, if not to Melville himself, Vavona was "a solitary Mardian; who seldom went abroad; had few friends; and shunning others, was shunned by them" (II.321). Lombardo, though more sociable, was a hermit (II.327). The ancient bards were blind, Babbalanja explains, because it was "endemical. . . . Few grand poets have good eyes; for they needs blind must be, who ever gaze upon the sun. Vavona himself was blind; when, in the silence of his secret bower, he said— 'I will build another world' " (II.320-21).

Lombardo's great epic, "his grand Koztanza," is also an attempt at such a work, as is Melville's *Mardi*. The original impetus, Babbalanja explains, was "Primus and forever, a full heart:—brimful, bubbling, sparkling; and running over like the flagon in your hand, my lord. Secundo, the necessity of bestirring himself to procure his yams" (II.322). The physical process of writing also seems plausibly Melville's: "When Lombardo set about his work, he knew not what it would become. He did not build himself in with plans; he wrote right on; and so doing, got deeper and deeper into himself; and like a resolute traveller, plunging through baffling woods, at last was rewarded for his toils" (II.326). The chief critical objection to the Koztanza is that it "lacks cohesion; it is wild, unconnected, all episode" (II.329). The answer would seem to hold a playful clue as well as an æsthetic justification: "And so is Mardi itself:—nothing but episodes; valleys and hills; rivers, digressing from plains; vines, roving all over; boulders and diamonds; flowers and thistles; forests and thickets; and, here and there, fens and moors. And so, the world in the Koztanza." If *Mardi* merits Abrazza's instant retort, "Ay, plenty of dead-desert chapters there; horrible sands to wade through," surely no one knew it any better than Melville himself.

Babbalanja's description of the Koztanza is marked by a series of mad fits which alternate with his more lucid explanations. Though Media specifically warns him against "incoherencies" at the outset of his story (II.322), Babbalanja can no more restrain himself than could the mad poet of the "crazy" epic or the author of *Mardi*. These outbursts serve as commentary on the story of Lombardo, presenting in him still another image of the questing hero, reflecting Babbalanja himself and Taji and, most important, involving Melville indirectly with his hero's character and situation. The first of these "incoherencies" is presented in terms of the symbolism of the old beldam and the little dwarf that heralded the moment of embarkation into unknown seas: "We have had vast developments of parts of men; but none of manly wholes. Before a full-developed man, Mardi would fall down and worship. We are idiot, younger-sons of gods, begotten in dotages divine; and our mothers all miscarry. Giants are in our germs; but we are dwarfs, staggering under heads overgrown. Heaped, our measures burst. We die of too much life" (II.323). In his next rage, Babbalanja furthers the notion of unequal struggle in terms of immortality and the potential self-destruction needed to achieve it:

No mailed hand lifted up against a traveller in woods, can so appall, as we ourselves. We are full of ghosts and spirits; we are as graveyards full of buried dead, that start to life before us. And all our dead sires, verily, are in us; *that* is their immortality. From sire to son, we go on multiplying corpses in ourselves; for all of which, are resurrections. Every thought's a soul of some past poet, hero, sage. We are fuller than a city. Woe it is, that reveals these things. He knows himself, and all that's in him, who knows adversity. To scale great heights, we must come out of lowermost depths. The way to heaven is through hell. We need fiery baptisms in the fiercest flames of our own bosoms. We must feel our hearts hot—hissing in us. And ere their fire is revealed, it must burn its way out of us; though it consume us and itself. Oh, sleek-cheeked Plenty! smiling at thine own dimples;—vain for thee to reach out after greatness. Turn! turn! from all your tiers of cushions of eiderdown—turn! and be broken on the wheels of many woes. At white-heat brand thyself; and count the scars, like old war-worn veterans, over camp fires. Soft poet! brushing tears from lilies—

this way! and howl in sackcloth and in ashes! Know, thou, that
the lines that live are turned out of a furrowed brow. Oh! there
is a fierce, a cannibal delight, in the grief that shrieks to multiply
itself. That grief is miserly of its own; it pities all the happy.
Some damned spirits would not be otherwise, could they.

(II.323–24)

All of Melville's basic concerns seem gathered here. The
scarred warriors of the earlier pages are merged now with
their figurative counterpart, the savage branded by fire, and
the call is to the "state-room sailors" of *Typee* to emulate
their hard "reach out after greatness." The image that follows
of Lombardo setting about his work, "like a resolute traveller,
plunging through baffling woods," indicates the closeness of
Melville himself to this definitive view of the hero. Whatever
the buried spirits that rose up against him like a "mailed hand
lifted up against a traveller in the woods" during the writing
of *Mardi*, they provided him with a frenzied energy and
power comparable to that of Babbalanja, who in his next
mad fit seems to take on dead Lombardo's rage, attacking his
"emasculated" critics with all of Ahab's furious hatred of the
White Whale.

Oh! that an eagle should be stabbed by a goose-quill! But at
best, the greatest reviewers but prey on my leavings. For I am
critic and creator; and as critic, in cruelty surpass all critics
merely, as a tiger, jackals. For ere Mardi sees aught of mine, I
scrutinize it myself, remorseless as a surgeon. I cut right and
left; I probe, tear, and wrench; kill, burn, and destroy; and
what's left after that, the jackals are welcome to. It is *I* that
stab false thoughts, ere hatched; *I* that pull down wall and
tower, rejecting materials which would make palaces for others.
Oh! could Mardi but see how we work, it would marvel more
at our primal chaos, than at the round world thence emerging.
It would marvel at our scaffoldings, scaling heaven; marvel at
the hills of earth, banked all round our fabrics ere completed.
—How plain the pyramid! In this grand silence, so intense,
pierced by that pointed mass,—could ten thousand slaves have
ever toiled? ten thousand hammers rung? —There it stands,—
part of Mardi: claiming kin with mountains; was this thing

piecemeal built? —It was. Piecemeal? —atom by atom it was laid. The world is full of mites.   (II.331–32)

The concept of the poet as demiurge is Emersonian and ultimately neo-Platonic, as is its corollary analogy between literary and divine creation, microcosm and macrocosm. Expressly, Mardi is the world. The author's sudden awe at the spectacle of his work ("There it stands,—part of Mardi: claiming kin with mountains") is echoed by Thoreau in *Walden,* the high art of which derives in part from an informing analogy between Walden Pond, actual and mythic, and Thoreau's own created *Walden.* Walden Pond "is perenially young, and I may stand and see a swallow dip apparently to pick an insect from its surface as of yore. It struck me again tonight, as if I had not seen it almost daily for more than twenty years,—Why, here is Walden, the same woodland lake that I discovered so many years ago. . . . It is the work of a brave man surely, in whom there was no guile! He rounded this water with his hand, deepened and clarified it in his thought, and in his will bequeathed it to Concord. I see by its face that it is visited by the same reflection; and I can almost say, Walden, is it you?"[7] The reflections in Melville's various waters are just as personal, but far darker and more elusive. Ishmael alludes in "Loomings" to the legend of Narcissus, whose "tormenting mild image" is "the image of the ungraspable phantom of life." At the end of *Mardi* it is the gleaming image pursued by Taji, "white and vaguely Yillah."

Babbalanja is both "critic and creator," and the former role reflects his maker as surely as does the latter. It has often been said that *Mardi* is actually two books in one, an allegory that gives way abruptly and without point to miscellaneous satires, general and specific. Such criticism is neither justified nor precise. *Mardi*'s flaws—and the "dead-desert chapters" are indeed numerous and "horrible sands to wade through"—result more from faulty execution than from lack of a controlling strategy. The image of the dwarf is used throughout to figure both man's smallness (the satiric) and his potential for the self-punishing heroism that Melville calls the "reach out after greatness" (the allegoric). The dynamic process of creation is analogous: a furious destruction of the known world precedes the erected "scaffoldings, scaling heaven." Like the blind Vavona, and his crazy descendant Lombardo, Melville builds "another world" that mirrors the real one, but the price of Vavona's demiurgic isolation is the loss of his humanity, and the new world of *Mardi* is built upon the rubble of the old. It is thus a single work conceived in terms of a twofold movement. As the voyagers search outwardly for Yillah and inwardly into the depths of mind and soul for the "mystery of mysteries," they are also looking carefully at the entire world in which they live. As they pursue, in other words, some bedrock truth, training down to what Babbalanja calls "the standard of what is unchangeably true," they are simultaneously engaged in eliminating everything that is changeable, untrue, or false. The moral purpose and method of satire is to expose human folly in its extreme instances so that fallible man may recognize in himself such tendencies and strive to correct them in accordance with implicit norms of social decency, if not ideals. Where such norms are blurred or nonexistent, or where the standards are set beyond the reach of every man, all human folly appears monstrous, and the satire becomes bitter, Swiftian, verging ultimately on the broad areas of tragedy. Although as a metaphysician Babbalanja is a discontent, he is also, in his satiric role, the traditional malcontent of bitter satire. "You, who run a tilt at all things," Media calls him (I.307). "You, who have so long marked the vices of Mardi, that you flatter yourself you have none of your own," Mohi echoes. And "with unwonted asperity," Yoomy adds, "You, who only seem wise, because of the contrasting follies of others, and not of any great wisdom in yourself" (I.325). The balance between philosophic and psychic discontent, between the allegory of quest and the satire of discovery, provides the work with an essential energy and logic.

"Ever osseous in his allusions to the departed" (II.17), Babbalanja from the outset also sees the skulls beneath the living skins; and the more he sees of Mardi, the more terrible his visions and the howling laughter that accompanies them. The malcontent's furies and the philosopher's despair come together at Abrazza's court. If the spirit is once more Hamlet's, the substance is Melville's own. Abrazza, the extreme instance of the self-indulgent landsman, "sleek-cheeked Plenty! smiling at thine own dimples," elicits Babbalanja's fiercest mockeries, and again the meanings are informed by the continuing distinction between the little dwarf who blindly complies with his suffering and the little dwarf who just as blindly attempts a grand defiance. The authority of "Ludwig the Fat," an old supper-loving king of Franko, clearly meant to signify Abrazza, is "far higher than the authority of Ludwig the Great:—the one, only great by courtesy; the other, fat beyond a peradventure. But they are equally famous; and in their graves both on a par. For after devouring many a fair province, and grinding the poor of his realm, Ludwig the Great has long since, himself, been devoured by very small worms, and ground into very fine dust. And after stripping many a venison rib, Ludwig the Fat has had his own polished and bleached in the Valley of Death; yea, and his cranium chased with corrodings, like the carved flagon once held to its jaws" (II.339).

The visible differences, though necessarily small, are crucial. Babbalanja, in fact, confronts them as he speaks. King Media, like King Abrazza, "would be merry": "Let us gain the sunny side," he urges as they approach the island, "and like the care-free bachelor Abrazza, who here is king, turn our back on the isle's shadowy side, and revel in its morning-meads" (II.316). But while Abrazza has luxuriated at home, Media has been voyaging with Taji and Babbalanja. Though he prefers the sunny side, he cannot finally choose it. In the chapter called "L'Ultima Sera," where all but Taji consider for the last time the imagined horrors of the grave, Media's stance is that of the kingly warrior. "Time to die, when death comes, without dying by inches. 'Tis no death to die; the only death is the fear of it. I, a demi-god, fear death not" (II.358). Serenia, a haven for the others, is for Media only a temptation, not unlike that presented by Abrazza's willful optimism. When the old man of Serenia preaches Love, "that heart of mild content, which in vain ye seek in rank and title," Media answers, "Wouldst thou unking me?" And though he briefly surrenders, Media is urged by Babbalanja himself to return: "Thy station calls thee home" (II.370).

Media, then, is the quester Taji's final analogue. In the last chapter, the warrior's course and Taji's merge. Mohi and Yoomy arrive at Hautia's island to find Taji on the verge of absolute darkness: "Taji lives no more. So dead, he has no ghost. I am his spirit's phantom's phantom" (II.398). Making one final attempt to save him, they drag him in a somnambulistic state to the boat and set out. "Soon—Mohi at the helm—we shot beneath the far-flung shadow of a cliff; when, as in a dream, I hearkened to a voice."[8] The voice which suddenly rouses Taji tells the story of Media's return to Odo, where the three avengers, furious at missing Taji, have stirred up a rebellion. Confronting them, Media achieves at once serenity and the heroic character of Melville's solitary seamen. "But one hand waving like a pennant above the smoke of some sea-fight, straight through that tumult Media sailed serene: the rioters parting from before him, as wild waves before a prow inflexible." Like Ahab, it is no fearless fool who stands here but a personality in full awareness of impending doom. "The state is tossed in storms; and where I stand, the combing billows must break over. But among all noble souls, in tempest-time, the headmost man last flies the wreck. So, here in Odo will I abide, though every plank breaks up beneath me. And then,—great Oro! let the king die clinging to the keel! Farewell!" The tale of Media's end directly triggers Taji's own farewell. Recalled to his quest by the mention of the three avengers, he seizes the helm though warned that "through yonder strait . . . perdition lies. And from the deep beyond, no voyager e'er puts back." Echoing

Media's earlier stance toward death, he also echoes his farewell: "And why put back? is a life of dying worth living o'er again? —Let *me*, then, be the unreturning wanderer. The helm! By Oro, I will steer my own fate, old man. —Mardi, farewell!" (II.398–99).

Though all the differences between Ludwig the Fat and Ludwig the Great are contained in a single syllable, the distinction between "a demi-john" and "a demi-god" will occupy Melville continually until *The Confidence-Man*. First raised as issues in *Typee* and *Omoo*, the terms of the polarity proliferate in *Mardi*, informing theme and structure, narrative mode and stylistic manner. Abrazza, for instance, is also threatened by revolution, but only by a "pale, ragged rout" that bursts in to beg politely for redress for serious grievances. Abrazza orders them immediately driven away and calmly returns to his cups, complaining to Media in the obvious tones of the effete decadent, "High times, truly, my lord Media, when demi-gods are thus annoyed at their wine." Emphasizing his points, as always, with reference to a basic recurrent symbolism, Melville portends the relevance of Abrazza's blind unconcern, and his looming fate as well, by describing the leader of this small inept rebellion as another incipient hero, "a tall, grim, pine-tree of a fellow, who loomed up out of the throng, like the peak of Teneriffe among the Canaries in a storm." When they are finally driven off, the last sight is of "The Peak of Teneriffe going last, a pent storm on his brow; and muttering about some black time that was coming" (II.341).

It is Abrazza's pretense of happy divinity that galls and embitters Babbalanja, his pose of jolly kingliness that provokes the satirist's fiercest attack. The rage specifically is against one who claims kinship with Prometheans though only a smug contented lordling.[9] Of all the affectations encountered, Abrazza's is the largest and the most profoundly galling, and Babbalanja's purpose is not to correct his stony self-conceit, but to destroy it. "My lord! my lord!" Abrazza finally cries out to Media. "This ghastly devil of yours grins

worse than a skull. I feel the worms crawling over me"
(II.339). For such success, however, Babbalanja pays an
awful price. His terrible vision of Abrazza rotting in his grave
is a mirror image, reflecting back his own maddening fate.
"In hell we'll gibber in concert, king!" he finally cries, affirming the grim kinship. "We'll howl, and roast, and hiss together!" (II.345).

For Melville, writing *Mardi,* there is a comparable cost.
Though he would, like his Babbalanja, be creator as well as
critic, leveling the false only to build the true and the enduring, he has involved himself too much in matters of this
fallible real world. Though he would be the ideal writer, like
Lombardo "rejecting materials which would make palaces for
others," he cannot escape continual confrontation with what
Babbalanja repeatedly calls jackals. The dominant impulse,
finally, is the satirist's. Yet even in this, though indirectly,
we may see foreshadowing of *Moby-Dick,* where, turning his
back on the landsman's world, Melville can also turn his back
to landsmen and confront not jackals but white whales. As
the smug bachelor, blind to the world's true workings,
Abrazza has his counterpart in *Moby-Dick* in the homeward-
bound ship, the *Bachelor,* whose captain urges Ahab to come
aboard to a party, promising to "take that black from your
brow." Though he has heard of the White Whale, the "gay
Bachelor's commander . . . don't believe in him at all"
(II.268). But where Babbalanja shrieks and goads, striving
to compel belief, Ahab is willfully indifferent: "thou art a
full ship and homeward bound, thou say'st; well, then, call
me an empty ship, and outward bound. So go thy ways, and I
will mine" (II.268).

The oddest of all the mysteries in this odd, mystery-ridden
book is that its author also seems to go his own peculiar way
before the story ends. Confronted finally with an impossible
choice between blind compliance and equally blind—and
blasphemous—deep-diving, Babbalanja breaks down. His
philosophic quest drives him nearly mad; his satirist's prob-

ings lead to an almost permanent despair. Just before Serenia, he is reduced to a tormented, beaten human being: "No coward he, who hunted, turns and finds no foe to fight. . . . Like the stag, whose brow is beat with wings of hawks, perched in his heavenward antlers; so I, blinded, goaded, headlong, rush! this way and that; nor knowing whither; one forest wide around!" (II.360). He is, of course, no cowardly Abrazza. By hard voyaging he has earned his Serenia. But neither is he a Taji; and though he has frequently spoken for the author, his final acceptance of Serenia is not Melville's. The alternatives are clearly articulated, if nothing more. On the one hand is Babbalanja's madness and despair, with Serenia as a symbolic possibility; on the other is Taji's deep descent into that void from which no traveler returns. Standing now behind the one character, now behind the other, Melville is finally content to let each separate line play out as a comment on its opposite. He has, however, already written off the whole effort.

One need not belabor the intriguing correspondence between Melville's description of his state of mind when beginning *Mardi* and the novel's central character and theme. As the notion of an ideal artistic creation is developed, the Icarian overtones of Melville's "longing to plume my pinions for a flight" become clearer. Moreover, the resemblances between fictional questing and the quest for an ultimate fiction are repeatedly underlined, the outright identification of Lombardo's Koztanza and Melville's *Mardi* being the most notable. All such instances indicate that, in addition to its more immediate concerns, *Mardi* is also a book about the writing of a book called *Mardi*. And in this regard, far more significantly than in *Typee*, Melville's peculiar use of two distinct first-person narrative presences—one a character's, one a detached author's—is of special interest.

The evolving narrative voices are difficult to trace accurately, but certain broad patterns are evident. The nameless narrator who begins the story in the first person is, like Ishmael, one who survives the experience and returns to tell of it.

Melville makes this clear at the outset in an apostrophe to the *Arcturion,* of which "no word was ever heard, from the dark hour we pushed from her fated planks." He goes on, more-over, to pray that "the spirit of that lost vessel . . . may never haunt my future path upon the waves" (I.29–30). The voice is not that of the transfigured Taji, last seen embarking on an endless quest into the "deep beyond . . . from which no voyager e'er puts back." The possibility that the unreturning wanderer has somehow wandered back to civilization to in-quire about the *Arcturion* and to write the story of his exploits is patently absurd. The conventional first-person narration lasts only until the voyage through Mardi is actually under way. As they embark, the voice is first-person singular; once they land at their first stop, it is first-person plural and in-creasingly as much an editorial "we" as the collective voice of the participants. As the initial voice disappears, so does the character of Taji, save in those chapters when his quest for Yillah is of immediate concern, and then Melville also reverts to the first person. Apart from such moments, it is only at Pimminee, the land of the bourgeois Tapparians, that Taji is allowed any role apart from his actual quest. The re-version is abrupt and emphatic. Between Mondoldo and Pimminee, Taji is mentioned only in the single chapter that concerns his quest (II, Ch.14); suddenly, upon landing at Pimminee, they all begin to talk about him and to him again. The strategy, though obscure, has a certain logic to it. The "ir-reclaimable Tapparians" are Taji's own people, the emerging American middle class, and they have as little understanding of him as he has liking for them. The substance of his visit is a conversation with an old Tapparian Begum who cannot see how an ostensibly civilized, middle-class landsman like Taji could have become involved in such wild doings. "The Begum was surprised that he could have thus hazarded his life among the barbarians of the East. She desired to know whether his constitution was not impaired by inhaling the unrefined atmosphere of those remote and barbarous regions." The thematic relevance is insistent. The mere thought of

Taji's travels makes the old lady "faint in her innermost citadel; nor went she ever abroad with the wind at east, dreading the contagion which might lurk in the air" (II.99).

Following this encounter, Taji is once more virtually invisible, except for the recurrence of his quest, and even then he is no longer used as a narrator save at the very end when he is alone. The split between the two narrators thus coincides with a direct encounter between Taji and the world in which the author himself must live, and this too has its own suggestive logic. In the novels prior to *Mardi,* as in those immediately following it, the subject is invariably approached through a youthful neophyte who moves gradually toward a crucial experience, understanding and absorbing something of its essential meanings, and who finally returns, somewhat altered, to write of it in a story that includes the drama of his own involvement. Tommo's journeys to Typee on the *Dolly* and to Tahiti aboard the *Julia* are essentially the same in concept as Ishmael's to the vortex of the sinking *Pequod.* In the first two novels, the narrators are imperfectly initiated; they keep their distance from the experience that could at least potentially engulf them. Tommo finally retreats each time, affected but not transfigured. In *Mardi,* where Melville pushes his hero through the outer reaches of experience to its virtual center, two narrators are needed because there are two distinct dramas, parallel to a point but not identical. The parting of the ways would seem to take place at Pimminee because the Tapparians, however degraded, represent the only society to which the initiate can return. The spirit is akin to Johnson's *Rasselas* and Swift's *Gulliver,* the two chief models for the satiric portions of *Mardi.* Rasselas finally returns to his Happy Valley because all other places have proved corrupt or tedious; Gulliver returns because as a mortal man he is a Yahoo among Houyhnhnms. Yet the returning narrator of *Mardi* seems neither maddened like Gulliver nor wearily resigned like Rasselas. He is, instead, an ambitious young writer who by hard, bold work has gained important knowledge of himself and who is ready to begin again.

If the use of narrators is sometimes confusing, there is no question about when the voice is Melville's own. In four chapters, he speaks out directly, using an author's first person, and although these are digressive, the tone, the content, and the careful placing of them in the sequence of the journey make it clear that Melville is deliberately suggesting a personal experience comparable and even schematically parallel to that of his characters. The first of these, "Time and Temples," is Melville's first assertion of the builder-poet's pursuit of eternal works and of his need to travel sunward to achieve them. Significantly, it is placed just after the questers have encountered the miserably landlocked, effeminate, heirless Donjalolo. The second, titled "Faith and Knowledge," is more personal and more revealing. It serves to introduce Samoa's "Tale of a Traveler," the account of his ability to transform warriors into pigs, and hence it properly heralds the beginning of the satires. The chapter begins with a dispassionate, pedantic discussion of the tensions and contradictions between faith and knowledge, real and apparent, and a conventional distinction is made between things only apparently true and things grandly and genuinely true. In order to achieve the higher truth, man must reject the lower. Consequently, Melville argues, "dissenters only assent to more than we. Though Milton was a heretic to the creed of Athanasius, his faith exceeded that of Athanasius himself; and the faith of Athanasius that of Thomas, the disciple, who with his own eyes beheld the mark of the nails." Though Melville's analogy between the savage Samoa and Milton is playful, underlying it is a wild presumption of his own equality with Milton both as poet and as heretic. With the general argument established, Melville suddenly bursts out in a ringing assertion of his own personality and demiurgic powers.

In some universe-old truths, all mankind are disbelievers. Do you believe that you lived three thousand years ago? That you were at the taking of Tyre, were overwhelmed in Gomorrah? No. But for me, I was at the subsiding of the Deluge, and helped swab the ground, and build the first house. With the

Israelites, I fainted in the wilderness; was in court, when
Solomon outdid all the judges before him. I, it was, who sup-
pressed the lost work of Manetho, on the Egyptian theology,
as containing mysteries not to be revealed to posterity, and
things at war with the canonical scriptures; I, who originated
the conspiracy against that purple murderer, Domitian; I, who
in the senate moved that great and good Aurelian be emperor.
I instigated the abdication of Diocletian, and Charles the Fifth;
I touched Isabella's heart that she hearkened to Columbus. I
am he, that from the king's minions hid the Charter in the old
oak at Hartford; I harbored Goffe and Whalley: I am the
leader of the Mohawk masks, who in the Old Commonwealth's
harbour, overboard threw the East India Company's Souchong;
I am the Veiled Persian Prophet; I, the man in the iron mask;
I, Junius. (I.345)

The stunning, climactic "I, Junius" prefigures what immediately does take place in *Mardi*—the assumption of the satirist's
role as well as the mystery of authorship.[10] Equally relevant
is the insistent, rhythmic egomania that accompanies the self-
expansion, intensified by contrast to the sophistic tangle of
words preceding it. The concept of the artist as a repository
of history's buried great will recur more pointedly at
Abrazza's court with Babbalanja's recognition that "woe it
is, that reveals these things." Here the surge is still upward,
the identification with bright power and unburdened greatness. Yet even at this moment when Melville's self-assertion
is proudest and least tinged with dark associations, the
tendency toward despair is implicit. The egomaniacal process,
however necessary, isolates the poet from his world and directs him against it. The climactic conjunction of Persian
prophet and imprisoned French king with the anonymous
satirist who shook an English government suggests at once the
terms and limits of the role Melville blocks out for himself,
involving frustration on the one hand and an ultimate heresy
on the other.[11]

The next such divagation extends and clarifies the implications of "Faith and Knowledge," again providing an almost

schematic parallel to the immediate drama. Following the revelation of Hivohitee, high priest of Maramma, who proclaims an omnipresent nullity instanced in the ensuing news of Jarl's senseless murder, Melville inserts a chapter called "Dreams" wherein the artist's condition is discussed with less confidence but far more presumption of divinity than in "Faith and Knowledge." The artist is first pictured as a warrior, dashing through endless prairies of golden dreams and striving with his "lance, to spear one, ere they all flee." The purpose is to transfix and thus perpetuate what is transitory. The world of dreams, however, is not only endless but embraces fundamental and potentially devastating contraries, leading the poet from gentle warming Mediterranean suns to the "Antarctic barrier of ice" and beyond to "deathful, desolate dominions . . . freighted with navies of icebergs,—warring worlds crossing orbits." The progress toward this chilling vision is inevitable; once pursued, the golden dreams prove to be nightmares. The urge for such a flight is trammeled by fear and by radical self-doubts: "But beneath me, at the Equator, the earth pulses and beats like a warrior's heart; till I know not, whether it be not myself. And my soul sinks down to the depths, and soars to the skies; and comet-like reels on through such boundless expanses, that methinks all the worlds are my kin, and I invoke them to stay in their course. Yet, like a mighty three-decker, towing argosies by scores, I tremble, gasp, and strain in my flight, and fain would cast off the cables that hamper" (II.52–53).

The heretical posture of divinity, if earthly bonds are cut and such a flight achieved, is a forecast of an ultimate shipwreck. The first image of the warrior becomes that of a ship, peopled by "a thousand souls" playing contrary roles and issuing "contending orders, to save the good ship from the shoals." These many souls in him, like sirens in concert, summon him from tropical calms to stormy flights: "Sometimes, when these Atlantics and Pacifics thus undulate around me, I lie stretched out in their midst: a land-locked Mediterranean, knowing no ebb, nor flow. Then again, I am dashed in the spray of these sounds: an eagle at the world's end, tossed skyward, on the horns of the tempest." The movement is recurrent, not absolute, an alternation of calm and storm, sea and land, like that of Ishmael periodically dispelling the damp Novembers from his soul: "Yet, again, I descend, and list to the concert (II.53). The voices that immediately inspire him are the great poets—Homer, Shakespeare, Milton, and, regrettably, Ossian, Waller, and Prior. But these are merely inspirational, for the voices of philosophers and theologians call as well, and from their impossibly conflicting wisdoms must come the enduring truth.

A third image of power initiates another movement. From the single warrior and the "mighty three-decker," he images himself as the great Mississippi, rushing like an emperor with his legions to the sea: "And as the great Mississippi musters his watery nations: Ohio, with all his leagued streams; Missouri, bringing down in torrents the clans from the highlands; Arkansas, his Tartar rivers from the plains;—so, with all the past and present pouring in me, I roll down my billow from afar." The martial images, suggesting some final battle, intensify the figure, underlining heretical implications to which Melville now reacts sharply, if not humbly: "Yet not I, but another; God is my Lord; and though many satellites revolve around me, I and all mine revolve around the great central Truth, sun-like, fixed and luminous forever in the foundationless firmament." Although he retreats here, briefly, from the·verge of Taji's ultimate heresy, he has already approached too close to the metaphoric sun and found it fire, not light. "Fire flames on my tongue; and though of old the Bactrian prophets were stoned, yet the stoners in oblivion sleep. But whoso stones me, shall be as Erostratus, who put torch to the temple: though Genghis Khan with Cambyses combine to obliterate him, his name shall be extant in the mouth of the last man that lives. And if so be, down unto death, whence I came, will I go, like Xenophon retreating on Greece, all Persia brandishing her spears in his rear." The heroic posture is familiar. What is extraordinary is the presumption of divinity. His imagined, anonymous assassin achieves immortality because, like the thief who stole the great rock of Pella, his defiance is of the godhead itself. The swift transition is from the ungodly, godlike man to God. Then, having built from feelings and aspirations of power to power itself and beyond to the audacious assumptions of omnipotence that are the extreme limit of such sensations, suddenly he breaks off and, as in "Faith and Temples," abruptly unveils the man behind the image. "My cheek blanches white while I write; I start at the scratch of my pen; my own mad brood of eagles devours me; fain would I unsay this audacity; but an iron-mailed hand clenches mine in a vice, and prints down every letter in my spite. Fain would I hurl off this Dionysius that rides me; my thoughts crush me down till I groan; in far fields I hear the song of the reaper, while I slave and faint in this cell. The fever runs through me like lava; my hot brain burns like a coal; and like many a monarch, I am less to be envied, than the veriest hind in the land" (II.54–55).

Where the movement in "Faith and Knowledge" was ascendant, an enormous all-inclusive "I" finally emerging from behind the mask of a wordy philosopher, in "Dreams" it is reversed. The warrior become deity is now only a scribbler, jumping at the sound of his own pen. If Melville seems at the end of *Mardi* to have taken on Ahab's heroic burden along with his anguish, the terms are notably modified. Where Ahab in "The Symphony" dreams of the green country, home and family, at the brink of the overwhelming vortex to which another sort of dream has brought him, Melville in his study listens to the farmers in the fields outside. They are analogous, perhaps, but not identical. The lord of his creation, he is not Lord of all creation, nor finally does he pretend to be. This is surely not to belittle. An Indian-hater par excellence arises but once in an age, his existence known only through the diluted Indian-hater whose own exploits are the stuff of legend. The values are relative, and the persistent image is the ladder to the sun. If a man's eyes are open to the rung immediately above, it is enough; something of whatever is at the top filters down. "Dreams," then, is an imaginative view of what it feels like to think oneself an Icarus, and not a self-portrait of Icarus as such. Melville is obsessed, not visionary, and such a novelist writes not about what he wants, but about what he is, might be, or might have been. The "iron-mailed hand" that forces him to write is seen by Babbalanja as well (II.323). It is also dramatically embodied in Taji's three avengers, whose physical presence is less terrible to him than the guilt they continually recall. Having viewed the farthest reaches of the possibilities within himself, Melville can write of those who like Taji and Ahab push themselves beyond the final limit. But he can also write of Babbalanja who, achieving knowledge through suffering, is able to accept the haven of Serenia.

Something of the quality of Melville's education in writing *Mardi,* as well as of its purposes, may be seen in the last of the four digressive chapters that present this personal drama. "Sailing On" is set between the satire's end and the beginning of the journey's final stage. The whole known world has been examined and found wanting. The travelers have completed a full circle, emerging like a "baffled hunter" from a "boundless prairie's heart" to confront "the universe again before us; our quest, as wide." In choosing this moment to assay the result of his soundings, Melville seems deliberately to be calling attention to the finality of the moment. For the first time, he interrupts a narrative already begun. As they sail on with "all the lands that we had passed . . . faded from the sight," the author's voice breaks in, moved to speak "by some mystic impulse."

> Oh, reader, list! I've chartless voyaged. With compass and the lead, we had not found these Mardian Isles. Those who boldly launch, cast off all cables; and turning from the common breeze, that's fair for all, with their own breath, fill their

own sails. Hug the shore, naught new is seen; and "Land ho!" at last was sung, when a new world was sought.

That voyager steered his bark through seas, untracked before, ploughed his own path mid jeers; though with a heart that oft was heavy with the thought that he might only be too bold, and grope where land was none.

So I. (II. 276)

Though Balboa is subsequently referred to, it is not far-fetched to assume here the spirit of Columbus as well. The historical new world, which is archetype to the "new world . . . of mind," is the same with both explorers. And if the direction is implicitly homeward, the tone also suggests rapprochement. Unlike previous declarations, the voice speaks directly here and with a quiet self-assurance. The view of the hero—still the bold seaman setting out from land—is similarly more restrained. Though he fills his own sails with his own breath, he now looks up to do so. The explorer fears only that he may be "too bold, and grope where land was none." Taji's ultimate boldness comes, like Ahab's, when he vows pursuit of an unattainable goal. Melville is both more cautious and less doubtful of the outcome. "Land ho!" was at last "sung, when a new world was sought." The possibilities at least are there, although in *Mardi,* he realizes, he has not achieved them: "And though essaying but a sportive sail, I was driven from my course by a blast resistless; and ill-provided, young, and bowed to the brunt of things before my prime, still fly before the gale;—hard have I striven to keep stout heart" (II.277). The anticipation of better work to come in his prime, coupled with the feeling of a job not badly done, allows him the quiet courage of his present failure.

The tone of "Sailing On" seems one of disengagement. Where previous chapters were written in a present tense, the tense here is past. We have the extraordinary image of an author turning away from his book with a hundred or so pages to go, sailing on, as it were, in one direction while his book continues on course to its end. But the direction is still that of Lombardo's ultimate fiction. New seas must be found because the old ones "have oft been circled by ten thousand prows," and if this should demand still harder striving than in *Mardi,* "much more the glory!" The departure is of course not a real one. However much he anticipates the work to come, Melville has a book to finish and, with uncharacteristic candor, in keeping with this outburst of straight speaking, he says so: "But fiery yearnings their own phantom-future make, and deem it present. So, if after all these fearful, fainting trances, the verdict be, the golden haven was not gained;— yet, in bold quest thereof, better to sink in boundless deeps, than float on vulgar shoals; and give me, ye gods, an utter wreck, if wreck I do" (II.277).

If Melville goes on immediately after *Mardi* to break this vow to sink pursuing lofty aspirations rather than to "float on vulgar shoals," it is because, as he wrote to Duyckinck in December 1849, "a hollow purse makes the poet *sink—* witness 'Mardi.' "[12] His contempt for the "beggarly" *Redburn* probably came in no small part from his feeling of having written it for money after the aspirations voiced in *Mardi.* To Lemuel Shaw, his father-in-law, he wrote in October 1849: "So far as I am individually concerned, & independent of my pocket, it is my earnest desire to write those sort of books which are said to 'fail.' "[13] His notion of such books, as described in the letter to Duyckinck, remains unchanged from that expressed throughout *Mardi*: "But we that write & print have all our books predestinated—& for me, I shall write such things as the Great Publisher of Mankind ordained ages before he published 'The World'—this planet I mean—not the Literary Globe." In Melville's own view *Mardi* was a forerunner of the predestinated book now looming immediately before him. "I am but a poor mortal, & I admit that I learn by experience & not by divine intuitions. Had I not written and published 'Mardi,' in all likelihood, I would not be as wise as I am now, or may be. For that thing was stabbed *at* (I do not say *through*)—therefore, I am the wiser for it." The figure itself looks back to *Mardi* and forward to *Moby-Dick*. *Mardi*'s creative process is imaged in the poet's wild attempts to spear the fleeting dreams that pass before him. With Ahab, the transformation is central and definitive: "If man will strike, strike through the mask."

PART TWO

DESCENT

★ 4 ★

THERE IS NO QUESTION that the "beggarly" *Redburn* and *White Jacket* are better novels—surer, more coherent, more substantial—than Melville thought. It is curious, however, that he should have been so vigorously contemptuous of works in which he had, perhaps despite himself, an important private investment. Melville's psychic involvement, growing out of his continuing obsession with the quester-hero theme, is in some ways actually deeper in these less ambitious efforts. *Mardi* reflects a mind newly fed by prodigious reading as it plays over basic existential questions. For all its noise and passion, it is essentially a work of the intellect. *Redburn* and *White Jacket,* especially when considered as a pair, embody private tensions and uncertainties that are, in some dim way, the product of all his recent intellectual ferment. Nonetheless, Melville's contempt for the two books is understandable. Whatever their merits, his "two jobs . . . done for money"[1] were done as hack work. It is easy to forget just how fast Melville wrote them. *Redburn* took him at most two months, and *White Jacket,* some seventy-five pages longer, roughly the same. One can estimate the actual writing time fairly closely. *Mardi,* which by contrast took him nearly two years to finish,[2] came out in the United States on April 14, 1849, and it is unlikely that Melville would have begun

Redburn before May 1, perhaps even somewhat later. There is every indication that he would not have written it at all had *Mardi* been successful, and though the English edition was published a month before the American, the initial reviews were largely favorable. Even as late as April 23 Melville appears to have been reasonably sanguine.[3] But as the unfavorable American reviews piled up, it was soon clear that *Mardi* would bring him neither fame nor money.

The first-known reference to *Redburn* comes in a letter of June 5 to Richard Bentley which would seem to be in response to low English sales figures. After justifying *Mardi* on artistic grounds, he goes on, "I have now in preparation a thing of a widely different cast from 'Mardi':—a plain, straightforward, amusing narrative of personal experience—the son of a gentleman on his first voyage to sea as a sailor—no metaphysics, no conic-sections, nothing but cakes & ale. I have shifted my ground from the South Seas to a different quarter of the globe—nearer home—and what I write I have almost wholly picked up by my own observations under comical circumstances."[4] Although it would not appear from this that Melville was very far along at the time, the book was completed by the end of June and *White Jacket* immediately begun, this time with Melville under the additional pressures of having to read proof for *Redburn* as he worked on its successor. By the end of August, *White Jacket* too was completed. A letter of December 14, 1849, to Evert Duyckinck attests to the painful drudgery of the work: "When a poor devil writes with duns all round him, & looking over the back of his chair—and perching on his pen & diving in his inkstand—like the devils about St. Anthony—what can you expect of that poor devil?—What but a beggarly 'Redburn!' And when he attempts anything higher—God help him & save him!"[5] Yet for all the self-contempt, it should be noted that he is still, like his heroes, bedeviled. The duns are small and pesky, to be sure, but in their way they are also deep-divers and they have had a like effect upon their harried victim.

The highest testimony to the worth of this odd pair of

novels is that one cannot imagine Melville's having written *Moby-Dick* without them. What we find in *Redburn* and *White Jacket* is a queer coincidence of financial and artistic needs. The letter to Bentley heralds a turning from romance to an essentially realistic mode of writing. Melville's primary reason for adopting a "plain, straightforward" manner was surely to attract a wide popular audience and also, perhaps, to reach that audience quickly.[6] Yet the consistently extravagant language of romantic allegory was a dead end and moreover, I suspect, was unnatural to him. In the letters and journals— where he is writing at his ease—the distinguishing energy of Melville's natural style derives from an effective balance of realistic fact and soaring fancy. I think, too, that this was how he lived and thought, steadily balancing "cakes and ale" with flights of poetry and metaphysics. It underlies, for instance, his first reaction to Hawthorne as man and writer. After praising *Twice-Told Tales* in a letter to Duyckinck as even better than the *Mosses*, he goes on to complain of "something lacking—a good deal lacking—to the plump sphericity of the man. . . . He doesn't patronise the butcher—he needs roast-beef, done rare. —Nevertheless, for one, I regard Hawthorne (in his books) as evincing a quality of genius, immensely loftier, & more profound, too, than any other American has shown hitherto in the printed form."[7] That Melville was aware of his own need for red meat as well as for nobler stuff may be inferred from his description of *Moby-Dick* in a letter to Richard Henry Dana, Jr., dated May 1, 1850: "It will be a strange sort of a book, tho', I fear; blubber is blubber you know; tho' you may get oil out of it, the poetry runs as hard as sap from a frozen maple tree;—& to cook the thing up, one must needs throw in a little fancy, which from the nature of the thing, must be ungainly as the gambols of the whales themselves. Yet I mean to give the truth of the thing, spite of this."[8] The ingredients in this oddly transcendentalist whale stew are by and large the same as those in *Mardi*. The difference is that the romance of *Moby-Dick* is firmly grounded in reality. Melville's turning away in *Redburn* from the South Seas to places "nearer home" thus serves a function far more serious than the immediate one of attracting a publisher's waning interest and a reading public's dollars. The move is permanent. The ultimate truths are now to be pursued in literal "things," and not in romances that have only allegoric reference.

His central concern, however, is still the intricate relation between the awakening neophyte and the Promethean hero. Redburn derives from Tommo and Taji, and he anticipates Ishmael and Pierre. Yet the stylistic and geographic relocation of the quester-figure necessarily alters to some extent the character and his situation. He must be literal now as well as generally representational; his goal, correspondingly, must have some plausible connection to his world as well as embody all his deepest longings. Ahab, a whaling captain from Nantucket, pursues the White Whale according to the real world's logic as well as his own metaphysics. The progression from Yillah to Moby-Dick thus involves extraordinary effort. Melville's perceptions remain the same; the radically different approach demands that he find new and more lifelike bodies for the creatures of his "world of mind." Because they are rooted so firmly in a realistic context, *Redburn* and *White Jacket* represent a crucial phase of the development.

The dominant spirit of *Redburn* is not its nominal hero but the incomprehensibly evil Jackson. The importance of Jackson as a direct forerunner of Ahab has been amply discussed, most notably by William Gilman,[9] but some restatement is called for, since in every physical respect Jackson is merely another embodiment of the figure portended in *Typee* and most fully described by Babbalanja at King Abrazza's court. Jackson has Ahab's overawing power and his strange, dictatorial magnetism. The authority derives from a primal malignance, signified by an evil eye, a "most deep, subtle, infernal-looking eye" that "must have belonged to a wolf, or starved tiger" (72). Like Ahab, Jackson is "gnawed within" as well as "scorched without." His sickness is the direct cause of his satanic misanthropy; he hates Redburn because he is young and healthy while "*he* was being consumed by an incurable malady, that was eating up his vitals." His spiritual alienation is frequently expressed by a complete withdrawal from the ship's society: "He was apt to be dumb at times, and would sit with his eyes fixed, and his teeth set, like a man in the moody madness" (74). This blasted isolato also has his symbolic scar: "He was a Cain afloat; branded on his yellow brow with some inscrutable curse; and going about corrupting and searing every heart that beat near him" (134).

Yet there is grandeur in Jackson's opposition to his inscrutable antagonist, and a concentrated energy that recalls Bembo and foreshadows Ahab: "He seemed to be full of hatred and gall against everything and everybody in the world; as if all the world was one person and had done him some dreadful harm, that was rankling and festering in his heart" (78). Jackson has Ahab's understanding of human nature—"He was by nature a marvelously clever, cunning man . . . and understood human nature to a kink, and well knew whom he had to deal with" (72)—and also something of his defiant intellectual vitality: "Though he had never attended churches, and knew nothing about Christianity; no more than a Malay pirate; and though he could not read a word, yet he was spontaneously an atheist and an infidel; and during the long night-watches, would enter into arguments, to prove that there was nothing to be believed; nothing to be loved, and nothing worth living for; but everything to be hated, in the wide world. He was a horrid desperado, and like a wild Indian, whom he resembled in his tawny skin and high cheek-bones, he seemed to run amuck at heaven and earth" (134). Living in full knowledge of his fate, Jackson has no fears of death. He mocks his shipmates, who dread the plague's contagion and quake before the mysteriously dead Portuguese sailor. His death, like Ahab's, is presented as a tremendous act of will. As they approach home port, Jackson suddenly shows up on deck determined to work. He seems to have risen from the tomb, from Babbalanja's lowermost depths: "His aspect was damp and death-like; the blue hollows of his eyes were like vaults full of snakes; and issuing so unexpectedly from his dark tomb in the forecastle, he looked like a man raised from the dead." But as Ahab rises out of a curious, deathlike trance in order to pursue his fate, so this Lazarus has returned only for a wilder and more fitting end: "For it was one of the characteristics of this man, that though when on duty he would shy away from mere dull work in a calm, yet in tempest-time he always claimed the van, and would yield to none; and this, perhaps, was one cause of his unbounded dominion over the men." The death itself resembles Ahab's, though White Jacket's climactic fall is specifically foreshadowed. "Like a diver into the sea," Jackson plunges from the yard-arm, his last word a "blasphemous cry," in a moment, Melville tells us, when sailors' "spirits seem . . . to partake of the commotion of the elements, as they hang in the gale, between heaven and earth," and when "they are the most profane" (381).

The metaphysical implications of Jackson's death are illuminated by a sharp, familiar contrast with the landsman's way of facing death. The plague which has killed a number of the emigrants in steerage has also killed one of the few cabin passengers, an elderly American woman "whose death, however, was afterward supposed to have been purely induced by her fears." Her fears reflect a general panic in the cabins, where an outbreak of extreme, hypocritical religiosity takes place. Redburn's own reaction is profoundly stoical, in the manner of Babbalanja's more reflective moments: "Strange, though almost universal, that the seemingly nearer prospect of that death which anybody at any time may die, should produce these spasmodic devotions when an everlasting Asiatic cholera is forever thinning our ranks; and die by death we all must at last." The reaction is "almost universal" because, Redburn goes on immediately, there are those few who, like Jackson, have full and pressing awareness of their mortality: "Sailors, officers, cabin passengers, and emigrants, all looked upon each other like lepers. All but the only true leper among us—the mariner Jackson, who seemed elated at the thought that for *him*—already in the deadly clutches of another disease—no danger was to be apprehended from a fever which only swept off the comparatively healthy. Thus, in the midst of the despair of the healthful, this incurable invalid was not cast down; not, at least, by the same considerations that appalled the rest" (373). Like both Queequeg and Ahab, then, Jackson at least dies game, possessing from the start the fearful awareness of mortality acquired by the travelers in *Mardi* only through hard voyaging.

The cabin passengers, throughout *Redburn* as contemptible as the state-room sailors of *Typee,* reflect the insidious, inhuman blindness of Abrazza and the old Tapparian Begum who, fainting in her "innermost citadel," never went "abroad with the wind at east, dreading the contagion which might lurk in the air" (*M,* II.99). And they are all Melville's versions of Hawthorne's presumptuous pilgrims traveling "The Celestial Railroad" to the Celestial City with Mr. Smooth-it-Away as their guide. The crucial fact, as with Hawthorne, is that they are doomed and do not know it. Once the danger of the plague is past, they instantly fall back into their impregnable smugness: "As for the passengers in the cabin, who now so jocund as they? drawing nigh, with their long purses and goodly portmanteaus, to the promised land, without fear of fate" (376). Yet their promised land is figuratively the same one for which Jackson is imminently destined. Literally, it is the world that had devastated young Redburn at the outset, and the world that will also devastate the emigrants now seeking it in the mistaken belief that the differences between New York and Liverpool are more than geographic.

The emigrants, a collective counterpart to young impoverished Redburn gone to sea to seek his fortune, approach the new land in a darker spirit. Those who have escaped the plague's effects "wore a still, subdued aspect, though a little cheered by the genial air, and the hopeful thought of soon reaching their port." Those who have experienced it directly are more severely shaken and have already taken on something of Jackson's consuming sickness, even his distinguishing brand: "But those who had lost fathers, husbands, wives, or children, needed no crape to reveal to others who they were. Hard and bitter indeed was their lot; for with the poor and desolate grief is no indulgence of mere sentiment, however sincere, but a gnawing reality that eats into their vital beings" (375). Redburn, poor and desolate throughout, has also been forced to confront the gnawing reality that he is truly orphaned. Even his dream of his father has been shattered, for his dead father's guidebook has proved useless in leading him through a Liverpool entirely transformed from what it had been. The leap from Redburn's recognition of his father's uselessness to Ahab's grand defiance of his "fiery father" (M-D,II.282–83) is a large one; but the lines are clearly drawn, and they indicate something at least of how it might be with poor Wellingborough Redburn should the red blush of innocence someday be transformed into the scorched face of the Promethean.[10]

If Redburn comes no nearer to Promethean status than Tommo did to the pure savagery of Typee, Jackson, the exemplar of satanic defiance, achieves at least metaphorically something of Ahab's stature along with the physical resemblances already pointed out. In the "democracy" of hell, Jackson will take his place beside Nero, Napoleon, and Milton's Satan, as well as Tiberius, "that misanthrope upon the throne of the world . . . who even in his self-exile, embittered by bodily pangs, and unspeakable mental terrors only known to the damned on earth, yet did not give over his blasphemies, but endeavoured to drag down with him to his own perdition all who came within the evil spell of his power" (356). From the outset, Redburn has tried to escape such moral contamination. Isolated from the others because of Jackson's enmity, he finds himself "a sort of Ishmael in the ship, without a single friend or companion; and I began to feel a hatred growing up in me against the whole crew—so much so, that I prayed against it, that it might not master my heart completely, and so make a fiend of me, something like Jackson" (79). Where Ishmael is overpowered by Ahab's passionate argument to hunt the whale, joining with the rest of the crew in the crusade, Redburn is never directly influenced by Jackson. Yet he is unquestionably affected, and in terms that suggest kinship as well as horror: "But there seemed even more woe than wickedness about the man; and his wickedness seemed to spring from his woe; and for all his hideousness there was that in his eye at times that was ineffably pitiable and touching; and though there were moments when I almost hated this Jackson, yet I have pitied no man as I have pitied him" (134). Ahab's great woe appears Christ-like, and something of the same strange association seems suggested, though vaguely, in Redburn's observation that "*his* [Jackson's] death was *their* [the crew's] deliverance" (383). Like Conrad's Waite, Jackson dies within sight of land. The day after his death is Sunday, and the weather, suddenly bright and calm after the storm, reflects the homecoming atmosphere.

Whatever Jackson's moral effect on Redburn's rapidly developing world-view, it literally makes of him an author. As Ishmael must ennoble "a poor old whale-hunter" in order to make of his plight high tragic drama, so must his young predecessor dignify Jackson: "And though Tiberius came in the succession of the Caesars, and though unmatchable Tacitus has embalmed his carrion, yet do I account this Yankee Jackson full as dignified a personage as he, and as well meriting his lofty gallows in history; even though he was a nameless vagabond without an epitaph, and none, but I, narrate what he was" (356). The relationship, in this respect at least, is once again that between the Indian-hater par excellence and the diluted Indian-hater who returns to tell the anonymous hero's story. The connection with Ishmael appears still more forcefully when, immediately following Jackson's death, Redburn discourses on the paucity of lifeboats aboard the *Highlander*: "To be sure, no vessel full of emigrants, by any possible precautions, could in case of a fatal disaster at sea hope to save the tenth part of the souls on board; yet provision should certainly be made for a handful of survivors, to carry home the tidings of her loss; for even in the worst of the calamities that befell patient Job, some *one* at least of his servants escaped to report it" (383).

As with his predecessors, Redburn's coming of age is neither conventional nor perfunctory. The frame of mind in which he sets out upon his quest for knowledge and experience is already darkened by present and portended misery. Seeing a "strange, romantic charm" in ship advertisements is only one aspect of the adolescent Redburn. The other side is his poverty, which is intensified by memories of happier times when his father was alive. The allure of travel is itself prophetic. He dreams of "how fine it would be to be able to talk about remote and barbarous countries; with what reverence and wonder people would regard me, if I had just returned from the coast of Africa or New Zealand; how dark and romantic my sunburnt cheeks would look; how I would bring home with me foreign clothes of a rich fabric and princely make, and wear them up and down the streets, and how grocers' boys would turn back their heads to look at me as I went by. For I very well remembered staring at a man myself, who was pointed out to me by my aunt one Sunday in church, as the person who had been in Stony Arabia, and passed through strange adventures there, all of which with my own eyes I had read in the book which he wrote" (4). The nameless romantic traveler, Redburn's first inspirational image, is neither sunburned nor richly clothed. All that distinguishes him from the others is his peculiar eyes, which make him the subject of a kind of children's horror tale: " 'See what big eyes he has,' whispered my aunt; 'they got so big, because when he was almost dead with famishing in the desert, he all at once caught sight of a date tree, with the ripe fruit hanging on it.' "

Although the significance of the visionary date tree is unspecified, the point of it is that it elicits an immediate and precisely comparable response from Redburn. "Upon this, I

stared at him till I thought his eyes were really of an un-
common size, and stuck out from his head like those of a
lobster. I am sure my own eyes must have magnified as I
stared. When church was out, I wanted my aunt to take me
along and follow the traveller home. But she said the constables would take us up, if we did; and so I never saw this
wonderful Arabian traveller again. But he long haunted me;
and several times I dreamt of him, and thought his great eyes
were grown still larger and rounder; and once I had a vision
of the date tree" (4). The inference that there is something
criminal in pursuing the figure is suggestive, especially in
light of the implications of the date tree and its ripe fruit.
More immediately to the point, however, is the relationship
established at the outset between vicarious and ultimate perception. Redburn's eyes grow large viewing the large eyes of
this mysterious traveler who has perceived something unnamed but clearly central and definitive. Redburn is similarly
"haunted" and permanently affected by Jackson, whose
dominant characteristic is his mysterious eye, and who has in
turn perceived some ultimately terrifying vision.

This schematic relationship between Redburn and Jackson,
although a convention of fiction, represents a major conceptual advance over the earlier work, one that finally enables
Melville to direct his basic story landward without the absurd
pyrotechnics and sheer mystifications of the previous narrative
schemes. The terms are simple, but for Melville's limited
purposes they are at least serviceable. The neophyte must resemble the hero in some degree because Redburn must be able
and willing to confront the awful fact of a Jackson; he must
also pass on Jackson's unholy reading of the world to the
mass of men who stand just this side of the land's extremest
limit. In himself Jackson is a comment on those who come
no closer to his experience than the reading of it; Redburn is
the means by which the comment, necessarily qualified, may
be made.

Redburn's first voyage is from the start, then, comparable
to those of his predecessors, even to the extent that he dimly

expects from his travels subjects for stories: "As years passed on, this continual dwelling upon foreign associations bred in me a vague prophetic thought, that I was fated, one day or other, to be a great voyager; and that just as my father used to entertain strange gentlemen over their wine after dinner, I would hereafter be telling my own adventures to an eager auditory" (6–7). Just as the large-eyed stranger indicates something of the extreme results of great voyaging, so the glass ship, which specifically fixed Redburn's longings on the sea, presents some of the important characteristics of the process. Like the glassy surface of water, alluring Narcissus to plunge in and discover its deep secret, the glass ship has elusive mysteries to be dived for. As a child, Redburn had dreamed that it held buried gold, a notion inspired by legends of Captain Kidd's treasure ship supposedly lying at the bottom of the Hudson River near the Highlands. The location of this sunken treasure may be merely coincidental; it is surely deliberate, however indirect the statement, that the figurehead of the *Highlander,* like the figurehead of the glass ship, which falls from its perch "the very day" Redburn leaves home, is identified both with Redburn and with the heroic quester-figure: "As for steering, they would never let me go to the helm, except during a calm, when I and the figure-head on the bow were about equally employed. . . . He was a gallant six-footer of a Highlander *'in full fig,'* with bright tartans, bare knees, barred leggings, and blue bonnet, and the most vermilion of cheeks. He was game to his wooden marrow, and stood up to it through thick and thin; one foot a little advanced, and his right arm stretched forward, daring on the waves. In a gale of wind it was glorious to watch him standing at his post like a hero, and plunging up and down the watery Highlands and Lowlands, as the ship went foaming on her way. He was a veteran with many wounds of many sea-fights; and when he got to Liverpool a figure-head builder there amputated his left leg, and gave him another wooden one, which, I am sorry to say, did not fit him very well, for ever after he looked as if he limped" (147–48).

Though becalmed and as lacking in vital energy as his wooden, red-cheeked counterpart, Redburn in Liverpool will undergo a similar, though metaphoric, amputation, confronting his own isolation from his father as well as a suffering humanity's separation from a benign divinity. Also like the figurehead, he will be only altered, not finally transfigured, by his acquired knowledge. Both can be repaired and repainted, the figurehead literally. Jackson, by contrast, is irreparable. His analogue is the figurehead of a doomed ship: "Brooding there, in his infernal gloom, though nothing but a castaway sailor in canvas trowsers, this man was still a picture, worthy to be painted by the dark, moody hand of Salvator. In any of that master's lowering sea-pieces, representing the desolate crags of Calabria, with a midnight shipwreck in the distance, this Jackson's would have been the face to paint for the doomed vessel's figure-head, seamed and blasted by lightning" (355).

It is through such omens, ironies, and symbols that Redburn's fate as a voyager may be read at the very beginning of his journey. Like his predecessors who desert their ships, he leaves home because it has already proved intolerable. "At that early age . . . as unambitious as a man of sixty" (10), he goes to sea already a "misanthrope . . . with the warm soul of me flogged out by adversity." The terms of his departure adumbrate Ishmael's setting out, but there is neither knowledge of the life ahead nor high spirits. "It was early on a raw, cold, damp morning toward the end of a spring, and the world was before me; stretching away a long muddy road, lined with comfortable houses, whose inmates were taking their sunrise naps, heedless of the wayfarer passing" (11).

The innocent departs no longer innocent, and the garden is no Eden but the familiar sleepy world of the sightless landsman. Though he leaves appropriately clad in a shooting jacket and armed with a gun, he will point it not at sea monsters but at his fellow travelers on the ferry to New York. The mere thought of his neighbors sleeping comfortably at such a time is galling to him, and as he walks, his "fingers worked moodily at the stock and trigger, and I thought that this indeed was the way to begin life, with a gun in your hand." Already he is an outcast among landsmen. The well-fed passengers on the ferry "all cast toward me their evil eyes and cold suspicious glances, as I sat apart, though among them" (12). His first antagonist, the ticket seller to whom he must confess that he has miscalculated the fare and does not have enough to pay his way, is an effeminate "captain's clerk, a slender young man, dressed in the height of fashion." This humiliation passed, "the most insolent" of the gaping passengers is a "short fat man, with a plethora of cravat round his neck." If it was mere bravado that previously made Redburn flaunt a patch on his trousers, it is this and a good deal more that make him first return the fat man's stare defiantly and then abruptly point his gun at him. The gesture is no playful one. He clicks the gunlock and aims carefully, "point-blank, full in the left eye." When accused of being crazy, he agrees, though only to himself: "So I was at that time; for otherwise I know not how to account for my demoniac feelings, of which I was afterward heartily ashamed, as I ought to have been, indeed, and much more than that" (14–15).

Much worse than shame, presumably, is fear that such an action will be repeated, and with more serious consequence. His shipboard prayer is that burgeoning hatred will not make of him "a fiend . . . something like Jackson." Temporarily at least, he has been pulled back from the verge of murder, yet not without some insight. On the night of his arrival in New York, comfortable and well fed, with "the devil that had been tormenting me all day" finally gone, he can marvel at his behavior on the ferry: "That night I went to bed thinking the world pretty tolerable, after all; and I could hardly believe that I had really acted that morning as I had, for I was naturally of an easy and forbearing disposition; though when such a disposition is temporarily roused, it is perhaps worse than a cannibal's" (17). However he tries to make it so, the world he confronts is not even pretty tolerable, and more and more he is roused to cannibal thoughts if not actions. His most humane act, his attempts to feed a starving woman and her daughters, elicits his most murderous thoughts, and these are not directed against the society that has abandoned the woman. Having descended into the hell-like cellar where they sit dying of hunger, he thinks briefly of trying to get them out but rejects the possibility, because "they would only perish in the street, and here they were at least protected from the rain." If this is merely sensible and not the heartless sophism of the spurious do-gooder, what follows nullifies the virtues of the act. "I crawled up into the street, and looking down upon them again, almost repented that I had brought them any food; for it would only tend to prolong their misery, without hope of any permanent relief; for die they must very soon; they were too far gone for any medicine to help them." Finally the reaction is pushed to a logical and revealing extreme. "I hardly know whether I ought to confess another thing that occurred to me as I stood there; but it was this—I felt an almost irresistible impulse to do them the last mercy, of in some way putting an end to their horrible lives; and I should almost have done so, I think, had I not been deterred by thoughts of the law" (235–36). Although still not entirely outside society, he is not far from its edge. It has been suggested that Redburn moves steadily toward a broadly humanitarian character and outlook.[11] Yet his humanities, such as they are, are really incidental. His generosity is increasingly tempered by a corrosive anger, and at times outright revulsion, against the sufferer as well as the society that makes him suffer. His friend Harry Bolton, for instance, is as friendless and impoverished in New York as Redburn himself was in Liverpool, but Redburn quickly deserts him after putting him in touch with someone who might get him work.

Though his likely end is an isolato's, Redburn is simply too young to be more than a tentative version, at most, of the Promethean hero. "May I never be a man," he thinks, taunted and isolated by the crew at the start of the voyage, "if to be a boy is to be such a wretch. And I wailed and wept, and my heart cracked within me, but all the time I defied them through my teeth, and dared them to do their worst" (66). Although the posture is Jackson's, the antagonist is quite different. Already scarred and orphaned, Redburn may eventually become a Jackson or a Taji, but his first voyage is, in effect, Melville's portrait of the hero as a boy. From the beginning, however, the only possible direction for him is Jackson's, and the question is only how far toward Jackson's lonely fate he will be driven. As he walks to the ferry carrying his gun, the later Redburn, whose voice frequently intrudes directly, characterizes his youth in terms that portend his future as a "blasted" warrior with so deep "a scar that the air of Paradise might not erase it" and with only the possibility that he may someday reach "the stout time of manhood, when the gristle has become bone, and we stand up and fight out our lives, as a thing tried before and foreseen" (11–12).

The budding warrior goes through various rituals that are by now familiar. The night before taking ship, he cuts his long hair short, thinking it will make him lighter running aloft. No sooner is he on board than the chief mate gives him a new name: "I'll baptize you over again . . . henceforth your name is *Buttons*" (34). As the ship departs, he confronts the fact of his mortality: "For when I looked up at the high, giddy masts, and thought how often I must be going up and down them, I thought sure enough that some luckless day or other, I would certainly fall overboard and be drowned. And then, I thought of lying down at the bottom of the sea, stark alone, with the great waves rolling over me, and no one in the wide world knowing that I was there. And I thought how much better and sweeter it must be, to be buried under the pleasant hedge that bounded the sunny south side of our village graveyard, where every Sunday I had used to walk after church in the afternoon" (41). The terms echo Babbalanja's on true immortality, and the substance is prophetic of Jackson's end. As the *Highlander* passes through the

Narrows toward the open sea, Redburn, quickly reversing himself, makes a similar resolution: "After casting a last look at some boys who were standing on the parapet, gazing off to sea, I turned away heavily, and resolved not to look at the land any more" (46). The ensuing suicide of a drunken sailor, "raging mad with the delirium tremens" (63), indicates the symbolic aspect of Redburn's resolve. After the death, he goes below for his first night's sleep and discovers that there is no place for him to sleep but the suicide's bunk (64). A similar connection is made later. Two of the three books with which "he endeavours to improve his mind" belonged originally to the dead sailor: "One was an account of shipwrecks and disasters at sea, and the other was a large black volume, with *Delirium Tremens* in great gilt letters on the back" (109). The third book is Smith's *Wealth of Nations,* which was given him by his brother's friend Mr. Jones with the admonition to study it well, for "it would soon discover hidden charms and unforeseen attractions; besides teaching me, perhaps, the true way to retrieve the poverty of my family, and again make them all well-to-do in the world" (110). The book, it develops, is Jones's legacy from his father, and it is as useless to Redburn as his own father's guidebook proves to be. Soon afterwards, he draws a compass on one of its blank leaves in order to learn how to steer the ship and studies that "every morning, like the multiplication table" (150).

As with Ishmael, then, Redburn's turn to the sea and concomitant rejection of the land is essentially a moral act, instancing a willingness to undertake a course that in every key respect accords with that of the quester-hero. His childhood desire to visit "remote and barbarous countries" is fulfilled at the outset of his journey as he realizes that going to sea is "like going into a barbarous country, where they speak in a strange dialect, and dress in strange clothes, and live in strange houses" (82). To Larry, the primitivist who has asked him, "Are *you* now, Buttons, any better off for bein' snivelised?" (129), Liverpool "beats the coast of Afriky, all hollow; nothing like this in *Madasky"* (162–63). London then offers the budding hero a quick look at the Orient. "Aladdin's Palace," the gambling den he visits with Harry Bolton, is alive with sensuous, Eastern images comparable in spirit if not in substance to those in *Mardi.* In *Redburn,* however, the journey is wholly figurative: the real world of Liverpool and New York embodies the significance of Typee and of Mardi, and Redburn's travels result in a direct, if a familiar, moral judgment on that world. "We talk of the Turks, and abhor the cannibals; but may not some of *them* go to heaven before some of *us?* We may have civilised bodies and yet barbarous souls. We are blind to the real sights of this world; deaf to its voice; and dead to its death. And not till we know that one grief outweighs ten thousand joys will we become what Christianity is striving to make us" (379).

The Christian ideal remains just that, a Serenia hardly to be realized. The actual alternatives that the maturing hero confronts are those of the fundamental land-sea polarity, savage sailors, Turks, and cannibals on the one hand and, on the other, the deadened landsman whose existence is perpetual calm. Redburn may speculate on a truly Christian way of facing death, but the examples before him are the terrified hypocrites in the cabins and Jackson. Similarly, his whole journey has provided him with few images to measure himself against except those involving a choice between a false civilization and a genuine savagery. As Jackson dominates the forecastle, so Captain Riga is absolute dictator over the entire ship, and Riga is Melville's first sharp portrait of a confidence man par excellence. The alternative to Jackson in the forecastle is Max the Dutchman who repeatedly takes pious exception to Jackson's blasphemies. Though "perhaps the best-natured man among the crew," and the kindliest toward Redburn, Max is a fussy, womanish sort, "a great scold and fault-finder," whose proudest self-assertion is his acquired American citizenship and whose most noteworthy achievement is that he has two wives, interchangeable in every respect. An epitomized landsman, this "bachelor of a sailor" sails back and forth between domestic situations, with a "decent, civil woman" in each port to clean and mend his clothes. Initially, Max appears as a full-grown Redburn, providing, like the *Highlander*'s figurehead, a possibly prophetic image of what Redburn will become. "His hair, whiskers, and cheeks were of a fiery red; and as he wore a red shirt, he was altogether the most combustible-looking man I ever saw" (101–2).

Yet Max is only "combustible-looking." The genuinely combustible sailor is the mysterious Portuguese who is brought aboard at Liverpool, apparently drunk but actually dying if not already dead. It is Jackson who first notices that the man, "fast locked in his trance" (315), is dead, and it is Max the Dutchman who denies it. " 'No, he's not dead,' he cried. . . . But hardly had the words escaped, when, to the silent horror of all, two threads of greenish fire, like a forked tongue, darted out between the lips: and in a moment, the cadaverous face was crawled over by a swarm of worm-like flames" (316). This "Living Corpse," in contrast to the corpselike, living landsman, has the essential symbolic attributes of the Promethean and is even called so: "The eyes were open and fixed; the mouth was curled like a scroll, and every lean feature firm as in life; while the whole face, now wound in curls of soft blue flame, wore an aspect of grim defiance and eternal death. Prometheus, blasted by fire on the rock" (317). This blasted figure, as Jackson has also called him, is, like other analogues of Redburn, branded and emphatically red: "One arm, its red shirt-sleeve rolled up, exposed the man's name, tattooed in vermilion, near the hollow of the middle joint; and as if there was something peculiar in the painted flesh, every vibrating letter burned so white, that you might read the flaming name in the flickering ground of blue." Again, Melville would seem to be playing word games with his readers—the image of "the flaming name" carries an obvious association. At any rate, Redburn himself has already seen a comparable image of the sailor's fate in a Liverpool "Dead House" for drowned sailors: "A sailor stretched out, stark and stiff, with the sleeve of his frock rolled up, and showing his name and date of birth tatooed upon his arm. It was a sight full of suggestions: he seemed his own headstone" (230). Redburn is clearly witnessing here his own possible fate, the anonymous death of the tattooed sailor who has permanently renounced the land. And just as the initial renunciation of the land was conceived as a kind of suicide, accompanied by a literal one, so the effects of the knowledge acquired in Liverpool and London have brought about a kind of death symbolized by the burning Portuguese.

The dead Portuguese, of course, merely suggests the extreme possibilities of Redburn's development. It is Jackson's fate which is specifically foreshadowed. Jackson is the first to note that the sailor is dead, and it is Jackson who claims to have seen other instances of "animal combustion." Whereas the death tends to drive the others closer together, it isolates Jackson still further. "After the event, no one sailor but Jackson would stay alone in the forecastle, by night or by noon; and no more would they laugh or sing, or in any way make merry there, but kept all their pleasantries for the watches on deck. All but Jackson: who, while the rest would be sitting silently smoking on their chests, or in their bunks, would look toward the fatal spot, and cough, and laugh, and invoke the dead man with incredible scoffs and jeers. He froze my blood, and made my soul stand still" (318). In this last, the characteristic construction of *Redburn* may again be seen. Redburn, apart from the others, stares with horror at Jackson, similarly isolated, similarly staring at some more profound horror.

If Jackson is only foremost among the several examples set before Redburn, he would seem the likeliest to be imitated. The alternatives at sea are the bland confidence man, Captain Riga, and the landsman sailor, Max. Life on land, which he has renounced, offers him no better models than the smugly foolish Mr. Jones, the cabin passengers, the pawnbrokers, and their victims. The voice of the adult Redburn, heard now and again in the narrative, offers no conclusive view of the path he has followed after his first voyage. We know from the outset that, like the figurehead of the glass ship, he has not yet found his own legs though some years have passed (257). He remains both bitter (10) and impoverished, "a poor fellow, who have hardly ever known what it is to have five silver dollars in my pocket at one time" (314). We know too that he has followed the sea, had certain nameless adventures, in one of which he "expected to be killed every day" (27), and that he remains an unmarried isolato (277). In short, all his travels subsequent to his first voyage would seem to have made of Redburn only an older and more knowledgeable version of what he was, an Ishmael still seeking a definitive and transfiguring experience. In *White Jacket* the same sort of wandering hero, still undefined, encounters a figure entirely different from Jackson. With Jack Chase, Melville raises the possibility of a happier model for his young and still uncommitted neophyte.

WHITE JACKET *or The World in a Man-of-War* is the
most cheerful and accessible of Melville's novels. It
is also, in a way, the most difficult to evaluate. Written even
more hastily than *Redburn* and under greater pressures, it
nonetheless makes overt claim to high seriousness. As the
subtitle states, there is an allegorical correspondence between
the *Neversink* and the world, and the symbolic white jacket
that burdens and distinguishes the hero also names the novel.
Moreover, like *Omoo,* it seems to represent an emotional reaction to its immediate predecessor. The extreme leap from
the demonic Jackson to the benign Jack Chase reflects the
continuing tension in Melville between belief and disbelief,
hope and despair, and, more specifically, between recurrent
notions of voyage and return, sea life and land life. But where
Long Ghost is a foolish comic in a decayed and unheroic
world, Jack Chase is an unquestionably vital personality and,
on the surface at least, a substantial and heroic figure. Yet
what is most striking about Jack Chase and the man-of-war
world he dominates is that there seems to be a reaction not
merely against the mood of *Redburn* but against the entire
concept of the Promethean hero. The nature of the hero, his
relation to the developing neophyte—even the figurative machinery previously used to denote the Promethean character

and situation—all suddenly undergo a peculiar transformation. Everything in *White Jacket* is as upside down as its seasons—Christmas is "summered out" on the Equator, and the Fourth of July is spent in the "frigid latitudes of Cape Horn" (112).

Below decks, for instance, in emphatic contrast to the noble and comradely maintop men, the gunners are "a most unpleasant set of men," a "cross and quarrelsome" group. Yet they are described according to the patterns of heroic imagery already considered and have a special relevance to *Redburn*. All are of "the same dark brown complexion; all their faces looked like smoked hams" (55–56). Quoin is a "bitter, ill-natured, inflammable little old man." Priming has a harelip, and Cylinder both a stutter and a clubfoot. The chief gunner, the counterpart below decks to Jack Chase, captain of the maintop, is named Old Combustibles, and his place in the ranks of Melville's fiery, warrior-divers is unmistakable: "Among all the persons and things on board that puzzled me, and filled me most with strange emotions of doubt, misgivings, and mystery, was the gunner—a short, square, grim man, his hair and beard grizzled and singed, as if with gunpowder. His skin was of a flecky brown, like the stained barrel of a fowling-piece, and his hollow eyes burned in his head like blue lights. He it was who had access to many of those mysterious vaults I have spoken of. Often he might be seen groping his way into them, followed by his subalterns, the old quarter-gunners, as if intent upon laying a train of powder to blow up the ship" (159). Needless to say, the chief gunner also has his "frightful" scar, having once been "almost mortally wounded" in battle (161).

The differences between Old Combustibles and Jack Chase stem primarily from occupational factors, Melville blandly asserts at one point, citing a "most merry and companionable" maintop man who is transferred below to a quarter-gunner's berth and abruptly becomes ill-tempered and gloomy from being surrounded by cannon and "subject to the orders of those deformed blunderbusses, Priming and Cylinder" (56).

The point of view, as it is developed from this example, is the complete reverse of the basic beliefs most fully articulated by Babbalanja at Abrazza's court:

> The truth seems to be, indeed, that all people should be very careful in selecting their callings and vocations; very careful in seeing to it that they surround themselves by good-humoured, pleasant-looking objects, and agreeable, temper-soothing sounds. Many an angelic disposition has had its even edge turned, and hacked like a saw; and many a sweet draught of piety has soured on the heart from people's choosing ill-natured employments, and omitting to gather round them good-natured landscapes. Gardeners are most always pleasant, affable people to converse with; but beware of quarter-gunners, keepers of arsenals, and lonely lighthouse men. (56)

The ironies are obvious, though inconclusive and perplexing. Although Melvillé is surely not advancing Abrazza's mode of life as a preferable alternative to the Nantucket whaling man's, whose island home is "more lonely than the Eddystone lighthouse" (*M-D*, I.77), neither is he being pointlessly sarcastic or untruthful. Reflected here, and throughout *White Jacket,* are pressing, perhaps crucial, emotional needs. "It would be advisable for any man," Melville pontificates at one point, "who from an unlucky choice of a profession, which it is too late to change for another, should find his temper souring, to endeavour to counteract that misfortune by filling his private chamber with amiable, pleasurable sights and sounds" (57). White Jacket, heeding such advice, goes to the maintop with Jack Chase. Reacting to like pressures, Melville, it would seem, tried to sweeten his temper by writing *White Jacket*.[1]

As with Redburn and Jackson, White Jacket's exposure to Jack Chase determines both the subject and the spirit of his written narrative: "I feel persuaded in my inmost soul that it is to the fact of my having been a main-top man, and especially my particular post being on the loftiest yard of the frigate, the main-royal-yard, that I am now enabled to give such a free, broad, off-hand, bird's eye, and, more than all, impartial account of our man-of-war world" (59). Whether or not impartiality is realized, the view from the main-royal-yard is a strange one for Melville to be taking, and he takes it in a strange way.

> The reason of the mirthfulness of these topmen was, that they always looked out upon the blue, boundless, dimpled, laughing, sunny sea. Nor do I hold that it militates against this theory, that of a stormy day, when the face of the ocean was black and overcast, that some of them would grow moody, and chose to sit apart. On the contrary, it only proves the thing which I maintain. For even on shore there are many people, naturally gay and light-hearted, who, whenever the autumnal wind begins to bluster round the corners, and roar along the chimney-stacks, straight become cross, petulant, and irritable. What is more mellow than fine old ale? Yet thunder will sour the best nut-brown ever brewed. (59)

The argument is striking: indecisive, illogical, half-mocking, and, above all, atypical. Redburn's final awareness that "one grief outweighs ten thousand joys" has hitherto been for Melville both a world-view and a working principle. It may also be recalled that King Abrazza, determined to live only in sunlight, is taunted by Babbalanja as "sleek-cheeked Plenty! smiling at thine own dimples; vain for thee to reach out after greatness," and urged to "turn! turn . . . and be broken on the wheels of many woes. At white-heat brand thyself; and count the scars, like old war-worn veterans, over camp fires" (*M*, II.324). The chief gunner, branded by the fires of war, is far closer to Melville's previous beliefs: "And with that booming thunder in his ear, and the smell of the powder in his hair, he retired to his hammock for the night. What dreams he must have had!" (161). The description of the Koztanza as a thunder rolled by Lombardo through Mardi antedates by over three years the famous letter to Hawthorne of April 1851: "There is the grand truth about Nathaniel Hawthorne. He says NO! in thunder; but the Devil himself cannot make him say *yes*. For all men who say *yes*, lie."[2] One can hardly believe that this central and consistent position

would be so abruptly reversed, especially during the un-
usually lonely and harried period of July-August 1849, when
Melville was writing *White Jacket*. Yet the chief gunner and
those like him, hitherto Melville's heroic thunderers, are in
White Jacket incidental and even inconspicuous figures. The
focus throughout is on the maintop and Jack Chase.

Melville's new, apparently optimistic viewpoint is no lie,
however, but rather a tentative, almost wistful yearning to say
yes against all the logic of his senses and his mind. Jack
Chase, though a happier model for the developing youth to
emulate, is neither heroic nor even very useful, but merely one
admirable man in a very bad world. That he lacks both stature
and substance would seem clear enough and no matter of
concern, were it not for interpretive views like that of Richard
Chase which posit him as Melville's explicit moral alternative
to Ahab, as, in Richard Chase's term, a "true Prometheus,"
a genuine savior, not a spurious one.[3] There is actually no
indication that Melville intended to picture Jack Chase as
anything more than a handsome, engaging, much-loved
human being. "A frank and charming man," he calls him at
the outset. If Jack Chase is at all representational, it is as a
conventional democratic ideal, a "gentleman . . . though his
hand was hard" who "would have done honour to the Queen
of England's drawing-room" (14). The image throughout
is of a sociable, self-educated man with "an abounding air of
good sense and good feeling." There are, however, suggestions of a comparison with previous heroes, and these seem
clearly to connote a figure appreciably diminished in stature
if correspondingly more humane. He is, for instance, only "a
little bit of a dictator" (16), and, although another mutilated
hero, he is missing only "a finger of his left hand, which
finger he had lost at the great battle of Navarino" (13).
Chase has also deserted his ship in port—in order to fight for
Peru in her war against Bolivia—and like Tommo and Taji
he has undergone a change of rank, clothes, and name, becoming Don John, an officer in the Peruvian navy. But where
the real Jack Chase returned to his ship of his own volition

and after the fighting had stopped,[4] his fictional counterpart is spotted by Captain Claret of the *Neversink* during an accidental meeting at sea and peremptorily ordered to return, which he immediately does, and so gracefully that the desertion is overlooked and Chase is returned to his former post as captain of the maintop.

Jack Chase is, in fact, Promethean only in the ship's Fourth of July theatricals, in which he plays the leading role of Percy Royal-Mast, savior of sailors, rescuing no fewer than "fifteen oppressed sailors from the watch-house, in the teeth of a posse of constables" (118). Though White Jacket marvels sarcastically at the officers mixing so democratically with the crew to applaud "matchless Jack," on the following morning everything is back to normal, with another flogging at the gangway. The irony becomes more pointed later when White Jacket himself is threatened with flogging, and Jack Chase, the theatrical savior of sailors, merely stands by until a corporal of marines named Colbrook, hitherto of no importance, steps forward and, in an "almost unprecedented" action, speaks to the captain in White Jacket's defense. Only then does Jack Chase step forward too, "taking heart, perhaps, from Colbrook's example . . . and in a manly but carefully respectful manner, in substance repeated the corporal's remark, adding that he had never found me wanting in the top" (353–54). As a Prometheus, Chase's sole action for the general benefit of his fellows consists of his flattering the commodore into granting them all a day's shore leave. Confronted with a major challenge, the general order for "the great massacre of the beards," he fails rather markedly. Though he is initially furious and vows defiance, prudence quickly prevails: "In his cooler moments, Jack was a wise man; he at last deemed it but wisdom to succumb" (453).

If Jack Chase has nothing of Ahab's characteristic energy and power, it is partly because the world of the *Neversink* is expressly of the land and not the sea. The point is made early in the book when White Jacket, in what is obviously Melville's voice and mood, bewails his separation from the sea:

"Oh, give me again the rover's life—the joy, the thrill, the whirl! Let me feel thee again, old sea! let me leap into thy saddle once more. I am sick of these terra-firma toils and cares; sick of the dust and reek of towns. Let me hear the clatter of hailstones on icebergs, and not the dull tramp of these plodders, plodding their dull way from their cradles to their graves. . . . But when White Jacket speaks of the rover's life, he means not life in a man-of-war, which, with its martial formalities and thousand vices, stabs to the heart the soul of all free-and-easy honourable rovers" (97).[5] The atmosphere aboard the *Neversink* is that of the calm in *Mardi,* but though much of his time is spent in port, White Jacket does not even consider deserting a ship that is even more prisonlike than the *Dolly* or the *Arcturion.* Its specific analogue, in fact, is Sing-Sing Prison, according to a sailor named Shakings who has been there. Released from prison after many years, Shakings found it so difficult to cope with the demands of the outside world that "he almost wished he was back again in Sing-Sing, where he was relieved from all anxieties about what he should eat and drink, and was supported, like the President of the United States and Prince Albert, at the public charge" (217). A man-of-war, according to Shakings, is "a sort of state prison afloat," and White Jacket himself immediately echoes the view: "Immured as the man-of-war's man is, serving out his weary three years in a sort of sea-Newgate, from which he cannot escape, either by the roof or burrowing under ground, he too often flies to the bottle to seek relief from the intolerable ennui of nothing to do, and nowhere to go" (218).

Much of Melville's seeming divergence in *White Jacket* from basic previous positions becomes comprehensible when it is considered in light of the land atmosphere and land values of the work. The practice of flogging, for instance, is unquestionably a social evil, and yet Melville portrays it in terms of the overwhelming transcendent force against which the mutilated hero must strive: the old beldam and the little dwarf, the White Whale and Ahab.

"All hands witness punishment, ahoy!"
To the sensitive seaman that summons sounds like a doom. He knows that the same law which impels it—the same law by which the culprits of the day must suffer; that by that very law he also is liable at any time to be judged and condemned. And the inevitableness of his own presence at the scene: the strong arm that drags him in view of the scourge, and holds him there till all is over; forcing upon his loathing eye and soul the sufferings and groans of men who have familiarly consorted with him, eaten with him, battled out watches with him—men of his own type and badge—all this conveys a terrible hint of the omnipotent authority under which he lives. Indeed to such a man the naval summons to witness punishment carries a thrill, somewhat akin to what we may impute to the quick and the dead, when they shall hear the Last Trump, that is to bid them all arise in their ranks, and behold the final penalties inflicted upon the sinners of our race.   (167)

The four victims of this initial flogging represent four distinct responses to the ordeal. The first reacts like Stubb, bravely but mindlessly, smiling afterwards and saying, "D—n me! it's nothing when you're used to it! Who wants to fight?" The second, a Portuguese, responds in the manner of Jackson, "pouring out a torrent of involuntary blasphemies. Never before had he been heard to curse. When cut down, he went among the men, swearing to have the life of the captain." The third "only cringed and coughed under his punishment. . . . He became silent and sullen for the rest of the cruise." The last, a young boy scourged for the first time, seems permanently and seriously affected: "I don't care what happens to me now! . . . I have been flogged once, and they may do it again if they will. Let them look out for me now!" (170–71). When White Jacket himself is finally summoned "to the dread tribunal" with no knowledge of his crime, his reaction, like this young boy's, is that of a potential Indian-hater, recalling Bembo and foreshadowing Pierre:

There are times when wild thoughts enter a man's heart, when he seems almost irresponsible for his act and his deed. The captain stood on the weather-side of the deck. . . . I stood a little to windward of him, and, though he was a large, powerful man, it was certain that a sudden rush against him, along the slanting deck, would infallibly pitch him head-foremost into the ocean, though he who so rushed must needs go over with him. . . . I cannot analyse my heart, though it then stood still within me. But the thing that swayed me to my purpose was not altogether the thought that Captain Claret was about to degrade me, and that I had taken an oath with my soul that he should not. No, I felt my man's manhood so bottomless within me, that no word, no blow, no scourge of Captain Claret could cut me deep enough for that. I but swung to an instinct in me— the instinct diffused through all animated nature, the same that prompts even a worm to turn under the heel. Locking souls with him, I meant to drag Captain Claret from this earthly tribunal of his to that of Jehovah, and let Him decide between us. No other way could I escape the scourge. (352–53)

The reference to Jehovah is curious. In Melville's previous writings the angry God has not been notably just to the human worms beneath His heel. The issues, however, are unresolved. Colbrook and Jack Chase step forward, and the same capricious judgment that had unjustly accused now arbitrarily exonerates, saving White Jacket from "being a murderer and a suicide" (354). Again it should be emphasized that what he is saved from is the fate of Melville's characteristic hero. Redburn begins his journey with murderous impulses and spends his first night at sea sleeping in a suicide's bed. Taji's abdication from the world is conceived as a symbolic suicide; the murder he commits is literal and necessary to the attainment of heroic stature.

For all its surface amiability, the world of *White Jacket* is a dark one, as criminal and savage as Redburn's. The dominant fact of life in this "city afloat" (94), rolling through the sea "like the world in its orbit" (144), is the "almost incredible corruption pervading nearly all ranks" (225). Even the amusements of the crew are those of the jungle. The games and sports described in the chapter entitled "Fun in a Man-of-War" all have to do with beating:

"Single-stick, as everyone knows, is a delightful pastime, which consists in two men standing a few feet apart, and rapping each other over the head with long poles" (344). "Sparring" and "Hammer-and-Anvil" are similar games, and *"Head-bumping,* as patronised by Captain Claret, consists in two negroes (whites will not answer) butting at each other like rams." Strict regulations are necessary; otherwise "a man-of-war's crew would be nothing but a mob" (7). But the rules, emanating from the effete and incompetent Captain Claret, are arbitrary, capricious, and unjust. The Negro gladiators who entertain Claret with their head-bumping are flogged when immediately afterwards they fight in earnest, and Claret himself makes the distinction: "I'll teach you two men that, though I now and then permit you to *play,* I will have no *fighting"* (346).

The laws that order this society are administered through a hierarchy equally frivolous and unjust. The midshipman "lords it over those below him, while lorded over himself by his superiors. It is as if with one hand a schoolboy snapped his fingers at a dog, and at the same time received upon the other the discipline of the usher's ferule" (274). Above Captain Claret is the nameless commodore, and though in *White Jacket* Melville seems to be avoiding metaphysics in accordance with his pledge to Richard Bentley, everything suggests that above the commodore is an equally capricious ultimate authority. The indictment is comprehensive and corrosive: "Through all the endless ramifications of rank and station, in most men-of-war there runs a sinister vein of bitterness, not exceeded by the fireside hatreds in a family of step-sons ashore. It were sickening to detail all the paltry irritabilities, jealousies, and cabals, the spiteful detractions and animosities, that lurk far down, and cling to the very kelson of the ship. It is unmanning to think of" (472–73). The influence of a Jack Chase on such a world is clearly not very great, though Melville tries to make what he can of it. "Jack Chase, old Ushant, and several more fine tars that might be added, sufficiently attest, that in the *Neversink,* at least, there was more than one noble man-of-war's man who almost redeemed all the rest" (486). Even this qualified respect is soon diminished: "We have seen that a man-of-war is but this old-fashioned world of ours afloat, full of all manner of characters—full of strange contradictions; and though boasting some fine fellows here and there, yet, upon the whole, charged to the combings of her hatchways with the spirit of Belial and all unrighteousness" (493).

If the contempt for organized society and the revulsion from essential human evil are akin to Babbalanja's, White Jacket himself is notably different from Tommo and Taji in that he is not adventuring but returning home. This narrative distinction underlies the significance of the symbolic white jacket. Where young Redburn undergoes a transfiguring experience without assuming the burden of his acquired knowledge, his older counterpart in *White Jacket* would clearly seem to have the burden without the experience that determines it. The white jacket is in every respect analogous to the Melvillian hero's characteristic brand. Repeatedly termed "infernal," the jacket's basic associations are with death and an isolating guilt. It is "white as a shroud" (1), and nearly proves to be one. Aloft, it seems at one point a ghost (98) and, at another, an albatross (5). It makes of its wearer a "Jonah," blamed by the others for the sudden rash of deaths and accidents aboard the *Neversink* (419). Where Redburn's overlarge hunting jacket shrinks to his size when wet, indicating figurative growth, White Jacket's is like a sponge and makes of him "a universal absorber" (2). The jacket also makes him instantly recognizable so that when there is work to be done, he is always singled out for it. His attempts to paint it over fail for want of paint: Like Lem Hardy's tattoo, the jacket is ineradicable. Nor can he, despite great efforts, sell it or give it away. "There was no getting rid of it, except by rolling a forty-two-pound shot in it, and committing it to the deep. But though, in my desperation, I had once contemplated something of that sort, yet I had now become unaccountably averse to it, from certain involuntary superstitious considerations. If I sink my jacket, thought I, it will be sure to spread itself into a bed at the bottom of the sea, upon which I shall sooner or later recline, a dead man" (253). When we recall that the white jacket gives the narrator his name, Babbalanja's definition of anonymous heroic immortality becomes immediately relevant. White Jacket does not finally carve his name into a stone and sink it, however. Instead his climactic fall frees him from the jacket; it sinks and he returns.

The fall is clearly a rite of initiation, a symbolic death and rebirth. Babbalanja's image seems about to be fulfilled as White Jacket falls "down, down, with lungs collapsed as in death . . . toward the infallible centre of this terraqueous globe." His return to life is pictured as a struggling for birth. The jacket pulls him down, and he must literally cut himself from it. "I whipped out my knife . . . and ripped my jacket straight up and down, as if I were ripping open myself. With a violent struggle I then burst out of it, and was free" (498).[6] In keeping with the homeward movement of *White Jacket,* this birth is the opposite of Taji's, whose similar moments force him farther and farther away from civilization. Freedom from the jacket is for White Jacket freedom to be indistinguishable from his comrades and, ultimately, to land at home and take his place in society. Membership in civilized society, however, according to the insistent analogy between the *Neversink* and the world, is at best a doubtful honor, as Melville himself, exhausted and despairing at this point, well knew.[7]

Though White Jacket manages to see the sunny side of things, he does so against both the evidence of his eyes and the underlying logic of life in the man-of-war world. The order for "the great massacre of the beards" is specifically an attempt by an arbitrary authority to emasculate its followers. However mock-heroic in character, the issues are those of the scornful old beldam and the little dwarf. Jack Chase, after brief protest, complies out of prudence, even ironically absolving the barber of this "sin" against his "manhood," and blessing him "in token that I cherish no malice" (454–55). Old Ushant, who refuses to be shaved, suffers first flogging and then imprisonment, but attains "a glorious conquest over the Conqueror himself, as well worthy to be celebrated as the battle of the Nile" (462). Confronting two such models, White Jacket chooses the prudent, unheroic course. He expressly rejects the idea of Nelson's burial at sea in a coffin made from the mainmast of a French ship destroyed at the battle of the Nile, preferring himself to "be urned in the trunk of some green tree, and even in death have the vital sap circulating round me, giving of my dead body to the living foliage that shaded my peaceful tomb" (398). Seeking a peaceful life and death, no different from other men, he finally manages to lose his only distinguishing badge, in effect his only identity. Once he is free of it, the jacket itself is mistaken for a white shark, pierced through with a number of harpoons, and sunk. Whatever the judgment on White Jacket's ensuing safety, it is for Melville only temporary. In his next work, the white jacket rises symbolically once more and is again pierced through with harpoons, though the results are as different as the two books themselves.

White Jacket, then, reflects Melville's strivings for some kind of honest accommodation with the world in which he had to live and make a living. Because he was writing without plan or special preconception, the work is by turns hopeful and doubting, fervent and sarcastic. It embodies, in brief, all the fluctuating tensions and conflicts of a man who had returned to a world in which he was not entirely at home. Hawthorne's striking characterization of Melville as a man who "can neither believe, nor be comfortable in his unbelief"[8] is as applicable to the Melville of 1849 as it was to the older, wearier traveler who visited Hawthorne in Liverpool in November 1856, just after completing *The Confidence-Man.* *White Jacket* is Melville's strongest assertion of positive belief, but the mood is shaky and fleeting, at least as a subject for fiction. It has, however, served a special purpose. The affirming spirit, so tentative and doubtful when Melville philosophizes in *White Jacket,* is sure and sharply felt within the dramatic scheme of *Moby-Dick.* Given concrete expression in the Ishmael-Queequeg relationship, it harmonizes Ahab's darker story without significantly undermining its awful grandeur. And the differences, of course, are those between an imperfectly realized work and a very great one.

★ 6 ★

IN MOBY-DICK, all previous concerns—personal and novel-istic—come to a rich fruition. The great work that R. W. B. Lewis has so aptly termed "the supreme instance of the dialectical novel—a novel of tension without resolution"[1] derives from and is inherently compact with its imperfect precursors. It is thus at once and inseparably both an artistic and a psychic apotheosis, fulfilling all that *Mardi* expressly promises, integrating the divergent moods of *Redburn* and *White Jacket*. As always, there is clear connection between Melville's literary style and his fluctuating states of mind. The extravagant shape and language of *Mardi* reflect the exuberant young knowledge-seeking Melville, the enthusiast-explorer, putting to instant use all his new readings. The tortured, self-mocking style of *Pierre*—and the still more eccentric, self-nullifying prose of *The Confidence-Man*—measure an increasing bitterness. So, too, the high art of *Moby-Dick* cannot be understood without reference to the mellowed state described so eloquently to Hawthorne in a letter of June 1851. "My development has been all within a few years past. I am like one of those seeds taken out of the Egyptian Pyramids, which, after being three thousand years a seed and nothing but a seed, being planted in English soil, it developed itself, grew to greenness, and then fell to mould.

So I. Until I was twenty-five, I had no development at all. From my twenty-fifth year I date my life. Three weeks have scarcely passed, at any time between then and now, that I have not unfolded within myself. But I feel that I am now coming to the inmost leaf of the bulb, and that shortly the flower must fall to the mould."[2] Though there is grim prophecy in the image of impending decay, such a declaration reflects a man at least momentarily at ease in the depths of himself, poised for a time between the fluctuations of belief and disbelief, reconciling and harmonizing all the galling existential ambiguities that will reverberate through *Pierre* as title, theme, and refrain.

Moby-Dick, then, is the product of a state of mind at once complex and harmonious, a synthesis of Melville's most urgent concerns informed by a temporary quietude and expressed with a new craft. "I stand for the heart," he wrote Hawthorne in that same memorable letter of June 1851. "To the dogs with the head! I had rather be a fool with the heart, than Jupiter Olympus with his head." The declaration, however forceful, is less a conscious choice than a condition he has arrived at. The feeling man has become so not because he has denied the intellect, but because he has come to terms with its discoveries, rooting in himself all the important lessons of existence afforded by his brief but ample education. The willful avoidance of metaphysics ("no metaphysics, no conic sections") and concomitant turn to subjects "nearer home" result also, finally, in an intense personalization of his subject, a narrowing of the distance between perception and feeling. And the consequence for his art is the complete absorption of theme into story. As Ahab incorporates for the first time all the separate qualities of his several predecessors, so the story of *Moby-Dick,* like the *Pequod* itself, federates "along one keel" all those divergent convictions previously asserted intellectually.

On April 23, 1849, Melville wrote to his father-in-law Lemuel Shaw that, whatever the immediate critical response,

"Time, which is the solver of all riddles, will solve 'Mardi.' "[3] The pride, if somewhat defensive, is genuine. In *Redburn* and *White Jacket* he had no confidence whatever, as we have seen; even his private feelings about them were contemptuous.[4] Yet if the less ambitious works pose no coherent philosophic riddles, they reflect—perhaps because of the very pressures that constrict them—a man deeply perplexed by all the riddling mysteries of life and striving to work himself toward some kind of certainty. In *Mardi,* the perceptions are intellectual, even bookish, and the stance, for all its conceptual confidence, is finally inconclusive. Melville's basic themes are there: the interfusion of light and dark, the oneness of good and evil, the necessity of ennoblement through savagery, and an ultimate, heretical self-assertion, the absence of heroic possibility within the boundaries of conventional society, and so on. But Taji, Yillah, and Hautia are merely concepts, as thinly fleshed as they are absurdly named. Only Babbalanja, whose name implies at least something of his maker's self-mockery, has a viable humanity, and though he suffers real pain, he is reprieved, finally, from the great tests that might make of him an Ahab. Galled, insulted, and injured, he has the Melvillian hero's mind, the awful exacerbation, and often something of the language, but he lacks a fitting antagonist and hence the possibility for an ultimate redemptive action. In part, this is simply because Melville has not yet found an effective way to verbalize the transcendent force that is the cause of man's suffering and the object of his enmity. For Babbalanja, it is existence itself that galls and, though vaguely, God who is to blame. He agonizes and he screeches, asking all the proper questions, but he has only social ills and affectations to combat. And so, finally worn down—as his maker must have been too by the depthless dive that is *Mardi*—he accepts a very ordinary and totally unconvincing sort of salvation.

The White Whale, then, is not merely a fresh symbol but actually stands for something new to Melville's fiction. Whatever the figurative connections between the White Whale and white Yillah, shadowed by dark Hautia, the important point is that Yillah no sooner arrives as an actual character than she disappears into vague symbol. There is no true confrontation between the questing Taji and his goal, no dramatic relationship, no collision. Taji ends, in effect, where Ahab begins, having separated himself from his fellow men to follow his lonely, self-dooming destiny. The unnamed horrors seen only by *Redburn's* Jackson are akin, one must assume, to the symbolic terrors buried in the anonymous, watery grave with White Jacket's white jacket. But whatever other meanings these contribute, they add only a slight drama to their respective stories. In *Redburn,* as in *Typee,* the essential dramatic relationship is between the neophyte and some nameless dark transcendent force experienced only vaguely in the first and vicariously in the second. In *White Jacket,* as in *Omoo,* the young hero returns to his familiar world from a symbolic wilderness that has had no significant impact on his story. In *Moby-Dick* the dramatic scheme is truer to the conception. Ishmael and Ahab are each given their full play and if, unlike the preceding novels, it is Ahab's story that predominates, this is now both more logical and much closer to Melville's persisting concerns and obsessions. His craft has finally caught up with his intellectual and psychic needs.

In a sense Melville's novelistic progress is almost programmatic. To Tommo's vaguely symbolic situation, Melville adds a Jackson, in terrible solitary traffic with invisible devils. And then, to the Redburn-Jackson relationship, he adds a white whale standing, whether as agent or as principal, for all the inscrutable forces lurking behind the pasteboard masks. The resultant shift in focus affects, in one way or another, every aspect of *Moby-Dick,* but nowhere more notably than in Melville's new sense of his hero. By pushing the basic situation one step beyond *Mardi*—to a direct contest with the symbol of hostile force—Melville manages to humanize the quester even as he idealizes him. Much of the resonance of *Moby-Dick* derives from a single fresh perception. In fleshing out the Promethean character, Melville also underlines the heaviness of the burden. The grand, ungodly, godlike figure is also a man—and with his humanities too. Once he is entirely committed to the sea, the hero's longing turns instantly landwards, and the yearning, occasional as it is, is comparable to White Jacket's wish simply to be like other men, to live quietly without terror and to die without rage and be buried in familiar earth. In this regard, the importance of *White Jacket* is incalculable.

It may be said, very broadly, that the dark side of *Moby-Dick* derives from *Redburn* and the light side from *White Jacket*. The dark side, of course, is decisive, and the connections between Jackson and Ahab can be clearly seen. The effects of *White Jacket* are much harder to measure, having more to do with tone and spirit than with substance. Yet it is the lingering affirmative mood of *White Jacket* that informs Ishmael's humanities and, especially, Ahab's. The redeeming bond between Ishmael and Queequeg has no analogue in *Redburn,* where comradeship is limited and incomplete. Redburn's one friendship, with Harry Bolton, is based more on common interest than affection. They are not chummies, freely and fully communicating with no secrets between them, but only temporary companions. On the *Neversink,* however, for all the radical corruption, comradeship is widespread and deeply felt, not only between White Jacket and Jack Chase but generally, in all quarters.

So, too, on the *Pequod.* The Ishmael-Queequeg relationship generates much of the work's humane spirit, but its effects are reflected everywhere. The wedding of cannibal and Christian in "a joint stock company of two" joined together by the "elongated Siamese ligature" in "The Monkey-Rope" (II.48) offers dramatic evidence that conflicting black and white may in fact be happily reconciled, both literally and symbolically. Yet Ahab offers similar testimony and in the same terms. "Thou art tied to me by cords woven of my heart-strings," he tells Pip on adopting him, and when Pip calls upon the blacksmith to "rivet these two hands together; the black one with the white," Ahab movingly concurs, recognizing Pip's special kinship with "the sweet things of love and gratitude" (II.302). If Ahab must battle steadily against his human ties and instincts, he also frequently gives way to them. Though he throws away his pipe, a "thing that is meant for sereneness," (I.160), he also carries with him to the end "a small vial of sand . . . filled with Nantucket soundings" (II.268).

Nowhere is this illuminating benignity more telling—or more moving—than in the treatment of Starbuck. In the long line of Melville's heroes who point guns, Starbuck stands a failure, the prudent man who dares not thrust himself beyond the circle's relatively safe perimeter. The scheme is, on the surface, no less simplified than its opposite in *White Jacket,* where the gunners are infernal creatures, living in gloom below decks. Starbuck's inability to kill Ahab when he has the chance—and thereby save the *Pequod* from destruction through a sacrifice of his own humanity—offers a specific, if intolerable, moral gloss on Ahab's dark, predestined course. However difficult for us to accept, Ahab's awful vengeance is also a heroic self-sacrifice, an act of renewal and redemption affirming ultimate human possibility. The analogies, as indicated earlier, are with the epic saviors of humanity: Perseus and St. George, Davey Crockett and Anarcharsis Clootz, and even, though it strains credulity, Christ. Thus Ahab in effect brings about what Starbuck in his separate sphere cannot manage. Still, however closed and definitive the conceptual scheme, it is Starbuck to whom Ahab turns for brief communion in the magnificent chapter "The Symphony" just before the final cataclysm. And they confront each other momentarily as comrades, each responding to the other's needs, the old man and the young, both doomed now but briefly gentle with one another, rooted in the same sweet harmony.

Redburn and *White Jacket,* then, may in a sense be considered as two halves of the fundamental ambiguity of light and dark which pervades *Moby-Dick.* And the separate explorations surely in some way allowed Melville to get closer to each aspect and to bring something of the spirit of each to his great work. The ambiguity of "ungodly, godlike" Ahab, "darkness leaping out of light," is everywhere clarified by comparable images: the Negro church Ishmael stumbles into; black Fleece and innocent little Pip; the three savage squires in all their power and humanity; the ironies of Father Mapple's sermon by which we dimly understand that Ahab—the *Pequod*'s Jonah—is also the hero who does the Almighty's bidding "To preach the Truth to the face of falsehood," the man who is true "even though to be false were salvation." The White Whale, of course, offers similar testimony from the other direction—lightness leaping out of darkness. ("Light though thou be, thou leapest out of darkness; but I am darkness leaping out of light, leaping out of thee!") (II. 282). Ahab has a "sweet mother," as well as a "fiery father," though as he says he knows her not, and therein lies his "puzzle." If Ahab's story is in the fullest sense darkly tragic, there is also throughout a persistent sense of grace, a mood only, a feeling that is without structure and without intellectual conviction but that complements—and to some extent directs—the conscious metaphysical speculations. It is as if the sudden will to optimism that made Melville posit a benign Jack Chase as the potential savior of sailors were still operative in *Moby-Dick,* even though Melville had specifically denied that possibility by the end of *White Jacket.*

What is finally denied in *White Jacket,* however, is not the existence of benignity but its dominance and its ultimate redemptive powers. *White Jacket* is thus a more extensive and a more intensely personalized treatment of those essential issues left hanging at the end of *Mardi.* Taji and Babbalanja—rejecting and accepting their Serenia—represent a kind of unresolved debate; Ishmael and Ahab, in their very different setting, reflect an acceptance of the impossibility of any genuine resolution. Melville's new ease with existential ambiguities is reflected everywhere in the richly paradoxical texture of *Moby-Dick.* It underlies both his exclusion of materials previously important to him and his ability to absorb into drama matters previously treated intellectually. With the incidental figure of Samoa in *Mardi*, for instance, Melville explores more fully the complex sexual implications of Tommo's mysterious, unmanning lameness at Typee. Badly wounded in his successful defense of his ship, Samoa has been forced to amputate his own arm. "In Polynesia," we are told in a coy aside, "every man is his own barber and surgeon, cutting off his beard or arm, as occasion demands" (I.88). The association of limb and beard, symbol of manhood and manliness, hints unmistakably at castration fears, one source of which is woman and domestic life in general.[5] "Though manly enough, nay, an obelisk in stature," Samoa "is far from being sentimentally prepossessing" (I.112). This "most terrible fellow to behold" is also a henpecked husband, and his heroic capabilities are considerably impaired thereby: "What, though a hero in other respects; what, though he had slain his savages, and gallantly carried his craft from their clutches:—Like the valiant captains Marlborough and Belisarius, he was a poltroon to his wife" (I.87). At its simplest, the polarity of sea and land corresponds to conventional notions of masculinity and effeminacy, *Omoo's* Bembo and Lady Guy, and in this limited sense, the domestic threat is specifically directed at the questing isolato's moral purpose and his unrelenting, vestal dedication. Samoa's shrewish wife is thus also an affront and threat to the as yet unnamed Taji and his chummy Jarl, and so they plot to kill her. Fortunately, a storm comes up to serve this purpose, at which point the proper business of *Mardi* can begin. In *Moby-Dick*, there is similar domestic threat, but having blocked out his position, Melville now locates it in the drama of Ahab's steady battle against the homeward pull of his humanities. Ahab "has a wife—not three voyages wedded—a sweet, resigned girl; hold ye, then," Peleg goes on to ask Ishmael, "there can be any utter, hopeless harm in Ahab? No, no, my lad; stricken, blasted, if he be, Ahab has his humanities!" (I.100). The female presence thus remains, but its effect is to humanize the hero's dilemma and to underscore his intractable dedication. Ahab's momentary longing for land and home in "The Symphony" creates compelling poignance just before the cataclysm, but his view of himself and his mission remains unalterably fixed: "Wife? Wife? —rather a widow with her husband alive! Ay, I widowed that poor girl when I married her" (II.328).

The progress from the peripheral Samoa's domestic situation to Ahab's reflects considerably more than an advance in novelistic skills. As Ahab passes by the frivolous *Bachelor* with hardly a glance, let alone the fierce harangues that Babbalanja directs at the bachelor King Abrazza, so Melville himself now pursues his story with a new single-mindedness and purity, apparently indifferent to matters hitherto of moment. "Trained down," in Babbalanja's words, "to the standard of what is unchangeably true" (*M,* II.81), he also fulfills one of Babbalanja-Lombardo's ultimate artistic aims by "rejecting materials which would make palaces for others" (*M,* II.331). In *Moby-Dick,* he pays little attention, for instance, to the world of "state-room sailors" that has previously furnished grounds for relevant satires. Save for certain of the gams, where contrast is the purpose, there are in *Moby-Dick* no Abrazzas and no Rigas. All such are left standing in faceless conglomerate at the land's "extremest limit" in the opening chapter, and the result is at once a world genuinely heroic and a work which is that world's most perfect distillation. The invention of the White Whale is again the decisive factor. If Babbalanja has only an ultimate nameless mystery of living to pursue, so he has only people to direct his rage against. Thus the image of a specific English king, called Bello, is invested with a tentative, irrelevant, but notably suggestive symbolism foreshadowing *Moby-Dick*: "In stature, Bello was a mountaineer; but, as over some tall tower impends the hill-side cliff, so Bello's Athos hump hung over him. Could it be, as many of his nobles held, that the old monarch's hump was his sensorium and source of strength: full of nerves, muscles, ganglions and tendons? Yet, year by year it grew, ringed like the bole of his palms. The toils of war increased it" (*M,* II.179-80). If Ahab piles a great deal

more upon the "whale's white hump" than does Babbalanja
on King Bello's, it is in large part simply because the balance
of forces has allowed him a fit antagonist.

Another measure of the changes in craft and outlook underlying *Moby-Dick* may be seen in Melville's diminished
and notably altered use of what he termed the allegorical.
Both *Mardi* and *White Jacket* are built upon elaborate
schemes of allegorical correspondences between the real
world and the literary work expressly titled to embody it.
Ishmael, like his forerunners, begins his actual journey with
a hint that some similar allegorical framework is to follow.
"I want to see what whaling is. I want to see the world," he
tells Captain Peleg before signing on. "Want to see what
whaling is, eh?", Peleg answers. "Have ye clapped eye on
Captain Ahab?" (I.88). The world as Mardi is in fact the
kind of puzzle Melville described in 1849 writing to Lemuel
Shaw. The world as Ahab is a mystery and is intended to
remain so. Something of Melville's own feelings on this score
may perhaps be inferred from a letter to Sophia Hawthorne
dated January 1852, in which, with no little irony, he praises
that good lady's "spiritualizing nature" which enables her to
"refine" all that she sees "so that they are not the same things
that other people see, but things which while you think you
but humbly discover them, you do in fact create them for
yourself. Therefore, upon the whole, I do not so much marvel
at your expressions concerning *Moby-Dick*. At any rate your
allusion for example to the 'Spirit Spout' first showed to me
that there was a subtile significance in that thing—but I did
not, in that case, *mean* it. I had some vague idea while writing it, that the whole book was susceptible of an allegoric
construction, and also that *parts* of it were—but the speciality
of many of the particular subordinate allegories, were first revealed to me, after reading Mr. Hawthorne's letter, which,
without citing any particular examples, yet intimated the part-
and-parcel allegoricalness of the whole."[6] Babbalanja, pursuing an answer to life's ultimate mysteries, represents finally
only an especially thoughtful and exacerbated metaphysician.

Ahab, himself a kind of answer, embodies a mystery inaccessible at its core. Like the doubloon he nails to the mast, he is all things to all men, depending on the nature of the beholder. From the special wisdom of his madness, Pip supplies the only decisive explication. "I look, you look, he looks; we look, ye look, they look" (II.194).

Even the narrative authority from which we, as readers, receive the story is limited and partial. Ishmael provides us with general guidelines toward interpretation, but only as a kind of overview, reiterating and amplifying the meanings of the opening chapter but always precluding any easy judgment of the *Pequod*'s emblematic mission. The following is characteristic: "Were this world an endless plain, and by sailing eastward we could for ever reach new distances, and discover sights more sweet and strange than any Cyclades or Islands of King Solomon, then there were promise in the voyage. But in pursuit of those far mysteries we dream of, or in tormented chase of that demon phantom that, some time or other, swims before all human hearts; while chasing such over this round globe, they either lead us on in barren mazes or midway leave us whelmed" (I.300).[7] The White Whale is always there, he tells us, whether or not man pursues it, but once man puts out to sea, his decision is irrevocable and its end grimly ordained: "For as this appalling ocean surrounds the verdant land, so in the soul of man there lies one insular Tahiti, full of peace and joy, but encompassed by all the horrors of the half known life. God keep thee! Push not off from that isle, thou canst never return!" (I.349). Such safety is ephemeral, however, residing only in untested innocence. And whether for Taji in his calm or Redburn and Ishmael in their drizzly, damp Novembers, or Melville himself, bored with his Tahitian romances and yearning for Icarian flight in *Mardi*, the seaward pull—as "Loomings" tells us—is universal and decisive, however mutilating.

Ishmael can thus comprehend and narrate "what the White Whale was to Ahab" and he can also reveal something of "what, at times, he was to me" (I.234), but he cannot actually decipher either and, significantly, he does not try to do so.

Such a crew, so officered, seemed specially picked and packed by some infernal fatality to help him to his monomaniac revenge. How it was that they so aboundingly responded to the old man's ire—by what evil magic their souls were possessed, that at times his hate seemed almost theirs; the White Whale as much their insufferable foe as his; how all this came to be— what the White Whale was to them, or how to their unconscious understandings, also, in some dim, unsuspected way, he might have seemed the gliding great demon of the seas of life,—all this to explain, would be to dive deeper than Ishmael can go. (I.233)

Ishmael, then, is the first of Melville's "thought-divers" who recognizes from the start his own radical limitations, and behind Ishmael's self-confessed inadequacies we may infer a notable lessening of Melville's old ambition to write all-comprehendingly about the ultimate mysteries of existence. Like the sub-sub-librarian compiling from world literature his extracts on the whale—and like Melville himself—Ishmael is only a researcher into whaling, however closely connected to its important actions. "The more I dive into this matter of whaling, and push my researches up to the very spring-head of it, so much the more am I impressed with its great honorableness and antiquity; and especially when I find so many great demi-gods and heroes, prophets of all sorts, who one way or other have shed distinction upon it, I am transported with the reflection that I myself belong, though but subordinately, to so emblazoned a fraternity" (II.101). To compare this characteristically quiet mood, so accepting of its human frailties, with the aggressive, often strident, voice of *Mardi*'s narrator, continually asserting an author's equality with great demigods and heroes, is again to locate the source of basic differences between the two works in Melville's self-proclaimed maturity. In *Moby-Dick,* the correspondence between whales and books is offered in a playful spirit, underscoring the inadequacy of books and not their primacy.

I would suggest, then, that the limitations specifically imposed on Ishmael as narrator reflect Melville's diminished sense of his own role and its boundaries. "Why ever since Adam," he wrote Hawthorne in November 1851, "who has got to the meanings of this great allegory—the world? Then we pygmies must be content to have our paper allegories but ill-comprehended."[8] The posture is familiar—as is the implicitly heretical analogy—but the tone is markedly lighter, even self-critical. Though he is still well up the ladder from his readers, the mature author who has "read Solomon more and more, and every time see[n] deeper and deeper and unspeakable meanings in him"[9] is no longer making overt claim to kinship with his heroes. Like Ishmael, he has in a sense been subsumed into Ahab's character and absorbed by his lofty, purposeful drama. The consequences of such a transmutation are again discernible in the craft of *Moby-Dick*. One tends to forget just how small is Ishmael's actual role aboard the *Pequod* once it puts to sea. The disappearance of the first-person narrator accords with his diminished activities as a participant, and this is both logical and necessary. The richness of the *Pequod*'s collective life derives not only from its cunningly structured varieties but also from a balance of fragmented forces coherent and completed finally only in the aggregate. Thus Bulkington appears briefly, earns an eloquent salute as premature epitaph, and disappears for good. The point is not, as has been argued, that such a spirit must either vanish or dominate, but rather simply that the brief appearance helps define the grandeur of the general quest. Bulkington's "apotheosis" is earned by his membership in the fraternity of whaling men, and in turn, as do so many of his fellow isolatos, Bulkington graces and legitimizes Ahab's mission. Like Ishmael, he is subsumed in Ahab, a true follower of a truly overpowering leader.

In this regard it is surely to the point that Ishmael has no direct contact with his captain, a narrative fact that once again illuminates both the remarkable differences and the underlying similarities between *Moby-Dick* and Melville's previous work. As has been pointed out, the young man's quest for paternity and for paternal models has been—and will again be—Melville's basic story. By the recurrent logic of the hierarchical ladder, Ahab not only has a "fiery father," but also is himself one. Thus he presides over the officers' dinner table "like a mute, maned sea-lion . . . surrounded by his war-like but still deferential cubs" who are "as little children before Ahab" (I.186). The domestic figure takes on a certain poignance with Ahab's refusal to make any kind of table talk. As at so many family tables, "in the cabin was no companionship; socially, Ahab was inaccessible. Though nominally included in the census of Christendom, he was still an alien to it" (I.190). The alienation, as always, cuts both ways. The sons are denied a father; the father lacks connection with his sons. When Ahab refuses to help the *Rachel*'s captain search for his lost son, it is with specific denial of his own actual fatherhood and in a spirit of marked sadness. And when Ishmael becomes that lost, orphaned child, the implication is of an unrealized paternity necessarily transferred from Ahab—a symbolic father lost, a foster father found. An important difference, then, between Ishmael and Redburn is that for Ishmael there is no vitalizing contact with the father-figure. That is reserved only for Pip, and with good reason, since Pip is the definitive castaway, the innocent irrevocably transfigured by his literal plunge into that endless and appalling sea. Yet even here, Melville refuses to be categorical. Pip, too, represents finally only another threat to Ahab's purpose. For Pip, the adoption is specific, reflecting basic filial desires: "had poor Pip but felt so kind a thing as this, perhaps he had ne'er been lost" (II.302). But though the one "is daft with strength, the other daft with weakness," the moving familial symmetries only portend the cataclysm. The father, to fulfill his purpose, must reject even his proper son. Ahab's paternal feelings—like his memories of home—are "too curing to my malady . . . and for this hunt, my malady becomes my most desired health" (II.316).

We touch here on a buried drama of major consequence

and interest, but one as essentially impenetrable as any of Melville's willfully created ultimate mysteries. Ahab's "fiery father" is in effect the mythic and symbolic extension of that literal paternal authority sought by young Redburn, image of the fatherless Melville. Though they tend toward a complex symbolism, the issues in *Redburn* are relatively simple, located in familiar psychological and social matters. In *Pierre*, however, the psychological drama reveals unmistakably the oedipal roots of Ahab's cruel puzzle. The "sweet mother" Ahab does not know finds a contrary kind of expression in Pierre's fiercely mannish mother. His "fiery father" is embodied quite literally in the revered parental portrait Pierre burns on discovering his father's secret sin. The symbolic aspects of the Glendinning family patterns will be considered in the next chapter. What is important for the present is some consideration of the kind of massive psychic tensions temporarily purged in *Moby-Dick* to create so perfect a distillation of its author's theme and state of mind.

Once more, *Mardi* offers an instructive contrast. Before she vanishes to become symbolic object of the quest, Yillah plays a curious domestic role. Again the implications accord somewhat with the oedipal configuration. Taji wins his pure albino bride by killing the old priest, who represents a literal, as well as a divine, paternity. The subsequent pursuit by Aleema's three avenging sons is reproduced in *Pierre* in virtually the same terms when the virginal Lucy Tartan's brother and Glendinning Stanly, Pierre's only male relation, seek vengeance on Pierre for having, as they think, corrupted Lucy. The three emissaries of dark Hautia, operating in conjunction with the avengers, add stark suggestions of the sexual sins that marriage necessarily entails. Yillah is thus the tarnished virgin of Puritan marriage fears, the fallen innocent necessarily corrupted by her lawful mate through the institution of marriage itself. Hence the inescapable oneness of Yillah and Hautia which Taji eventually comes to recognize. In this sense, Taji's quest may be seen as a hopeless effort to recreate the original connubial purities, the harmonious innocence of his brief idyllic island life with Yillah before her disappearance. Melville's occasional digressive attacks on marriage and domesticity underscore the private relevance of this aspect of his allegory.[10] In *Mardi,* however, such matters are only tentatively—perhaps even subconsciously—articulated. In *Pierre* they are explosive. Pierre, who has sworn—perhaps in jest, we are told—to kill any suitor of his widowed mother's hand, calls his mother sister. Mrs. Glendinning, who also plays this game, calling her son brother, is pleased with Lucy Tartan as Pierre's prospective bride precisely because she is weak and malleable. Pierre's half-sister, Isabel, a dark Hautia to white Lucy, is cast in Mrs. Glendinning's own dark image, and the ensuing incest between brother and dark sister may properly be viewed as a dislocation of Pierre's sexual ambitions toward his mother.[11] And, of course, he must first desecrate and then destroy his father's image in order to release his sexual energies and fulfill his darkest needs.

I would suggest that even in *Pierre,* such matters are not Melville's subject but his burden. The urge to the exclusively male life of the sea, with its constant homosexual element and its explicit definition of landlife in female terms, is in effect also an escape from the most troubling kinds of personal entanglements. To recognize, however partially and imperfectly, that Ahab's grim dilemma also has such unarticulated psychological sources is to sense as well how stunningly Melville managed this one time to transcend potentially crippling limitations, making from the stuff of private torment, epic literature. Some falling off was surely inevitable, though the quickness of it is surprising, even in so volatile and complex a man as Melville. The emotional equilibrium that results in *Moby-Dick* is terribly tenuous and fragile, and the inherently conflicting elements balanced so delicately in *Moby-Dick* virtually explode in *Pierre.* Whether or not Melville actually intended *Pierre* as the "rural bowl of milk" he promised Sophia Hawthorne in January 1852,[12] it is clear enough that once he turned to it a contrary sort of spirit quickly developed, fed by all the deep destructive elements previously held in check. In *Pierre,* the psychological turmoils finally surface, revealing themselves with an awful clarity. The spirit of the sub-sub-librarian, chronicling the deeds of larger men, turns sourly self-contemptuous, even anti-literary. And feeding and shaping the inchoate despairs, there emerges a new intellectual decisiveness, not about the Promethean hero—good or bad—but about his uselessness in an increasingly nonheroic world. The last three novels chronicle the hero's attrition and eventual disappearance. After *Moby-Dick,* the work gets steadily more bitter, simultaneously darker and more constricted, until it stops entirely.

PART THREE

RETREAT

★ 7 ★

THE LAST THREE NOVELS are a letdown, whatever their intrinsic worth. Recent critical admiration for *Pierre*, and less so for *The Confidence-Man*, stems in large part, I suspect, from continuing interest in a man whose single major work has been studied almost to the point of no returns. Yet the last novels do have their own distinction and interest. In terms of his career, Melville's final triad is his most compelling, for he is trying there to break free from his novelistic past, trying in effect to follow up *Moby-Dick*. There is, for instance, a use of new techniques, a clear effort to write differently. For all its verbal peculiarities, which in themselves instance a kind of stylistic groping, *Pierre* is a conventional third-person novel, Melville's first. *Israel Potter* is popular historical fiction, written for serialized publication in *Putnam's Monthly*. *The Confidence-Man* is patently experimental. What we confront, then, in this last phase is a man trying to move away from previous forms and styles, and yet, necessarily, always telling something of the same familiar story. The old obsessions persist, and they inhibit, even frustrate, the new gambits. As with the novels preceding *Moby-Dick*, there is a pattern to the progress, but here the logic is that of withdrawal, of slow, awkward return from wild wanderings and deep divings. The thrust is now steadily landward, marked by a significant shift in Melville's continuing symbolic use of land and sea. *Pierre,* though a fresh bold effort, a striking out in the mode of *Typee* and *Redburn,* takes place entirely on land. *Israel Potter,* a clear retrenchment and even, eventually, a homecoming story, is in large part sea-borne. And brilliantly fusing his latest concerns, Melville locates *The Confidence-Man* entirely on shipboard but on a land-bound river.

This landward movement is at once a chronicle of progressive disillusion and an abdication. Until *Pierre,* Melville's fiction had consistently mirrored his perceptions about the world; *Pierre* seems to reflect a last perception that the world no longer offered meaningful subjects for his fictions and that the act of writing was itself a fruitless act, as deeply unsatisfying as it was unremunerative. Perhaps the most curious development in these last novels, taken together, is the increasing distance between the author and his subject, a distance implicit in the shift to detached, third-person narrations. The writer who had always been so integral a part of all his work steadily refines himself away until, at the end of *The Confidence-Man,* he abruptly takes his leave entirely. "Something further may follow of this Masquerade" are the last cryptic words of that odd—and oddly final—book. And, of course, nothing does.

Pierre, or The Ambiguities, in many ways the most complex of Melville's novels and surely the most difficult to judge, is at once an end and a beginning. To Henry Murray, whose introduction to the Hendricks House edition is a brilliant consideration of Melville's private involvement in the life of his last substantial hero, *Pierre* represents Melville's final assault on his one great theme: "Through the Ahab of his imagination he had cursed God and drowned, but on waking from the dream, discovered that he was still among the quick. Ishmael survived the wreck; and in Ishmael there was still some energy, some grief, some hate—'deep volcanoes long burn ere they burn out.' *Pierre* is the burning out of

Melville's volcano."[1] The image itself is of course central to Melville, and an apt and expressive one. However, Melville's Promethean "combustibles" do not burn out but up, consumed by the fires of that inferno to which they voluntarily descend in full knowledge of impending annihilation. Pierre, though, unlike Ahab and the others, unquestionably does burn out. Although he embodies all the essential characteristics of the Promethean hero, his mission is performed under markedly different conditions and with distinctly altered consequences.

What Murray describes as "the performance of a depleted puppeteer" is actually a new kind of performance for Melville, just as the very role of puppeteer is also new. With *Pierre* he discards permanently the narrator who has both told his story and exemplified its meanings. He writes, instead, a more conventionally shaped third-person novel,[2] the setting of which is a familiar, constricting land atmosphere where the basic laws and terms of life are those of contemporary American society. The Promethean hero now lives and functions within the society he must by definition shun. Taji rejects the world as he gradually gains awareness of it, and finally he abandons it entirely for the mythic role of the eternal quester. Ahab, conceived at the outset on a mythic scale, looks back in poignant moments of resurgent humanity to the world he has had to renounce in order to enact his vengeful mission. In sharp contrast, Pierre looks seawards from a literal world in which the only possibilities for an Ahab-like defiance are expressly criminal.

There is, of course, a profound connection between this new view of the hero and Melville's increasing personal despair as he tried to make salable fictions out of deep emotional and intellectual dilemmas that grew more unmanageably complex the more he puzzled over them. The numerous biographical similarities between author and character discussed by Murray[3] merely enhance the painfully explicit portrait of Pierre as an overreaching, Melville-like young author, vowing to "gospelise the world anew, and show them deeper

secrets than the Apocalypse!—I will write it, I will write it!"
(381).[4] Pierre's presumptuous literary ambitions are as self-
destructive as his heroic decision to assume the burden of his
father's illegitimate daughter, Isabel, renouncing by that hard
choice all happiness and worldly expectation. Moreover, as
in *Mardi,* the author's proud calling is implicitly heretical,
and the quester's self-sacrifice is increasingly suspect, darkened, in Pierre's case, by incestuous complications. Eventually
Pierre has for each of his two roles far more self-contempt
than pride. Near the end, he receives two similar letters in the
same mail. The first, from his publisher, begins, "You are a
swindler. Upon the pretence of writing a popular novel for
us, you have been receiving cash advances from us, while
passing through our press the sheets of a blasphemous rhapsody, filched from the vile Atheists, Lucian and Voltaire"
(497). The other letter, from his cousin Glendinning Stanly
and his once-prospective brother-in-law Frederic Tartan,
sharpens this mocking self-contempt into something like self-
loathing: "Thou, Pierre Glendinning, art a villainous and
perjured liar. . . . Separately, and together, we brand thee, in
thy every lung-cell, a liar;—liar, because that is the scornfullest
and loathsomest title for a man; which in itself is the com-
pend of all infamous things." That such disgust is not merely
his enemies' view of Pierre, but also in some curious way his
own and his creator's, is suggested throughout. There is, for
instance, an earlier moment when Pierre suddenly suffers an
attack of vertigo returning home from one of his nightly
wanderings and passes out on the street, to waken finally
"lying cross-wise in the gutter, dabbled with mud and slime"
(475). The implication is of a Christ in some way defiled,
even self-polluted, and thus seems to support a view that
Pierre has somehow corrupted a course initially pure. But
though Pierre has from the first assumption of his burden
been specifically associated with Christ, his meanings are not
that easily deciphered. The self-loathing that characterizes
his end also marked his beginnings, when Isabel's letter revealed to him the personal relevance of the *Inferno* and

Hamlet and provoked him to "high deeds": "Now indeed did all the fiery floods in the *Inferno,* and all the rolling gloom in *Hamlet* suffocate him at once in flame and smoke. The cheeks of his soul collapsed in him; he dashed himself in blind fury and swift madness against the wall, and fell dabbling in the vomit of his loathed identity" (239). If the self-abuse here recalls similar outbursts of the malcontent philosopher Babbalanja, there is good reason for it. Like that often-unhappy predecessor, Pierre is driven to see too much of human wickedness and woe, but in his case the goad is neither intellectual nor heroically self-assertive. Where the earlier heroes suffer willfully, impelled by entirely private needs, Pierre undergoes his ordeal with reluctance and eventually with deep regret. What Taji, Redburn, and Ishmael choose, Pierre inherits. He must confront a fallen world because he must fall, and it is, ultimately, his maker who condemns him thus. "Now Pierre stands on this noble pedestal," Melville intones with heavy, unrelenting sarcasm at the very outset; "we shall see if he keeps that fine footing; we shall see if Fate hath not just a little bit of a small word or two to say in this world" (14). The tone is characteristic of *Pierre,* as is the posture. From the start, Pierre is viewed from the perspective of an ironic puppeteer whose stance toward his creation is fixed and admits of no drastic self-questioning. Melville the author has, in effect, already voyaged where his fictional counterpart is going, and the special knowledge gained serves to make of *Pierre* something like a parable of deep-diving—not, as in the preceding novels, a dramatized embodiment.

Yet if this version of the story lacks immediacy, and even conviction, it has its special depths and, as will be seen, its own distinctive urgency. The conception of the novel is in its way as complex as that of *Moby-Dick.* Onto the conventional story of the prodigal's fall from wealth and high station, Melville has grafted the old Promethean symbolism, directly analogous now to the nature and meaning of literary creation. Pierre's descent to penury and prison is also unquestionably a fulfillment of Babbalanja's summons to "reach out after greatness," and he does so both by enacting his hard course and by writing a novel about it. Specifically, the model is Dante, who is pictured as a Melvillian Indian-hater writing a Melvillian work: "The man Dante Alighieri received unforgiveable affronts and insults from the world; and the poet Dante Alighieri bequeathed his immortal curse to it, in the sublime malediction of the *Inferno*. The fiery tongue whose political forkings lost him the solacements of this world, found its malicious counterpart in that muse of fire, which would forever bar the vast bulk of mankind from all solacement in the worlds to come" (235–36). Inspired by Dante, and with the alternative example of Hamlet urging him to action, Pierre both takes the symbolic journey and writes an *Inferno* of his own, according to his one friend, Charlie Millthorpe, who calls the work in progress "the Inferno" and observes that "one is apt to look black while writing Infernoes" (441).[5] And of course the work is a wretched failure, and Pierre's course is increasingly shabby and finally criminal.

Whatever Melville's emotional stake in Pierre's dark journeying, his own book is hardly more successful than the "blasphemous rhapsody" that is in part its record. Whether or not one agrees with Newton Arvin that *Pierre* "is one of the most painfully ill-conditioned books ever to be produced by a first-rate mind," there can surely be no questioning his judgment that "*Pierre's* badness is an active and positive, not a merely negative one . . . the badness of misdirected and even perverted powers, but not of deficiency or deadness."[6] The perversities, such as they are, derive from Melville's obsessive identification with his hero's plight. In light of the many links between author and character, the often-savage ironies directed at Pierre throughout are also a kind of continuous self-mockery, informing, if not entirely explaining, the consistent tonal bitterness of the novel's oddly mannered prose.[7] Somewhat easier to chart, and perhaps more useful to recognize, are the tensions and uncertainties that result from Melville's effort to relocate the Promethean story in a familiar, realistic social context. The problems are in a sense comparable to those Melville faced writing *Mardi*, and in many ways the two books are similar. But *Mardi* is the work of a man who had yet to absorb the full implications of his theme, and *Pierre* is that of a man who has absorbed them all too thoroughly. *Mardi*, for all its flaws, is an exuberant work, heralding things to come. *Pierre*, for all its virtues, is a tired work, that of a man who has tested his powers and found them, in some dim private way, inadequate to his ambitions.

The failure of *Mardi* is in part due to Melville's inability to balance the conflicting demands of romantic allegory and social satire. *Pierre* presents similar problems, which Melville resolves in comparably haphazard ways. The attempt to endow familiar social realities with deep symbolic resonance results throughout in a blurring of distinctions between literal and symbolic, worldly and otherworldly, which indicates something of the difficulty involved in transplanting the Promethean story to familiar ground. Located in society, Pierre is not only unheroic but unconvincing, and often a target for corrosive mockery. There is, for instance, a long, inflated description of the Promethean Pierre wandering the city's streets alone in "the utter isolation of his soul" on stormy nights only in a mood of "dark triumphant joy; that while others had crawled in fear to their kennels, he alone defied the storm-admiral, whose most vindictive peltings of hailstones,—striking his iron-framed fiery furnace of a body,—melted into soft dew, and so, harmlessly trickled from off him" (474). The familiar portrait, however, is this time instantly deflated by the climactic irony and also by a decisive gloss in which Melville tells how Pierre quickly tires of such storms and retreats to local pubs where he drinks his half-pint of ale among the other "social castaways who here had their haunts from the bitterest midnights." The temper here, as elsewhere through the novel, is satiric, but there is no laughter whatever, and the result is a grim foreshadowing of the bleak, unfunny satire of *The Confidence-Man.*

Not surprisingly, the genuine Promethean in *Pierre* appears only in Pierre's "remarkable dream or vision" of "Enceladus the Titan, the most potent of all the giants, writhing from out the imprisoning earth;—turbaned with upborne moss he writhed; still, though armless, resisting with his whole striving trunk, the Pelion and the Ossa hurled back at him . . . still turning his unconquerable front toward that majestic mount eternally in vain assailed by him, and which, when it had stormed him off, had heaved his undoffable incubus upon him, and deridingly left him there to bay out his ineffectual howl" (480). The vision is of Ahab, and his predecessor Taji, even to the oriental turban, and the struggle pictured is that of the defiant combustible who "despairing of any other mode of wreaking his immitigable hate, turned his vast trunk into a battering-ram, and hurled his own arched-out ribs again and yet again against the invulnerable steep." The moral, moreover, is that of Ahab confronting his fiery father in order that he may "glory in [his] genealogy": "For it is according to eternal fitness, that the precipitated Titan should still seek to regain his paternal birthright even by fierce escalade. Wherefore whoso storms the sky gives best proof he came from thither! But whatso crawls contented in the moat before that crystal fort, shows it was born within that slime, and there forever will abide." The connection with Pierre is explicit. On the face of the grim phantom, suddenly the dreaming Pierre sees that "his own duplicate face and features magnifiedly gleamed upon him with prophetic discomfiture and woe," and in trembling, he wakes "from that ideal horror to all his actual grief" (482–83).

The familiar figure retains its previous power, but it is now only a dream. Pierre may imagine himself an "iron-framed fiery furnace" and his world of the city a ship on a stormy sea, but, as Harry Levin has aptly observed, "It is a far cry from a sailor's existence to Pierre's *ménage à trois* with his two heroines, neither of whom he is in a position to love."[8] The results generally are as grotesque and confused as Pierre's domestic situation. Isabel and Lucy Tartan, his erstwhile fiancée, have literal roles that seriously compromise their symbolic functions. According to the underlying rule of continual ambiguity by which *Pierre* is written, it is probably justified that the obvious light-dark symbolism of Yillah and Hautia should be reversed, that Lucy, the blonde celestial angel, should be rejected for the higher goal and truth of the dark sensual Isabel. But otherworldly Lucy becomes in time only an unworldly naïf, like Pierre, thinking to sell drawings and so support them all. And supernatural Isabel, Melville's extreme mystery of mysteries, offers to sell her hair and teeth for the same purpose. Throughout, there is this sort of disparity between literal fact and symbol, and what worked so well and naturally with white whales is unsatisfactory when applied to people. The literal tensions are those between two jealous and uncertain women in constant if unverbalized contest over an undeserving and not very sensible young man. But however apt the psychological insights, and however penetrating and coherent the full portrait, the actual drama is invariably subordinate to the symbolic machinery. Isabel is not merely the temptress from the other side of the tracks. Like Yillah, she embodies "the unsuppressable and unmistakable cry of the godhead through her soul, commanding Pierre to fly to her, and do his highest and most glorious duty in the world" (243). She is in fact quantitatively more mysterious even than that ultimate "mystery of mysteries" pursued by Babbalanja:

> Mystery! Mystery!
> Mystery of Isabel!
> Mystery! Mystery!
> Isabel and Mystery!
> Mystery! (178 and 211)

Yet her reactions once Lucy appears are entirely worldly, at times luridly romantic and even comical. First hearing of Lucy's intention to live with them, she responds pointedly: "My bed; lay me; lay me! . . . Fan me! fan me! . . . Oh! that feminine word from thy mouth, dear Pierre:—that *she,* that *she!"* (434–35). Later, when Pierre makes a public announcement that she remains first in his heart, "a triumphant fire flashed in Isabel's eye; her full bosom arched out" (449). She becomes, finally, no divine inspiration, but like Lucy a partner and specific counterpart to Pierre, "one in whom the most powerful emotion of life is caught in inextricable toils of circumstances, and while longing to disengage itself, still knows that all struggles will prove worse than vain; and so, for the moment, grows madly reckless and defiant of all obstacles" (464).

Just as Isabel—through whom the godhead summons Pierre to a hero's duty—is humanized and hence less effective as transcendent symbol, Pierre himself is a similarly diminished Promethean hero. The causes are historical as well as "powerfully symbolical" (376). Anticipating his view of the new America in *Israel Potter* and *The Confidence-Man,* Melville suggests that Pierre is a lesser figure, in part at least, because he lives in a diminished world. "In the peaceful time of full barns," the grandson of two generals can fight only against "Life . . . and three fierce allies, Woe and Scorn and Want," against "the wide world . . . banded against him." His grandfather's "hard bed of war" has "descended for an inheritance to the soft body of Peace," and sleeping in that bed, Pierre must continually confront the "humbling" realization that even his "most extended length measures not the proud six feet four" of his "grand John of Gaunt sire" (377). Like Redburn, Pierre as a boy had his own symbolic jacket to grow into, his grandfather's military vest which would always be too large for him. With his assumption of responsibility for Isabel, he attains such growth, at least metaphorically. The new figurative coat, however, proves to be more akin to White Jacket's isolating burden than to his

Indian-fighting grandfather's martial mail. With his first thoughts of Isabel's mysterious face, "a coat of iron mail seems to grow round, and husk me now; and I have heard, that the bitterest winters are foretold by a thicker husk upon the Indian corn; so our old farmers say. But 'tis a dark similitude" (57).

A bright similitude is offered by the example of his grandfather's Christian way of life, but the image is tarnished from the start, undermined by Melville's characteristic sarcasm. All those fierce military actions were done by "the mildest-hearted, and most blue-eyed gentleman in the world, who, according to the patriarchal fashion of those days, was a gentle, white-haired worshipper of all the household gods; the gentlest husband, and the gentlest father; the kindest of masters to his slaves; of the most wonderful unruffledness of temper; a serene smoker of his after-dinner pipe; a forgiver of many injuries; a sweet-hearted, charitable Christian; in fine, a pure, cheerful, childlike, blue-eyed, divine old man; in whose meek, majestic soul, the lion and the lamb embraced— fit image of his God" (39). Although the extent of the sarcasm is difficult to gauge at first, something of its quality becomes immediately apparent as Pierre goes on to chronicle the later life of "grand old Pierre," a tag repeated over and over as the grandfather-hero himself grows older and fatter till finally grand old Pierre can no longer even ride his horse but must go for his morning drive in a specially built phaeton, "fit for a vast General"; now he is merely "old Pierre," drawn forth by two horses "as the Chinese draw their fat god Josh, once every year from out his fane" (41). This coarsening of the patriarchal image, sapping it of whatever spiritual vitality it may originally have had, becomes comprehensible in the next generation in terms of hypocrisy and secret sinfulness. In matters of religion, Pierre's father is his grandfather's equal, the apparent embodiment of "the primeval gentleness and golden humanities of religion" (6). And that steadfast exemplar of the "kingly style of Christian" has had an illegitimate daughter and denied her.

At most, Pierre's grandfather represents only the dim memory, deeply suspect, of an operable Christian truth. As the defiant hero shrinks to human scale, an ideal image receding into history and dream, Melville does not fall back, like his Babbalanja, on any of the easy pieties of acceptance. He remains a nay-sayer, though the thunders gradually cease. The primitive faith of Pierre's grandfather is no more influential in his grandson's America than is his savage, Indian-fighter's vitality: "Say, are not the fierce things of this earth daily, hourly going out? Where now are your wolves of Britain? Where in Virginia now, find you the panther and the pard? Oh, Love is busy everywhere. Everywhere Love hath Moravian missionaries. No Propagandist like to Love. The south wind woos the barbarous north; on many a distant shore the gentler west wind persuades the arid east" (45–46). However tangled and confusing the answers prove to be, the question itself is strikingly clear-cut. The "fierce things" hourly vanishing from this earth are its Ahabs. Throughout the novels, the wolf has been a specific animal counterpart to the savage hero. In *Mardi* the opposite to the wolflike hero is the jackal, the fearful carping landsman whom Babbalanja steadily opposes. A basic premise of *The Confidence-Man* is that "in new countries, where the wolves are killed off, the foxes increase" (*C-M*, 2). In *Pierre* the issue is posed in question form—as if Melville were not yet entirely convinced—and the novel itself is in one respect an attempt to assess the possibilities for an Ahab-like hero in a world where "the stature of the warrior is cut down to the dwindled glory of the fight" (377).

Although thus diminished from the archetype, Pierre is in a sense Melville's most comprehensive version of the Promethean hero. However it obfuscates the symbolic statement, the resetting of the action in a realistic context does allow for a thorough, psychologically astute case history of the mythic figure. One result of the choice of an omniscient third-person narrator is that Pierre is made to assume the roles of both the narrator and his subject—Ishmael and Ahab, Redburn and

Jackson. He is both the young initiate and the full-grown hero, beginning as an innocent and proceeding to the opposite extreme of an incestuous murderer whose victim is virtually a brother to him. The youthful Pierre who has never known grief (55) must with the advent of Isabel thrust, like Ahab, through the mask: "If thou hast a secret in thy eyes of mournful mystery, out with it; Pierre demands it; what is that thou hast veiled in thee so imperfectly, that I seem to see its motion, but not its form? It visibly rustles behind the concealing screen. . . . If aught really lurks in it, ye sovereign powers that claim all my leal worshippings, I conjure ye to lift the veil; I must see it face to face" (56). The mere image of her still unidentified face makes of him a kind of Tommo, "wandering" in his soul (65), and it "almost unmans" him (67). Once he has read the explanatory letter, however, more of the hero's characteristics are assumed. The letter is like a dagger, scarring him "with a wound, never to be completely healed but in heaven" (89). He becomes like a "mariner, shipwrecked and cast on the beach," and his new identity is asserted with an Ahab-like resonance:

> With myself I front thee! . . . falsely guided in the days of my Joy, am I now truly led in this night of my grief?—I will be a raver, and none shall stay me! I will lift my hand in fury, for am I not struck? I will be bitter in my breath, for is not this cup of gall? Thou Black Knight, that with visor down, thus confrontest me, and mockest at me; lo! I strike through thy helm, and will see thy face, be it Gorgon!—Let me go, ye fond affections; all piety leave me;—I will be impious, for piety hath juggled me, and taught me to revere, where I should spurn. From all idols, I tear all veils; henceforth I will see the hidden things; and live right out in my own hidden life? (90–91)

He becomes like the trunk of a green tree blasted by lightning (123)[9] and is likened to a cripple (126); his body, already figuratively mutilated, becomes "only the embalming cerements of his buried dead within" (132). Like Taji, he sets out on his journey with "corpses behind me, and the last sin before" (286).

An orphaned isolato, Pierre is also "an infant Ishmael [driven] into the desert, with no maternal Hagar to accompany and comfort him" (125). Both Redburn's glass ship and Pierre's Memnon Stone have the same analogue, "Captain Kidd's sunken hull in the gorge of the river Hudson's Highlands" (186). But where Redburn's thoughts of this fabled pirate ship inspired dreams of diving for its buried gold, Pierre—the hero updated—has a darker sense of it. Like something out of *Typee,* the Memnon Stone is located in "the dense deep luxuriance of the aboriginal forest." In his most perceptive moments, "wrought to a mystic mood by contemplating its ponderous inscrutableness, Pierre had called it the Terror Stone. Few could be bribed to climb its giddy height, and crawl out upon its more hovering end" (188). Pierre has climbed the Terror Stone as a boy. What he had not yet done was to crawl under it to "that spot first menaced . . . should it ever really topple." The image of a huge rock, the shadow of which portends an imminent death, was used throughout *Mardi,* and Taji himself attained final stature as a quester in the shadow of such a rock. Pierre, specifically daring the Terror Stone to fall, eventually crawls beneath it and, surviving the ordeal, he returns to Isabel more dedicated if not actually initiated into herohood.

The quality of Pierre's calling is ideally no less lofty and ennobling than Ahab's: "Thus, in the Enthusiast to Duty, the heaven-begotten Christ is born; and will not own a mortal parent, and spurns and rends all human bonds" (149). He acts, moreover, in full awareness of the ultimate consequences: the choice is "Lucy or God" (253); Isabel can be recognized and his father's sin kept secret only by "the son's free sacrifice of all earthly felicity" (247). Nevertheless, it is the differences between Ahab and Pierre that are finally most striking and most relevant. The conception of the hero's course is significantly altered. There is no quest as such in *Pierre,* but rather the necessity of the hero's enacting a high duty. Isabel is less a goal than a responsibility inherited from his father. She is an incentive to Pierre to "do his highest and most glorious duty in the world." Though Isabel is "steeped a million fathoms in a mysteriousness wholly hopeless of a solution" (180), and though Pierre has taken a vow to sound the unfathomable depths, he soon renounces such deep-diving, determining "to pry not at all into this sacred problem" (199). Consequently, where Yillah beckons and runs away, eternally elusive, Isabel must be lived with. Pierre's fulfillment lies not in pursuit but in his decision to renounce his former life and happiness for her. Once the move is made, he is more pursued than pursuing, reacting to insult and poverty and not against first causes. Where Ahab's methodical purging of his humanities adds a moving element of human drama to his lonely course, Pierre's happier remembrances steadily undermine his sense of purpose. Isabel is an economic burden as well as a symbolic cross and an infernal temptation to sin. If Lucy's willingness to live with Isabel reflects a symbolism out of *Mardi,* it is equally important that she is another mouth to feed. Ahab is the hero burdened with his humanity; Pierre is man overwhelmed by the assumption of a hero's duty.

The issues are specifically formulated at the outset. "Sprung from heroes" on both sides, Pierre should not be other than his ancestors. His mother, though recognizing that he cannot be both docile and heroic, prays to heaven that some middle path may nonetheless be possible, that "he show his heroicness in some smooth way of favouring fortune, not be called out to be a hero of some dark hope forlorn . . . whose cruelness makes a savage of a man" (26). There is of course no smooth way, no favoring fortune, and, as seen in time, no heavenly presence. Pierre, like his predecessors, must "be broken on the wheels of many woes" (*M,* II.324). Yet his mother's wish is not entirely idle. Pierre is in fact just such a compromise, and that is the crux of his dilemma. Ahab, his humanities forcibly cast aside, knows his fiery father but not his sweet earthly mother. Like his mythic analogue Enceladus, Pierre is a doomed product of both Heaven and Earth, neither one nor the other but "mixed, uncertain, heaven-aspiring, but still not wholly earth-emancipated" (483). An interesting gloss on the special nature of Pierre's conflicting literal parentage is provided by his distinction between his mother's "hate-grief unrelenting" and his father's "sin-grief irreparable," both of which resulted in insanity and death, a "remarkable double-doom" that gives Pierre himself deep "presentiments concerning his own fate" (400). The sexes, significantly, are reversed with regard to their symbolic meaning. The hate-grief of his mother is that of Ahab's defiance of Moby-Dick. His father's "sin-grief irreparable" is of the earth; it is guilt without rebellious resentment, implicitly the response of the nondefiant dwarf. Governed by both strains, Pierre can neither ignore the sin he has inherited from his father (thereby, in a sense, accepting it) nor hate implacably without regret or lapse.[10] At the very end he is neither human nor inhuman, godly nor ungodly: "Pierre is neuter now" (503). At the actual moment of his death, he becomes a child. Grasping Isabel, he speaks his last words: " 'In thy breasts, life for infants lodgeth not, but death-milk for thee and me!—The drug!' and tearing her bosom loose, he seized the secret vial nestling there."[11]

According to the terms of Plinlimmon's pamphlet, the novel's central thematic document, Pierre may thus be considered as the heavenly, Christ-like chronometrical and the earthly, human horological inextricably intertwined. His tragedy is that he can neither practice the "virtuous expediency" of the horological nor make the heroic chronometrical's "complete unconditional sacrifice of himself in behalf of any other being, or any cause, or any conceit" (299). Terrestrial attachments continually threaten and mitigate Pierre's heavenly impulses, but they do not stem them. Lucy Tartan's coming to live with them, albeit as a "nun-like cousin" (431), is expressly conceived as his humanities come home to roost, as if Ahab in "The Symphony" had not finally rejected all hope of home and wife:

> If a frontier man be seized by wild Indians, and carried far and deep into the wilderness, and held there a captive, with

no slightest probability of eventual deliverance; then the wisest thing for that man is to exclude from his memory by every possible method, the least images of those beloved objects now forever reft from him. For the more delicious they were to him in the now departed possession, so much the more agonising shall they be in the present recalling. And though a strong man may sometimes succeed in strangling such tormenting memories; yet, if in the beginning permitted to encroach upon him unchecked, the same man shall, in the end, become as an idiot.

(427)

Pierre, as we learn right after this observation, has done his best to forget Lucy, but he has not entirely banished her image from his soul. Consequently, when her letter arrives announcing that she will shortly follow, he accepts it without question. And if he is not immediately "as an idiot," Lucy's arrival adds notably to his perturbed state and of course precipitates the final catastrophe.

Pierre's weary, unheroic end provides a striking contrast to the deaths of Melville's previous heroes. Taji, Jackson, and Ahab, each branded at the outset with the characteristic mark of the Promethean hero, move inexorably toward a fate wherein an ultimate defiance necessitates a suicidal act, literal in the case of Ahab, specifically symbolic with the others. Death is for them an enormous act of will by which they break conclusively through a final barrier toward the "deep beyond" from which "no voyager e'er puts back." Pierre acquires his literal scar just prior to his death, and it leads to no rebirth. Instead, he dies in a pitchblack prison cell, Melville's first actual prisoner since Tommo. His mood is one of tired resignation; his thoughts, characteristically, are with the happier life he willfully forsook to take on the burden carried so reluctantly to this end: "Here, then, is the untimely, timely end;—Life's last chapter well stitched into the middle! Nor book, nor author of the book, hath any sequel, though each hath its last lettering!—It is ambiguous still. Had I been heartless now, disowned, and spurningly portioned off the girl at Saddle Meadows, then had I been happy through a long life on earth, and perchance through a long eternity in heaven! Now, 'tis merely hell in both worlds. Well, be it hell. I will mould a trumpet of the flames, and, with my breath of flame, breathe back my defiance! But give me first another body! I long and long to die, to be rid of this dishonoured cheek" (502). The defiance, though couched in soaring terms, is brief and without conviction. Where Ahab's body, "all mutilated," is hurled against the White Whale for the last time, Pierre voices this curious but telling plea for a new and unscarred body.

When setting out upon his lonely course, Pierre had made a ringing declaration of "war on Night and Day," willing for himself Promethean character and powers: "Bind me in bonds I cannot break; remove all sinister allurings from me; eternally this day deface in me the detested and distorted images of all the convenient lies and duty-subterfuges of the diving and ducking moralities of this earth. Fill me with consuming fire for them; to my life's muzzle, cram me with your own intent. Let no world-syren come to sing to me this day, and wheedle from me my undauntedness" (150). World-sirens have nonetheless continually beset him, recalling to the very end the life of ease he might have led. And though he becomes metaphorically a gun and all proves false, as he feared, he can make war only on his fellow men. Like the very space around him, the grand defiance shrinks and narrows down to a small, unheroic murder followed by a suicide in prison to escape legal execution.

In keeping with the land orientation of *Pierre,* there is a strange metamorphosis of the White Whale back into a human being. Pierre confronts his cousin Glendinning Stanly and Lucy's brother Frederic in precisely the same way that Ahab confronts Moby-Dick. After their challenges and taunts have marked him prophetically with "the murderer's mark of Cain . . . burning on the brow," he plots an Ahab-like revenge which is specifically criminal:

Murders are done by maniacs; but the earnest thoughts of murder, these are the collected desperadoes. Pierre was such;

fate, or what you will, had made him such. But such he was. And when these things now swam before him; when he thought of all the ambiguities which hemmed him in; the stony walls all round that he could not overleap; the million aggravations of his most malicious lot; the last lingering hope of happiness licked up from him as by flames of fire, and his one only prospect a black, bottomless gulf of guilt, upon whose verge he imminently teetered every hour;—then the utmost hate of Glen and Frederic were jubilantly welcome to him; and murder, done in the act of warding off their ignominious public blow, seemed the one only congenial sequel to such a desperate career. (468–69) [12]

But confronting men, not whales, Pierre is the anti-Prometheus, no symbolic, outlawed Cain but a literal one. Examining his pistols, he cries with satanic glee, "Ha! what wondrous tools Prometheus used, who knows? but more wondrous these, that in an instant, can unmake the topmost three-score-years-and-ten of all Prometheus' making" (500). In accordance with the gentlemanly code, his cousin strikes him across the face, leaving "a half-livid and half-bloody brand." Pierre responds by shooting him on the spot: "Spatterings of his own kindred blood were upon the pavement; his own hand had extinguished his house in slaughtering the only un-outlawed human being by the name of Glendinning" (502).

The generic bonds between Pierre and Ahab are clear. Taking on the character and burden of the Indian-hater par excellence, Pierre becomes "this vulnerable god; this self-upbraiding sailor; this dreamer of the avenging dream" (253). But Pierre is earthbound, a sailor only metaphorically. An author and no whaling man or mystic quester, his demiurgic aspirations are more presumptuous than heretical. He shrieks and postures mightily, but he is only a writer, and no successful one at that. The professional failing is, of all his sins and crimes, surely the least consequential, but it links him inescapably to his maker. Something of Melville's own recognition of what had happened to *Pierre* is suggested by

Pierre's curious longing for the sea, reminiscent of White Jacket's yearning "to feel thee again, old sea! Let me leap into the saddle once more. I am sick of these terra-firma toils and cares; sick of the dust and reek of towns" (97). Near the end, Pierre voices an identical longing, though he has never been to sea: "Ere that vile book be finished, I must get on some other element than earth. I have sat on earth's saddle till I am weary; I must now vault over to the other saddle awhile. Oh, seems to me, there should be two ceaseless steeds for a bold man to ride,—the Land and the Sea; and like circus-men we should never dismount, but only be steadied and rested by leaping from one to the other, while still, side by side, they both race round the sun. I have been on the Land steed so long, oh I am dizzy!" (485–86).

Though cast in the role of the Promethean sun-seeker, Pierre gets only to the land's extremest limit. He and his two strange loves take a ferry ride to "a little hamlet on the beach, not very far from the great blue sluice-way into the ocean, which was now yet more distinctly visible than before" (495). Isabel, throughout a symbolic creature of the sea in contrast to Lucy, whose associations are wholly with the land, cries, "Don't let us stop here," and tries to jump overboard. Pierre and Lucy stop her "mechanically" and drag her back. The action is typical and revealing. Isabel may inspire Pierre to a hero's decision, but she cannot lure him from the land. As he has realized at the outset, it is "easy for man to think like a hero; but hard for man to act like one" (238). Where a Taji would emulate Narcissus and leap in after her, Pierre tugs her back calmly and meets his death on land. He cannot, finally, balance on two steeds any more than he could fulfill his mother's plea that he be granted a hero's stature without sacrifice of humanities, or any more than his mythic counterpart Enceladus could rest content half divine and half mortal.

The ties between Pierre and his creator are, as Murray has shown, extraordinarily deep, various, and complex. If Pierre is a lesser Ahab, functioning exclusively on land, he is also a kind of unredeemed Babbalanja whose malcontent reading of the world, reflecting Melville's own, leads to a logical antisocial extreme of murder and suicide. In *Mardi* the narrative movement is expressly twofold: satire levels all aspects of the known world so that new metaphysics may be built out of the debris. Babbalanja is both "critic and creator," killing, burning, and destroying for purposes that are essentially purgative and redemptive. *Pierre* begins on an identical premise, but it is one impossible of fulfillment though Pierre does not yet know it. "Nor now, though profoundly sensible that his whole previous moral being was overturned, and that for him the fair structure of the world must, in some then unknown way, be entirely rebuilded again, from the lowermost cornerstone up; nor now did Pierre torment himself with the thought of that last desolation; and how the desolate place was to be made flourishing again. He seemed to feel that in his deepest soul, lurked an indefinite but potential faith, which could rule in the interregnum of all hereditary beliefs, and circumstantial persuasions; not wholly, he felt, was his soul in anarchy" (121–22).

The tones are those of one whose soul, if not entirely in anarchy, is at least a good deal more so at this point than his young hero's. The novel's heavily ironic prose heralds the coming of *The Confidence-Man*, where "potential faith" such as Pierre's is real foolishness. Whatever Melville's efforts to sustain the thematic framework of metaphysical ambiguity, and to see in Pierre's fall from innocence something redemptive, something of substantial human worth, his own sense of things was by this time more cynical and much darker than his wavering metaphysics would indicate. Unlike Hawthorne's fortunately fallen innocents, Pierre's awakening into manhood is more debasing than enlarging. His discovery of inherent sinfulness, in his worshipped father and eventually in himself, would seem to argue a Calvinist theology, but there is no structuring faith, no belief in a God ordaining and controlling such a state of things. Though *Pierre* is finally indecisive on such ultimate issues, resting, as it were, on its ambiguities, Melville's direction is already clear, and the end is the awful final darkness of *The Confidence-Man.*

Pierre is thus at once a kind of summary of previous soundings and a turning toward new themes. To Ahab it does not matter whether the White Whale be agent or principal: " 'Tis enough. He tasks me; he heaps me" (I.204). In *Pierre,* Melville confronts the appalling fact of "that last desolation" to which Ahab in his energy and pride might be indifferent:

> Ten million things were as yet uncovered to Pierre. The old mummy lies buried in cloth on cloth; it takes time to unwrap this Egyptian king. Yet now, forsooth, because Pierre began to see through the first superficiality of the world, he fondly weens he has come to the unlayered substance. But, far as any geologist has yet gone down into the world, it is found to consist of nothing but surface stratified on surface. To its axis, the world being nothing but superinduced superficies. By vast pains we mine into the pyramid; by horrible gropings we come into the central room; with joy we espy the sarcophagus; but we lift the lid—and no body is there!—appallingly vacant as vast is the soul of man!   (396–97)

The discovery is in spirit akin to Tommo's at Tamai, where a mock-mystery was answered by a pair of tattered trousers. In *Pierre,* however, there is no levity. For the later hero, murder is the "one only congenial sequel to such a desperate career"; and afterwards, "nor book, nor author of the book, hath any sequel" (502). So, too, *The Confidence-Man* is the only logical sequel to a work that has described an empty, Godless world devoid of all useful heroic energy. First, however, in his characteristic way Melville pulls back from pressing concerns to write a sequel apparently lighter in tone and meaning, intended both to refill an empty purse and to relieve a gravely sagging spirit.

★ 8 ★

W ITH REDBURN AND WHITE JACKET, Melville turned from romance and romantic allegory to subjects, as he put it, nearer home. *Pierre,* though written in a strangely mannered, nonrealistic prose, is nonetheless a move still closer to a realistic way of looking at his subject. In *Israel Potter,* Melville abandons the self-conscious style of *Pierre,* but his retreat from the Promethean hero continues in what seems an orderly if not actually methodical way. The story is structured as in the previous novels. Israel, another wandering, outcast Ishmael, acquires a hard knowledge through involvement with heroes whom he comes partly to resemble. Only at the end of his life does he return to write of them, however, remaining till then a captive exile, imprisoned against his will. The hero encountered by Israel, moreover, is not merely diminished, as in *Pierre,* but is also fragmented into three historical Americans who, like all such heroes, serve specifically to inspire and educate an American Everyman to feats of emulation. From Franklin, Israel learns prudence, though the practice of it does him little good. From John Paul Jones, he momentarily absorbs a tigerish warrior's energy and daring, as well as an implacable hatred of the enemy. From Ethan Allen, he learns to be a captive in a strange land, and it is this lesson that ultimately prevails.

Melville acquired the *Life and Remarkable Adventures of Israel R. Potter* in the autumn of 1849.[1] In London he bought a map of the city during Potter's time specifically for use "in case I serve up the Revolutionary narrative of the beggar."[2] As late as July 1850, he was still thinking about the project and taking various notes for it.[3] That he waited four years before actually writing the book indicates something of the emotional needs and pressures that drove him to write *Moby-Dick* and then *Pierre*. But it is curious that, coming when it does, *Israel Potter* plays a role in Melville's development that could have had no meaning four years earlier. Moreover, the way in which he uses Potter's *Life* would seem to indicate that, whatever the original reaction to it, by 1854 its interest to him lay in its possibilities for direct comment on an America from which the wolves were hourly giving way to the universal love, faith, and confidence of the eternal yea-sayers. Whereas Israel's story is told in detail, often mechanically, directly from the *Life* up to his meeting with Franklin in France—roughly half the *Life* and a quarter of Melville's novel—the remainder is almost entirely Melville's own invention.[4] Franklin is briefly mentioned in the *Life*. Jones appears only by way of a digressive anecdote of his exploits, and Ethan Allen not at all. Melville's depiction of these revolutionary heroes and their influence on Israel is pointed and familiar. As an anonymous reviewer praising *Israel Potter* in the *Boston Post* was quick to complain, "Its *Paul Jones* and *Benjamin Franklin* . . . are not without a spice of Melville's former 'humors,' as they used to be called."[5] Jones looks back to Ahab; Franklin directly anticipates *The Confidence-Man*. Each is a lesser version, though somewhat more than a spice of the archetype.

Of the satiric portrait of Franklin, little need be said. His antecedents are the comic Long Ghost and the malevolent Captain Riga, but he is neither entirely comic nor entirely malevolent. Franklin anticipates the spirit, but not the epic substance, of the Confidence Man. His view of life, and his practice of it, underline the basic opposition of confidence man and Promethean hero, fox and wolf, which reflects almost precisely the earlier land-sea antinomy. "Sad usage," he tells Israel, "has made you sadly suspicious, my honest friend. An indiscriminate trust of human nature is the worst consequence of a miserable condition, whether brought about by innocence or guilt. And though want of suspicion more than want of sense, sometimes leads a man into harm, yet too much suspicion is as bad as too little sense" (52). In light of the indignities already undergone by Franklin's honest young friend, and considering the fearful sufferings to come, Melville's sarcasm is unmistakable and harsh, though the portrait itself is less so. The "sly, sly, sly" old diplomat (70) who counters the warrior-hero's stance of hopeless defiance with Falstaff's argument for a sensible expediency is not only nonheroic but, in Israel's case at least, wrong. "Bravery in a poor cause" may or may not be, as Franklin insists, "the height of simplicity" (56); for Israel, boldness and prudence have the same end and, whether he acts decisively or not at all, his fate is forty years in the City of Dis and then disappointment on returning home.

A distinctly American type, Franklin represents one path that his country and his countrymen might follow to maturity: "Printer, post-master, almanac maker, essayist, chemist, orator, tinker, statesman, humorist, philosopher, parlour man, political economist, professor of housewifery, ambassador, projector, maxim-monger, herb-doctor, wit: Jack of all trades, master of each and mastered by none—the type and genius of his land. Franklin was everything but a poet" (62). The respect, such as there is, is grudging, but the praise is not wholly a patriotic formality. Where the essential landsman has previously been scorned as effeminate or corrupt, Franklin is no enemy but at worst simply useless, to the poet and the Israel Potters both. *Poor Richard* is as worthless to Israel as the Paris guidebook he has bought but cannot use because of Franklin's prudent demand that he stay in his room. His reaction to *Poor Richard* is simpler and more worldly than was Redburn's to his father's outdated guidebook, but each reflects essentially the same perception of paternal—and hence divine—indifference.

John Paul Jones has "a bit of the poet as well as the outlaw in him" (72), but he is not entirely removed from the influence of *Poor Richard*. If the following description of his career suggests the earlier heroes, it also has the clear ring of an exemplum to a young man setting out to get rich quick in the America of the 1850s: "The career of this stubborn adventurer signally illustrates the idea that since all human affairs are subject to organic disorder, since they are created in and sustained by a sort of half-disciplined chaos, hence he who in great things seeks success must never wait for smooth water, which never was and never will be, but, with what straggling method he can, dash with all his derangements at his object, leaving the rest to Fortune" (151). When Israel follows this advice, however, in an excess of enthusiasm leaping to be the first to board an enemy ship in battle, it proves to be his undoing. Jones, more prudent, suspects "foul play" and pulls back, leaving Israel once again a captive (175). Jones has all the physical characteristics of Melville's typical hero, but these are diminished in ways that indicate more clearly Melville's steady progress toward complete rejection of his imagined hero's place in contemporary America.

Israel's first sight of Jones establishes both the familiar character and one aspect of its decline. Where Pierre's involvements with women were symbolic, as well as literally debilitating, Jones's are merely playful. His arrival is announced by a tittering chambermaid, roguishly pinched by one whose physical presence indicates clear kinship with all of his heroic predecessors.

> He was a rather small, elastic, swarthy man, with an aspect as of a disinherited Indian chief in European clothes. An unvanquishable enthusiasm, intensified to perfect sobriety, couched in his savage, self-possessed eye. He was elegantly and somewhat extravagantly dressed as a civilian; he carried himself with a rustic, barbaric jauntiness, strangely dashed with a

superinduced touch of the Parisian *salon*. His tawny cheek, like a date, spoke of the tropic. A wonderful atmosphere of proud friendlessness[6] and scornful isolation invested him. Yet there was a bit of the poet as well as the outlaw in him too. (72)

Though he has Pierre's enthusiasm and Jackson's savage eye, as well as the hero's tawny coloring, Jones is an isolato who is entirely at home in polite society. "A cross between the gentleman and the wolf" (125), Jones represents Melville's first depiction of the popular romantic stereotype of the cavalier-frontiersman, the Virginian gone west, moving gracefully between drawing room and forest primeval. There is, however, a basic difference in approach that undermines the image. Jones is a "disinherited Indian chief" and not, like Natty Bumppo, a Christian American at home among Indians. The distinction is, among other things, that between the epic whale-killer whose status is achieved by a willingly embraced savagery and a killer of human beings who is at heart a savage.

Nonetheless, Jones has all the mechanical attributes of the Promethean hero. His "bloody cannibal" savagery (121) is signified by "mysterious tattooings" such as are seen "only on thorough-bred savages—deep blue, elaborate, labyrinthine, cabalistic" (81). Repeatedly Jones is associated with fire: his "volcanic spirit" (74) is "flaming with wild enterprises"; going to sleep on the night of their meeting, with Jones still awake in the room, Israel feels "as if he had retired, not only without covering up the fire, but leaving it fiercely burning with spitting fagots of hemlock" (80). Jones's "uncompromising spirit" demands "supreme authority" (75). Though he claims to be "a democratic sort of sea-king" (128), he refuses to share a bed with Israel, being, like Ahab, a moody and restless insomniac who does not "sleep half a night out of three" (122). Yet this "lonely leader of the suit" (123) also has his humanities: "His wild, lonely heart, incapable of sympathising with cuddled natures made humdrum by long exemption from pain, was yet drawn toward a being, who in desperation of friendlessness, something like his own, had so fiercely waged battle against tyrannical odds" (120).

Even more than in *Pierre*, however, the physical resemblances to Ahab only underline the basic difference. Jones is finally no defeated, mythic "Coriolanus of the sea" (125), but only a worldly renegade whose success stems in large part from the kind of prudence that caused him to retreat from an apparently difficult battle, leaving his overzealous follower alone on an enemy ship. At the outset, Jones rejects any touch of Franklin's prudence: " 'Everything is lost through this shillyshallying timidity, called prudence,' cried Paul Jones, starting to his feet; 'to be effectual, war should be carried on like a monsoon, one changeless determination of every particle toward the one unalterable aim' " (74). But a later view of him emphasizes a prudence specifically like wily old Franklin's: "Seldom has regicidal daring been more strangely coupled with octogenarian prudence, than in many of the predatory enterprises of Paul" (131).

Something of the special quality of Jones's prudence is suggested by an episode that immediately precedes this definition of his character. Jones's "regicidal daring" is literal only and not that of the Promethean against his Maker. Confronted with the great crag of Ailsa, he immediately retreats. Pursuing a British ship into the "domineering shadow of the Juan Fernandez-like crag of Ailsa,"[7] Jones abruptly stops and, issuing "no more sultanical orders," abandons the chase. He has pulled back, he explains, not from the enemy or from King George himself, but from the "cock of the walk of the sea . . . yon Crag of Ailsa." The incident, though brief, is extraordinarily evocative and relevant. The image of the crag has throughout the novels indicated the transcendent force against which the potential hero must test himself. The whale-like rock of Pella, which provokes Babbalanja's definition of anonymous heroic immortality, typifies Melville's consistent use of the image. In the shadow of such a cliff, Taji achieves his apotheosis; Ahab's is in the jaws of an actual whale; Pierre crawls beneath the Terror Stone in order to test his new manhood's high resolve. In *Israel Potter,* the hero retreats: the great crag "dwarfed both pursuer and pursued into nutshells."[8]

As always, Melville is himself a curious and illuminating analogue to his hero. With *Israel Potter,* Melville finally fulfills a repeated promise to his publisher that his new book would have "very little reflective writing in it; nothing weighty."[9] He does so, however, not from laziness or caution, but rather because of a new, bitter conviction that "both war and warriors, like politics and politicians, like religion and religionists, admit of no metaphysics" (126). Like "young David of old," Jones can beard a literal "British giant of Gath" (125), but he cannot face its metaphysical equivalent, an inscrutable "giant of Gath" of the mind (128). Similarly, it would seem that Melville himself can at this point in his career confront a Jones but not an Ahab. The crag of Ailsa is a ghostly graveyard for what appear to be his own wrecked aspirations: "The crag, more than a mile in circuit, is over a thousand feet high, eight miles from the Ayrshire shore. There stands the cove, lonely as a foundling, proud as Cheops. But, like the battered brains surmounting the giant of Gath, its haughty summit is crowned by a desolate castle, in and out of whose arches the aerial mists eddy like purposeless phantoms, thronging the soul of some ruinous genius, who, even in overthrow, harbours none but lofty conceptions" (128).

Harboring less lofty conceptions, Jones turns immediately from the crag of Ailsa to launch his fierce assault against the land, attacking with a small band the entire town of Whitehaven, the specific source of his complaint against England. A familiar but loosely organized fire symbolism running through the scene underlines both the resemblances to previous scenes and the differences between an Ahab who confronts the sun with its own fire and an Old Combustibles who fires real guns at real human beings. Whitehaven, a mining town, is "now about to be assailed by a desperado, nursed, like the coal, in its vitals" (133). The image is of the gunner who rises from below decks to destroy, and not the titanic hero who "by fierce escalade . . . storms the sky" in order to give "best proof he came from thither" (*P,* 483). The effects of the entire scene are comparably scaled down. Jones's plan is to burn all the ships in the harbor and the fortifications as well and be gone before daybreak, but the "day-sparks" of the sun begin to appear, "forked flames" to Jones, and nothing has yet happened because the "incendiaries" have themselves run out of fire and cannot light the fuses. Jones calls on Israel to "prove [his] blood" by bringing fire, "a spark to kindle all Whitehaven's habitations in flames" (136). By a clever trick, Israel manages to fulfill his mission, thereby playing a kind of bastardized Prometheus to Jones, who then uses the fire "to put an end to all future burnings in America, by one mighty conflagration of shipping in England" (137).

The self-destruction of the mythic Promethean has an ultimately redemptive purpose. The hero confronting the godhead from the topmost rung of the ladder does so on behalf of all those on the lower rungs. When Jones burns Whitehaven in retaliation for British attacks on America, it is a "mutual obliteration." The climactic battle with the *Serapis,* like that at Whitehaven, takes place at night in fire, fog, and smoke so thick that friend cannot be told from foe. Ahab, in sharp contrast, fights his epic battle by day, returning each night to renew his strength and his resources. For all its verbal similarities to Ahab's final struggle, the magnificent sea fight in *Israel Potter* is conceived as Pierre against his cousin and Ishmael against Queequeg: "It seemed more an intestine feud, than a fight between strangers. Or, rather, it was as if the Siamese Twins, oblivious of their fraternal bond, should rage in unnatural fight" (165). Just as Ishmael and Queequeg are tied together when Queequeg descends into the whale's carcass, the lives of both depending solely on the "Siamese ligature" that makes of them "a joint stock company of two" (*M-D,* II.48), so it is with the embattled warships: "The belligerents were no longer, in the ordinary sense of things, an English ship and an American ship. It was a co-partnership and joint-stock combustion-company of both ships; yet divided, even in participation" (167). In this battle of Guelphs and Ghibellines, as it is characterized, "neither party could be victor. Mutual obliteration from the face of the waters seemed the only natural sequel to hostilities like these" (172). The losses do prove equal, and the historical irony of the victorious ship's sinking was not lost on Melville, who pointedly undermines the patriotic glory of the moment by likening the *Richard* to Gomorrah (173), with the *Serapis,* presumably, a Sodom already destroyed by its defeat.

If Jones is the least of Melville's several Ahab-like Prometheans, Israel is in a sense his most accomplished Ishmael, at times even exceeding his tutor, Jones himself, in warlike daring. When all seems lost at Whitehaven for want of a match, it is Israel who saves the day. In the battle with the *Serapis* he performs a similarly fiery feat, dropping grenades down the main hatchway of the enemy ship and doing her severe injury at a time when the battle seems lost to the Americans. The content, as at Whitehaven, is suggestive of similar moments in the previous novels. Perched high on the yardarm, a "bucket of combustibles" in his hand, his face "begrimed with powder," Israel himself seems for an instant about to become a deep-diver, descending into a vortex heavy with reiterated symbolic meanings. Instead, however, he hurls his grenade, becoming an especially murderous Old Combustibles. Something further of Israel's role as a symbolic combustible is suggested at Whitehaven, again in specific contrast to Jones. An angry crowd begins to gather on the pier as Jones's men are burning the last ship; partly to forestall them and partly from sheer bravado, Jones leaps to the ground and advances on them alone, pointing his pistol. Israel, going him one better, rushes madly at the disbelieving crowd, and when Jones calls him back, he answers, "Not till I start these sheep, as their own wolves many a time started me." His success is more notable than his wolflike captain's: "As he rushed bareheaded like a madman toward the crowd, the panic spread. They fled from unarmed Israel, further than they had from the pistol of Paul" (138). The situation is again illuminated by comparison with earlier instances. Redburn points a gun at his tormentors and is afterwards ashamed and seriously troubled by what he considers a momentary insanity. Pierre prays to be made into a gun that he may in himself combat the world's combined untruths, but, surrounded entirely by perplexing semitruths, he is finally only a shooter of pistols and no Enceladus hurling his battered trunk at an invulnerable godhead. In *Israel Potter* there is not even the sustaining vision of an Enceladus.

However accomplished and educable, Israel is an Ishmael without a future, foredoomed to captive exile in a land as barbarous as Typee and far less vital. He goes through all the motions of Tommo or Redburn, but he gets nowhere for his efforts. For all his escapes from captivity—and there are an extraordinary number of them—he is Melville's extreme version of imprisoned man. A brief comparison of the novel with its source provides some sense of the extent of this bitter irony. Where the largest part of Potter's *Life* concerns his sufferings as an impoverished exile, Melville invents for his hero a series of colorful adventures, often comic in character, during which he encounters and partakes of greatness only to have triumph snatched from him at every turning point by a ridiculous fate that returns him to his proper place as foredoomed victim of both divine and human authority. Waiting in a secret room at Squire Woodcock's while preparations are made for his return to Paris and then home, Israel suddenly realizes that he is being strangely ignored; eventually he emerges to discover that the good squire has died and with him all present hope of returning home. Later, miraculously escaped once more and now the confidant of John Paul Jones, by the same bizarre fortune he boards a ship too quickly and is left there when his captain has second thoughts.

Although the approach often seems comic with a happy ending just around the corner, the concerns themselves are basic to Melville's conception of Ishmael. Israel's long wait in Squire Woodcock's secret room, for instance, is a nightmare of immurement comparable to Tommo's and Redburn's, and especially to the eerie, Poe-like living death of the calm in *Mardi*. Yet his escape is both easy and comical; like Tommo in *Omoo*, he simply opens the door and leaves. The narrator of *Mardi* escapes the calm by a mock-death and genuine rebirth as a fallen Adam with the watery world all before him. Israel similarly feigns death in order to escape, putting on the dead squire's clothes and boldly walking out of the house as his ghost with everyone watching, including the dead man's horrified wife, who faints, in keeping with the sudden low comedy of the scene, and must be calmly stepped over. But for Israel there is never a rebirth, only a series of repeated opportunities, all of which prove futile and renew for yet another term his captive, deathlike life.

The consistent if sketchy identifications of Melville with his young author-narrators reach their climax in *Pierre*, and in *Israel Potter* there is a kind of obvious anticlimax, mechanical and not dramatic, more sad than enlightening. The association begins with the shift of the real Israel's birthplace from Cranston, Rhode Island, to "the eastern part of Berkshire, Massachusetts," and ends with Israel as a "bondsman in the English Egypt," making bricks to be used for "temporary temples." (Melville in *Mardi* once sought to build eternal temples with eternal stones.) The allegory of the bricks is itself perfunctory: "To these muddy philosophers, men and bricks were equally of clay. 'What signifies who we be—dukes or ditchers?' thought the moulders; 'all is vanity and clay.' So slap, slap, slap, care-free and negligent, with bitter unconcern, these dismal desperadoes flapped down the dough" (206). In the letter of June 29, 1851, to Hawthorne, where he talked of himself and Hawthorne as occasional Indian-fighters in the savage wilderness, returning necessarily to their lesser callings in the physical world, Melville characterized his state of mind in terms ominously prophetic of *Israel Potter*: "The 'Whale' is only half through the press; for, wearied with the long delay of the printers, and disgusted with the heat and dust of the babylonish brick-kiln of New York, I came back to the country to feel the grass—and end the book reclining on it, if I may."[10] Israel escapes the brick kiln as easily, but, setting out yet once more to seek his fortune, he goes directly to the City of Dis, where he is swallowed up for forty years. Melville's identification with Israel, such as it is, is of course not anticipatory—it looks back on a promise unfulfilled. He has not yet entered the Custom House or abandoned his calling. His general view of Israel's story, however, seems strikingly similar to his own situation: "One brief career of adventurous wanderings; and then, forty torpid years of pauperism" (23–24). Yet if it is no forecast of Melville's own impending captivity, *Israel Potter* is an accurate foreshadowing of his next and final fiction. The rebellious desperadoes who people the early works are "dismal desperadoes" in *Israel Potter*; in *The Confidence-Man* they are nearly gone.

Stripped of metaphysical interest, Jones is only the shell of Ahab. Nonetheless, Israel responds to him as Ishmael does to Ahab. "Fired by the contagious spirit of Paul, Israel, forgetting all about his previous desire to reach home, sparkled with response to the summons" to join in Jones's private vendetta against England (75). Later, specifically inspired by the sound of Jones's voice, Israel becomes a killer, first of several men—those on the disabled cutter he is rescued from by Jones[11]—and eventually of a great part of the crew of the *Serapis*. Like Ishmael, he takes on something of the hero's character as well as his grim mission. Yet Jones is worldly and barbaric both, and, while the example of Ahab leads to destruction, that of Jones promises a successful accommodation to society. Ishmael is saved from Ahab's fate because he is only a partial Ahab, retaining humanities that debilitate the hero but save the man. Israel, an imperfect Jones, meets his sorry fate also because of his imperfections. The conception is the same, but the perspective is that of the landsman, not the savage sailor. Where the Promethean hero's fate is that of the Indian-hater par excellence, the anonymous and awful immortality described by Babbalanja, in the land-oriented world of the last three novels the perfect worldly hero achieves historic fame, and his flawed student meets the fate of onetime heroes, now only a "Potter's Field" (223). The final comment blames both time and place, the new America, and underlines the resemblance of Melville, already thinking of a government position, to his hero, who has been as unsuccessful as an author as he was as a wandering Ishmael: "He was repulsed in efforts after a pension by certain caprices of law. His scars proved his only medals. He dictated a little book, the record of his fortunes. But long ago it faded out of print—himself out of being—his name out of memory. He died the same day that the oldest oak on his native hills was blown down."

Much has been made of the brief portrait of Ethan Allen, the third of *Israel Potter's* great Americans, as a benign counterforce to Jones. Yet the example he provides for Israel, one that is immediately followed in fact if not in quality of response, is of a captive in a foreign land. Where Jack Chase is an ineffectual savior of sailors, save in theatricals and cozening a day's shore leave for the men, Allen is seen as an imprisoned "Samson among the Philistines" (189), noble, raging, but literally bound and powerless. A huge figure who resembles "a great whale breaching amid a hostile retinue of swordfish" (190), Allen has Jones's "barbaric disdain of adversity" (198), and his "inevitable egotism" as well. But he is a "Christian gentleman" (193) with a cavalier gentility that is of the same romantic type as Jones's, but more instinctive, emblematic of a fundamental humanity and not a patina of civilization. He rages only against those who mistreat him, and Melville specifically observes that, if he acts like a wild beast, it is only because he has first been put into a cage. This God-fearing democrat is the essence of the Western spirit, and Melville voices the hope that "the Western spirit is, or will yet be (for no other is, or can be), the true American one" (198). Yet previously, and with better reason, he expressed the identical fear that Jones's battle with the *Serapis* might "involve at once a type, a parallel, and a prophecy. Sharing the same blood with England, and yet her proved foe in two wars—not wholly inclined at bottom to forget an old grudge—intrepid, unprincipled, reckless, predatory, with boundless ambition, civilised in externals but a savage at heart, America is, or may yet be, the Paul Jones of nations" (158). And still earlier the same thought was expressed about Franklin, though with more certainty: "Jack of all trades, master of each and mastered by none—the type and genius of his land . . . everything but a poet" (62).

Allen also combines contrary roles, but they are expressly mythic ones, in contrast to Franklin's useful trades: "Allen seems to have been a curious combination of a Hercules, a Joe Miller, a Bayard, and a Tom Hyer; had a person like the Belgian giants; mountain music in him like a Swiss; a heart plump as Coeur de Lion's. Though born in New England, he exhibited no trace of her character. . . . His spirit was essentially Western" (198). Whatever he was, Allen is already only a dream, a historical myth whose real self, like that of Pierre's grandfather, may well have once happily commingled the contrarieties of land and sea, Christian and pagan, civilized and savage. But he no longer represents a viable truth in contemporary America. His lesson is how to react to imprisonment; Franklin and Jones are guidebooks to success.

In *Israel Potter* Melville is writing of a young nation, whose national character, still unformed, might well have been molded in Allen's form or in Jones's or in Ben Franklin's. By 1854, however, an American mythology had been established, and, although his hopes and fears for his country lay in a theoretical choice between a debased and compromised Ahab and a captive Ethan Allan, Melville had special knowledge that Franklin, everything but a poet and a seafaring warrior, had surpassed both his contemporaries in the American pantheon of heroes. In his last work, appropriately his only Western novel, Melville confronts an America whose Ahabs are virtually extinct and whose confidence men have not merely inherited the world but become its gods.

★ 9 ★

THE DRAMA PLAYS OUT with characteristic strangeness in a surge of high imagination that fulfills the deadening logic and the cynical promise of the two preceding novels. *The Confidence-Man* is, in Perry Miller's words, "a long farewell to national greatness."[1] It is also, needless to say, Melville's own farewell to his profession, and the two, author and subject, go hand in hand into a final, obliterating darkness that is not Ahab's closing vortex, but rather something closer in spirit to the final imprisonments of Pierre and Israel Potter.[2] Continuing his identification with narrator-authors who both experience and describe Promethean heroes, Melville the novelist literally vanishes along with his fictional wolves. He does so, however, with an angry snarl and no whimper, and in a work of great ingenuity. It is, however, a depressing finale. One can see in *Mardi* the seeds of *Moby-Dick,* and for all its flaws, *Pierre* is the work of a man seriously attempting to realize a difficult amalgam of opposites, in both theme and style. But where *Mardi* had "dead-desert chapters" because its youthful author had overreached himself, *The Confidence-Man*'s reflect a tired author's vision of a world that was itself a dead desert. A satire without humor, a novel of ideas which denies the intellect all vitality other then its capacity to detect falsehood, *The Confidence-Man* is a grim book and a tedious one. It is the work of a man so lacking in conviction that he no longer takes even his angers seriously.

Yet the special interest of the novel lies precisely in the finality of its statement. In *The Confidence-Man,* the continuing process of self-revelation reaches its logical end. As before, the progress is coherent, phased, even programmatic. Melville's slow turning from the sea to the land, for instance, is completed in *The Confidence-Man.* Pierre longed for the sea; Israel Potter, contemporary with Pierre's almost mythic grandfather, traveled and fought on it. The location of *The Confidence-Man* is a landbound river down which the steamer *Fidèle* sails for New Orleans. The entire, bold conception, in fact, is a last, striking reformulation of Melville's one great theme entirely in terms of the land and its values. A society of yea-saying Abrazzas, seeking happiness and money, is pursued by a god in its own image, who is himself sporadically opposed by the bedraggled remnants of Melville's onetime heroes, still defiant nay-sayers but no longer speaking in thunder. The novel opens, appropriately, with a crowd congregated about a placard "offering a reward for the capture of a mysterious impostor, supposed to have recently arrived from the East; quite an original genius in his vocation, as would appear, though wherein his originality consisted was not clearly given." Moving through the crowd is a peddler selling biographies of legendary Western desperadoes, "one and all exterminated at the time, and for the most part, like the hunted generations of wolves in the same regions, leaving comparatively few successors; which would seem cause for unalloyed gratulation, and is such to all except those who think that in new countries, where the wolves are killed off, the foxes increase" (2). Although the Confidence Man is a new kind of deity, a new face on the wanted posters reflecting new, smooth faces in the crowd, the wolves are only "comparatively" absent. They are, however, peripheral to the action. Like the peddler of biographies, himself a debased image of the bard of hunted, wolflike heroes, they occasionally attempt to divert the crowd from its main interest, the "mysterious impostor" who hunts them even as they are hunting him.

The conception is that of the previous novels but scaled down, reversed, turned inside out. Instead of Ishmael seeking the sea, the loomings of *The Confidence-Man* posit the appearance of the Confidence Man on land as the Christ-like "man in cream colours," abruptly descended in the novel's opening sentence "like Manco Capac," a Peruvian deity mentioned in *Mardi* as an analogue to Alma, Mardi's Christ.[3] Though "in the extremest sense of the word a stranger" (1), he presents a physical image that is soft, smooth, placid, and suggestively foxlike: "His cheek was fair, his chin downy, his hair flaxen, his hat a white fur one, with a long fleecy nap." Though he has "the air of one . . . evenly pursuing the path of duty,[4] lead it through solitudes or cities," his course throughout the novel is to shun solitude and seek out crowds, who are also seeking him. The passengers on board the *Fidèle* comprise a group of "Canterbury pilgrims," representative of all questing humanity: "Farm-hunters and fame-hunters; heiress-hunters, gold-hunters, buffalo-hunters, bee-hunters, happiness-hunters, truth-hunters, and still keener hunters after all these hunters" (8). Through such a crowd the new savior calmly walks, up to the placard offering a reward for his capture. Just beside it, he places his own alternative message, *"Charity thinketh no evil"* (2), which attracts the attention of the assemblage. The revelation that he is "not alone dumb, but also deaf" (5) underlines the basic symbolic resemblances between hunters and hunted. No one on the *Fidèle* sees the truth, and no one on the *Fidèle* hears it except for occasional, scruffy outcasts who, as the ghosts of wolves, attempt a weak defiance.

The informing image is once more that of the ladder, but the perspective now is downward. Weary and rumpled, "as if, travelling night and day from some far country beyond the prairies, he had long been without the solace of a bed," the newly descended god in the cream-coloured suit falls asleep at the foot of an actual ladder. "His flaxen head drooped, his whole lamb-like figure relaxed, and, half-reclining against the ladder's foot, lay motionless, as some sugar-snow in March which, softly stealing down over night, with its white placidity, startles the brown farmer peering out from his threshold at daybreak" (5). The "far country beyond the prairies" is surely the same ultimate region toward which Taji set out at *Mardi*'s end to seek his Yillah.[5] The returning Confidence Man is no wanderer, however, but a transcendent force like white Yillah and the White Whale, now come to land to trouble placid farmers.

The primal figure is once again developed in terms of a carefully contrived system of symbolic blacks and whites, which now indicates, however, less the ambiguous, tormenting oneness of good and evil than the way in which such a mixture, in social terms, produces a neutral and nonmoral gray. The god's progression, like the hero's, is one of gradual constriction and descent from initial extremes to the common denominator of an ordinary, worldly Everyman. The Christ-like "man in cream colours" awakens as a crippled black, crawling like a dog, and his successful shipboard career begins with a plea for literal charity of the sort abstractly urged in his previous masquerade. The spurious cripple is a "black sheep," only the other side of the coin, and even at that he is "a half-frozen black sheep" (11). He is simply a "white operator, betwisted and painted up for a decoy" (15), a "white masquerading as a black" (40). In his next identity, as the man with the weed, he is a pale white man in mourning. He is seen next, seemingly "transformed into another being" (31), as a man in a "gray coat and white tie" (36), and finally as "the man in gray" (45). Blending in increasingly with his victims, he then appears as a "brisk ruddy-cheeked man in a tasselled travelling-cap" (60), peddling both the Black Rapids Coal Company and the New Jerusalem and preaching that the worst hypocrites of all are the "hypocrites in the simulation of things dark instead of bright" (63). This sociable and eminently unmysterious role culminates in that of the cosmopolitan, "the mature man of the world" who wears clothes of all colors and "federates, in heart as in costume, something of the various gallantries of men under various suns" (176–77).

The Confidence Man, then, is a kind of pursuing Yillah, a Moby-Dick come to land. Ubiquitous and protean, he promises all things to all men, and, if in this unheroic world he does not literally destroy his eager victims, he does steal what he can get and makes fools of them in the process. Though some are easier prey than others, all finally succumb; the more difficult the task, actually, the greater the Confidence Man's professional pleasure. The allegorical ship of faith and fools is the Confidence Man's environment and physical target. Typical of his means is a "Protean easy-chair . . . so all over bejointed, behinged, and bepadded, every way so elastic, springy, and docile to the airiest touch, that in some one of its endlessly changeable accommodations of back, seat, footboard, and arms, the most restless body, the body most racked, nay, I had almost added the most tormented conscience must, somehow and somewhere, find rest" (50).

These "most tormented," shadows of Ahab, are the only ones who find no rest through faith and submission. Their function throughout the novel is to oppose. The opposition, however, is weak and ineffectual. Since the wolves have disappeared, there is no human hero fit for struggle against the epic Protean. Like the *Pequod*'s crew, the travelers are "a piebald parliament, an Anacharsis Cloots congress of all kinds of that multiform pilgrim species, man" (9). There is, however, no visible captain of the *Fidèle*, no Cloots himself to lead, as Ahab does, his "Anacharsis Clootz deputation from all the isles of the sea, and all the ends of the earth . . . to lay the world's grievances before that bar from which not very many of them ever come back" (*M-D,* I.149–50). Yet several anachronistic wolves do arise to challenge the new deity, and there are stories told as well of distant heroes and vague legendary exploits no longer possible in the world of the *Fidèle*.[6]

The first of these bedraggled heroes is a "limping, gimlet-eyed, sour-faced person" (12) who denounces the supposedly crippled black man's plea for charity. Like Ahab, whom he resembles in physical detail if not in stature, he has a wooden leg and thus contrasts specifically with the Confidence Man as the true cripple to the false. This isolated outcast is the only one among the onlookers who sees that "charity is one thing, and truth is another" (15) and who recognizes the Confidence Man behind the mask of the crippled black. At first he manages to arouse suspicions against the black, but when, "emboldened by this evidence of the efficacy of his words" (13), he attempts a direct assault, trying to prove his accusation by stripping the black on the spot, the crowd turns against him. He is driven away by two clergymen who have taken charge of "this game of charity," which is to the *Fidèle* what games of brutality were to the *Neversink*. The Methodist clergyman, "a martial looking man," tries to teach the wooden-legged malcontent "charity on the spot . . . catching this exasperating opponent by his shabby coat-collar, and shaking him till his timber-toe clattered on the deck like a ninepin" (17). Thus humiliated, he leaves with fiery satanic scorn: " 'You fools!' cried he with the wooden leg, writhing himself loose and inflamedly turning upon the throng; 'you flock of fools, under this captain of fools, in this ship of fools!' " The Methodist minister comments: "There he shambles off on his one lone leg, emblematic of his one-sided view of humanity." The other, hearing this, turns "from a distance" and retorts, pointing to the crippled black, "But trust your painted decoy . . . and I have my revenge." This is dismissed, however, as only "the foiled wolf's parting howl," and the Methodist goes on to preach a sermon on behalf of the Confidence Man and against all Promethean Ahabs, now pictured wholly from the outside, like creatures in a zoo or a museum. "I have been in madhouses full of tragic mopers, and seen there the end of suspicion: the cynic, in the moody madness muttering in the corner; for years a barren fixture there; head lopped over, gnawing his own lip, vulture of himself; while, by fits and starts, from the corner opposite came the grimace of the idiot at him" (18).

His small, passive revenge so effortlessly achieved, the wooden-legged man returns shortly afterwards to gloat at the Episcopal clergyman, in the process of being bilked by the Confidence Man as the man in gray. Making no effort to denounce the new pose directly, he contents himself with a short sermon of his own, a bawdy anecdote about an old Frenchman who marries a beautiful young girl and, discovering a stranger in her bedroom, *begins* to suspect her. This told, "the wooden-legged man threw back his head, and gave vent to a long, gasping, rasping sort of taunting cry, intolerable as that of a high-pressure engine jeering off steam; and that done, with apparent satisfaction hobbled away." The Confidence Man himself then asks, "Who is he, who even were truth on his tongue, his way of speaking it would make truth almost offensive as falsehood. Who is he?" (39–40). If little more can be said of this strange, dim echo of Ahab, he is at least the hero of Father Mapple's sermon who "did the Almighty's bidding. . . . To preach the Truth to the face of Falsehood," the man who will "be true even though to be false were salvation" (*M-D*, I.58–59).

The wooden-legged man, according to the Confidence Man, is a menace to civilized society, "a bad man, a dangerous man; a man to be put down in any Christian community" (42). The next resurrected hero is apparently already such an outcast. The Confidence Man is now the herb doctor, selling a "Samaritan Pain Dissuader . . . warranted to remove the acutest pain within less than ten minutes" (110). The boat docks at a curious, primeval port, "a houseless landing, scooped, by a land-slide, out of sombre forests; back through which led a road, the sole one, which, from its narrowness, and its being walled up with story on story of dusk, matted foliage, presented the vista of some cavernous old gorge in a city, like haunted Cock Lane in London" (111–12).[7] Out of this almost mythological dusk ("story on story" of it) there steps an anachronistic, storybook figure, "a kind of invalid Titan in homespun; his beard blackly pendent, like the Carolina-moss, and dank with cypress dew; his countenance tawny and shadowy as an iron-ore country in a clouded day." A shaggy, suffering giant, he walks "with a step so burdensome that shot seemed in his pockets." His voice is "deep and lonesome enough to have come from the bottom of an abandoned coalshaft," though when he questions the herb doctor, it is "as when a great clock-bell—stunning admonisher—strikes one; and the stroke, though single, comes bedded in the belfry clamour" (114). He is a maimed warrior who vehemently denies that he is lame: "Why, there is no telling, but the stranger was bowed over, and might have seemed bowing for the purpose of picking up something, were it not that, as arrested in the imperfect posture, he for the moment so remained; slanting his tall stature like a mainmast yielding to the gale, or Adam to the thunder" (113). Recognizing that "in strong frames pain is strongest," the herb doctor tries to sell the invalid Titan some of his pain dissuader, but the "dusk giant," clearly suffering intolerably, refuses, calling him a liar because "some pains cannot be eased but by producing insensibility, and cannot be cured but by producing death" (115). The herb doctor then calmly passes on to other customers. In the midst of another sales-talk, the invalid Titan, for no apparent reason, suddenly strikes him a great blow. "With a countenance lividly epileptic with hypochondriac mania," he screams "Profane fiddler on heart-strings! Snake!" (116), and is about to add more when just as suddenly he stops, grown abruptly speechless; taking the mysterious child who accompanies him, he disappears. The child, a little Indian girl "not improbably his child, but evidently of alien maternity" (112), is curiously like Pip in *Moby-Dick*. "A little Cassandra in nervousness," with large black eyes that "would have been large for a woman," she has an instinctive aversion to the Confidence Man and a strongly mollifying effect upon the invalid Titan. No more is suggested and nothing whatever is stated; they come hand in hand and leave so. It would seem, however, that where Ahab deserted Pip in order to attack the White Whale, the invalid Titan abandons the assault and takes the child. No harm has been done by the one blow. The herb doctor in his benign "innocence" dismisses his assailant as "regardless of decency, and lost to humanity" and, after a sermon on faith and fellow-feeling, he goes once more about his business.

The invalid Titan seems to have stepped into the world from some long-forgotten mythic tale. The other heroic figures in *The Confidence-Man* appear only in stories, hazy interpolated tales of unsure authorship and questionable truth far removed from the immediate context and hence impossible for anyone to verify. The most notable of these, that of Colonel John Moredock, the Indian-hater, has already been discussed as a general formulation of Melville's basic attitudes toward the Promethean hero. That so final and authoritative a statement is made in *The Confidence-Man* is in itself an indication of the finality of Melville's mood in this bleak work. Moredock, a diluted Indian-hater, is roughly contemporary with Pierre's grandfather and Ethan Allen. Like them he manages to combine ferocious and implacable Indian-hating with Christian humanities and cavalier refinements. Though not himself a figurative wolf, Moredock appears for the first time asleep on wolfskins, and throughout the tale this sense of the character's dilution is maintained. To the Indian-loving cosmopolitan's suggestion that Moredock was insane and "must have wandered in his mind," his acquaintance answers, "Wandered in the woods considerably, but never wandered elsewhere, that I ever heard" (188). Though he has gone so far as to reject the governorship of Illinois in order to continue his lone warfare because "he was not unaware that to be a consistent Indian-hater involves the renunciation of ambition, with its objects—the pomps and glories of the world" (208), Moredock does not renounce society as such, and so attains a historical fame denied the pure archetype of his species. The telling point, however, is less what Moredock represents than the fact of

his absence from the novel proper.[8] The story is told by
Charles Noble, in the words of "his father's friend, James
Hall the judge" (190), and this specific naming of Melville's
actual source for the story would seem to suggest that Charles
Noble has read the same book. At any rate, it is the judge's
story we hear, and the events are so distant in time that they
are not merely legendary but debatable. Ethan Allen and
Pierre's grandfather may or may not have actually managed
to combine the conflicting qualities of Christian and savage.
On the *Fidèle* the cosmopolitan has the final word:

> If the man of hate, how could John Moredock be also the man
> of love? Either his lone campaigns are as fabulous as Hercules';
> or else, those being true, what was thrown in about his geniality
> is but garnish. In short, if ever there was such a man as More-
> dock, he, in my way of thinking, was either misanthrope or
> nothing; and his misanthropy the more intense from being
> focused on one race of men. Though, like suicide, man-hatred
> would seem peculiarly a Roman and a Grecian passion—that is,
> pagan; yet, the annals of neither Rome nor Greece can produce
> the equal in man-hatred of Colonel Moredock, as the judge and
> you have painted him.   (209)

The question is an apt one and one that has been asked repeatedly without answer in the novels preceding *The Confidence-Man*. In this last work, though, the issues are no
longer even relevant. In pagan times and lands, there may
have been men like Moredock; in cosmopolitan America,
there are none, and all such questions become moot.

Moredock appears in a story within a story retold by a
narrator at least twice removed from his source. The same
problems of precision and veracity occur in the separate
stories of Goneril and Charlemont, who for no clear artistic
reason are akin to Mary Glendinning and her son Pierre.
Goneril has an "Indian figure" which is "lithe and straight,
too straight, indeed for a woman," and a still more masculine
"trace of a moustache" (77). Her complexion, as with previous such figures, is "naturally rosy and . . . would have been

charmingly so, but for a certain hardness and bakedness, like that of the glazed colours on stone-ware." She is proud, icily inhuman, and seemingly insane. Yet she has the hero's characteristic independence and something of its metaphysical implications: "Those who suffered from Goneril's strange nature, might, with one of those hyperboles to which the resentful incline, have pronounced her some kind of toad; but her worst slanderers could never, with any show of justice, have accused her of being a toady. In a large sense she possessed the virtue of independence of mind" (78). A suggestive aspect of what is meant by a "large sense" of the character is her essential savagery. For one thing, she is lacking in the basic humanities of a soft, civilized life: "One hardly knows how to reveal, that, while having a natural antipathy to such things as the breast of chicken, or custard, or peach, or grape, Goneril could yet in private make a satisfactory lunch on hard crackers and brawn of ham. She liked lemons, and the only kind of candy she loved were little dried sticks of blue clay, secretly carried in her pocket. Withal she had hard, steady health like a squaw's, with as firm a spirit and resolution." In addition, "some other points about her were likewise such as pertain to the women of savage life": she is silent, rarely speaking at all before late afternoon, "it taking that time to thaw her . . . into but talking terms with humanity." She has the "evil eye" and "a strange way of touching" that has "the dread operation of the heathen taboo" (79). Possessed by "a calm, clayey, cakey devil" (80), she tortures her little innocent daughter in order to revenge herself on her husband, and because of her name we may well assume that her malignance is also in some way directed against a father.

It is virtually impossible, however, to tell what the story signifies or even if the facts, such as they are, are true. Goneril's injured husband, an "innocent outcast wandering forlorn in the great valley of the Mississippi" (81), turns out to be the Confidence Man himself as the man with the weed. Before reaching us, his story has been "filled out by the testimony of a certain man in a gray coat" (76), also the Confidence Man, and is now told again, to the Confidence Man in his pose as the man in the traveling cap, by a man who has already been taken in by the preceding poses. All that is reasonably certain is that a female with certain Ahab-like qualities is supposed to have opposed and defeated the Confidence Man at some time in the past and, doing so, won custody of their child. What the story means is perhaps less important than the fact of its obscurity. It may or may not have happened, but it does not happen on the *Fidèle*. Goneril herself, according to the story, has recently died and, having read of her death in the newspapers, the man with the weed is trying to raise money to return and claim his child.

A clearer and more pointed comment on would-be heroics is provided in the story of Charlemont, told by the cosmopolitan himself and specifically labeled a "romance . . . the fiction as opposed to the fact" (248). Charlemont recalls Pierre in more ways than his French name and descent. A wealthy young bachelor in his twenty-ninth year, happy and secure in his social position, Charlemont undergoes some cataclysmic upheaval. A "sudden, secret grief" turns him "from affable to morose," and after going bankrupt, he disappears completely for nine years (245). Asked to explain "the one enigma of his life," he hints broadly at a deep mystery analogous to Pierre's but with the significant difference that he was somehow able to return to the real world of earthly horologicals. Unlike Taji, Charlemont is a "restored wanderer," but the restoration is manifestly unheroic: "If ever, in days to come, you shall see ruin at hand, and, thinking you understand mankind, shall tremble for your friendships, and tremble for your pride; and, partly through love for the one and fear for the other, shall resolve to be beforehand with the world, and save it from a sin by prospectively taking that sin to yourself, then will you do as one I now dream of once did, and like him will you suffer; but how fortunate and how grateful should you be, if like him, after all that had happened, you could be a little happy again" (247). The story

is thus in some strange way a fulfillment of Pierre's own rei-
iterated wish to retrace his steps, returning to the happy life
at Saddle Meadows he had abandoned for Isabel and high
duty. It is, like all romance, a dream realization of an impossible might-have-been miraculously come true. Its special
pathos may be dimly inferred from the striking fact that in
Melville's twenty-ninth year *Mardi* was completed, and nine
years later, at the age when Charlemont managed his happy
return, Melville himself saw the publication of *The Confidence-Man,* his last novel.

Charlemont's renunciation of the hero's course, and his
humble return from such madness, is at most a wistful hope
and only a romance. The subsequent story of China Aster,
though told "at second-hand" (276) like all the rest, is
closer to the reality of *The Confidence-Man.* A young candlemaker (the ironic significance of the profession should be
noted) is quietly destroyed by a divine confidence man, and
his epitaph records the fate of one "RUINED BY ALLOWING
HIMSELF TO BE PERSUADED, AGAINST HIS BETTER SENSE,
INTO THE FREE INDULGENCE OF CONFIDENCE, AND AN
ARDENTLY BRIGHT VIEW OF LIFE TO THE EXCLUSION OF
THAT COUNSEL WHICH COMES BY HEEDING THE OPPOSITE
VIEW" (292). This lengthy epitaph, at the other extreme
from Babbalanja's requisite gravestone, proclaims the futility of a passive Faith and the absence of genuine safety
even on land. The renunciation of heroic opposition to trans-
human forces merely makes the dwarf's ultimate defeat that
much easier.

The extinction of the honest candlemaker is prelude to the
novel's end, where a final lamp is extinguished, the "last
survivor of many" that "the commands of the captain required . . . to be kept burning till the natural light of day
should come to relieve it." The symbolism is as obvious as
the physical situation. The final victim, a benign, white-
haired old man reading the Bible, is, like China Aster, meek,
honest, and believing. With the look of "a well-to-do farmer,
happily dismissed, after a thrifty life of activity, from the

fields to the fireside," this old man has never voyaged, never quested, never even opened his eyes. He is as one "to whom seclusion gives a boon more blessed than knowledge, and at last sends them to heaven untainted by the world, because ignorant of it; just as a countryman putting up at a London inn, and never stirring out of it as a sight-seer, will leave London at last without once being lost in its fog, or soiled by its mud." Seated in the dazzling light of this single remaining "solar lamp" at a round white marble table, the old man is a vision of Christian brightness from *Mardi's* Serenia: "A clean, comely, old man, his head snowy as the marble, and a countenance like that which imagination ascribes to good Simeon, when, having at last beheld the Master of Faith, he blessed him and departed in peace" (320–21).

Like the biblical Simeon, who could not die before seeing the infant Christ, this righteous old American meets quite another kind of "Master of Faith," a little-boy confidence man peddling useless gadgets who bilks him and then insults him for having been so foolish. This new aspiring god not only perfectly reflects the old, but also works with him. They operate on the old man almost as a team. The cosmopolitan first undermines the old man's faith by reading to him from the Apocrypha, the "word in black and white," the unread middle of his Bible between the "certain truth" of Old and New Testaments, and then pointing out that "fact is, when all is bound up together, it's sometimes confusing . . . calculated to destroy man's confidence in man" (324). The old man's confidence is already somewhat shaken by this when the little peddler appears, and he buys a special kind of lock to keep out thieves, as well as a theftproof purse. As a special bonus for buying so much, he is given a Counterfeit Detector, a piece of paper that supposedly tells how to distinguish true bills from false. This he immediately puts to use on his own money. He now doubts everything, including "the Creator," and the Confidence Man can resolve all these doubts with his characteristic brand of faith. The ending is sour as well as darkly symbolic. The Confidence

Man's last ploy is a scatological joke in which a chamber pot beneath a stool is passed off to the now idiotic old man as a life preserver with the recommendation that "in case of a wreck . . . you could have confidence in that stool for a special providence" (335).[9] His convert thus secured, the Confidence Man extinguishes the solar lamp, and in an enveloping darkness he "kindly" leads the simpering old Christian away.

In this final scene the hero makes his last appearance, but only as a disembodied voice from one of the curtained booths. His initial observation, the first of four such interruptions, is that the Bible which the old man is reading is "too good to be true" (322), a comment ignored by both the cosmopolitan and his victim but which serves to do the cosmopolitan's job for him. The cynic's voice interrupts next specifically to identify the cosmopolitan as the Confidence Man, the first and only such moment in the novel.[10] The first interruption merely provoked the cosmopolitan to observe that "someone talks in his sleep." This second one seems to surprise him: " 'Awake in his sleep, sure enough, ain't he?' said the cosmopolitan, again looking off in surprise. 'Same voice as before, ain't it? Strange sort of dreamy man, that. Which is his berth, pray?' " (323). If he has either suspicions or angry intentions, he soon learns that he has even less to fear from this bodiless voice than from the invalid Titan and the wooden-legged man. The next intrusion mockingly confuses Apocrypha with Apocalypse, and the cosmopolitan observes, "He's seeing visions now" (324), and goes right on with his business. In the final interruption, something of the nature of these visions is suggested. Speaking "more in less of mockery," he urges them to stop "keeping wiser men awake. And if you want to know what wisdom is, go find it under your blankets" (325). The willful indifference of this cynical, unprotesting voice is as stark a final comment as the darkness that ensues. The last opponent does not defy at all; instead he goes to sleep.

With this complete abdication of the hero's role, a new

figure appears, the little confidence boy who is, curiously, a kind of Redburn of the coming generation. He wears a "red-flannel shirt" that "flamed about him like the painted flames in the robes of a victim in *auto-da-fe*. His face, too, wore such a polish of seasoned grime, that his sloe-eyes sparkled from out of it like lustrous sparks in fresh coal. He was a juvenile peddler, or *marchand,* as the polite French might have called him, of travellers' conveniences" (325–26). The wheel thus comes full circle. What Tommo retreats from in Typee and Redburn fears he will become from contact with Jackson, this last of Melville's learning boys already knows and has become. The figure he emulates, however, is neither that of Ishmael nor Pierre nor even Israel Potter's John Paul Jones. In a world without wolves, the ideal of human excellence is necessarily the fox, and the boy, it would seem, will prove an eminently successful one. The disembodied voice that disappears beneath the blankets has taken with it all other heroic images. Whether from weariness or absolute despair or both, Melville the scrivener, like his Bartleby, also finally prefers not to.

Epilogue

MELVILLE'S STORY IS A FAMILIAR ONE, typically romantic, typically American. "We do not have great writers,"
Hemingway pontificates with special, private urgency in
Green Hills of Africa. "Something happens to our good
writers at a certain age." The judgment can be argued, and
the informing posture of the self-doomed American, hunger-
ing for greatness, sometimes verges on absurdity, but however one may scoff or disagree, both viewpoint and image
are important aspects of our literature and cannot be ignored.
Hemingway's distinction between the great and the merely
good, an implicit denigration, may be pointless, even senseless, but it nonetheless reflects an attitude prevalent since
Emerson that has had its effects on author and reader alike.
From Melville and Hawthorne to Hemingway and Faulkner
to Saul Bellow and Norman Mailer, the American writer's
aspiration is enormous and his sense of limitation binding.
The urge to greatness is both nourishing and detrimental,
sometimes even destructive. Something has unquestionably
happened to many of our good writers, and whatever its
forms, it has tended to hit novelists more frequently than
others. The social and economic reasons for this are numerous, some clear enough and some hardly fathomable. But
there is something, too, in the nature of the genre itself,

which is, of all literary forms, the most essentially uncontrollable and the most inherently imperfect. And, needless to say, until quite recently at least, there has been in America small tolerance for imperfection and even less for failure. That absurd and marvelous chimaera, the Great American Novel, spooks us all, novelist, critic, and common reader alike. The term is part of our national vocabulary, and not implausibly so, considering a training and tradition which proclaim the certainty of any ultimate achievement if only one acts rightly in pursuing his chosen course (any boy a president of something, any girl an ideal happy wife or movie queen). The idea of that impossible big one—the single largest, deepest, purest, most personal, national, universal, and uniquely truthful perfect fiction, slumbering at its deep depth, perched at its high height—has beckoned and allured and sooner or later invariably undone our finest, most ambitious novelists. If this dream has even less substance than the Holy Grail, to its pursuers it has always seemed a likely and a bodied thing, and that is really all that matters.

That Melville was of such company is abundantly clear, both from the fiction and from the surviving letters. Whether or not he actually considered *Moby-Dick* an ultimate accomplishment, in his high sense of a work of art akin to pyramids or mountains, it was surely an achievement large enough to make any subsequent effort seem a letdown. Of the many American novelists whose best work was done early and whose later creative lives were seriously trammeled, and often overwhelmed, by earlier success, Melville is surely pre-eminent. Given his ambitions and obsessions, the three novels following *Moby-Dick* have an awesome logic, and silence seems the only likely sequel to *The Confidence-Man*. It is pointless, if not wrong, to blame the Philistines who would not buy his books for his eventual refusal to provide them. From *Mardi* on, having already had no small acclaim, he knew what to expect by way of popular response. "So far as I am individually concerned, & independent of my pocket, it is my earnest desire to write those sort of books which are said to 'fail.' "[1] It is impossible to judge the importance to him of his lack of independent means and the need to feed his family. Surely it was a factor, and no slight one, in his decision to seek another trade. Yet he did not make a genuine try at any sort of worldly success, following Franklin's advice or Jones's example. Instead he deliberately chose an occupation which, like the U. S. Navy and its analogue in *White Jacket,* Sing Sing Prison, epitomizes the secure, unchallenging life of the irrevocably landlocked, sea-hungering American. On Melville's return from Europe and the Orient, a trip taken immediately after he wrote *The Confidence-Man,* his brother-in-law, Lemuel Shaw, Jr., wrote his brother Samuel, "Herman says he is not going to write any more at present & wishes to get a place in the N. Y. Custom House."[2] The Custom House, apparently, was not merely his choice, but a specific alternative to writing. He will write no more, and he will work in the Custom House; there is no hint of an intention to combine the two.

In this too, of course, there is an eloquent, familiar story. If so many American novelists, working always in the shadow of compulsive, impossible aspirations, have considered themselves failures, regardless of achievement, it may be said that to some extent at least their sense of failure was bred into them. The imaginative writer in America has always been suspect and often outcast, an odd one, a nonworker, even unmanly. Few writers, I think, have entirely escaped some feeling that such accusations are deserved. Their alienation, whether self-imposed or not, has often been cause for deep embarrassment as well as pride. Hawthorne's shame at being an effete, unproductive descendant of ancestors who cracked skulls and governed commonwealths finds fictional expression in Melville's Pierre, as do his exultations and his sense of special powers. Traditionally, bardic madness has been for American writers both a cross and an emblem of singular status. There is, for instance, that odd, recurrent figure of the well-adjusted poet nervously proclaiming a true kinship with his mad, flamboyant colleagues. We tend to make so much of William Carlos Williams' medicine and Wallace Stevens' insurance business, I suspect, because they contradict the shackling logic of the sellout, offering firm example that one may both belong and write well. Its symbolism aside, Melville's decision to enter the Custom House is a kind of rejoining of society, like White Jacket's and that dusty pair of grubbers, the pale consumptive usher and the sub-sub-librarian who provide the etymology and extracts for *Moby-Dick*. Among the hitherto contemptible landsmen, he takes a tedious job, the daily labor of which is as measurable as the regular paychecks that constitute its sole tangible reward. And, also in accordance with acceptable behavior, in his spare time, after hours and on weekends, as others golf or garden, he continues to write, save that now he writes only poetry. In July of 1858, the gossipy George Duyckinck, visiting Pittsfield, writes that Melville "is busy on a new book."[3] It is the last such reference and is unsupported either by contemporary accounts or by Melville's own statements.[4] Until *Billy Budd*, begun on November 16, 1888, all known references to Melville's writing are to poetry.

However one values Melville's verse, it was neither his first interest nor his profession. Denis Donoghue, one of the most perceptive and favorable of recent critics, finds among the "hundreds of poor poems" Melville wrote, only "about fifteen poems of the first order."[5] Even accepting the estimate, the achievement, while substantial enough, is hardly striking for thirty years of work and certainly not commensurate with the talent of the author of *Moby-Dick*. Nor is there any reason to believe that his poetry would have earned survival had it not been for interest in him as a novelist. Melville himself seems to have been uncomfortable with at least the public aspects of his new literary role, such as they were. It is perhaps understandable that he should have been so nervous about the preparation in 1860 of his first book of verse, but one might think that all his various dealings with publishers would have made him more knowing and less sanguine. Yet there is a hint of sarcasm in his self-deprecation at this time that seems to go beyond mere gentlemanly sophistication and mature humility. After compiling a long list of do's and don'ts for his brother Allan concerning publication, he ends, apologizing for being so finicky, "Of all human events, perhaps, the publication of a first volume of verses is the most insignificant; but though a matter of no moment to the world, it is still of some concern to the author."[6] Whatever his mood here, fifteen years later with *Clarel* the nervousness was far greater, and there was no longer the excuse of novelty.

Whatever its flaws—and its "dead-desert" portions are far more numerous even than *Mardi's*—*Clarel* was clearly a major effort for him. The overreaching novelist turned poet was attempting, in his own distinctive way, the Great American Poem, and if there is no little absurdity in the result, there is also considerable poignance. Though he had the old ambitions, Melville had few of the requisite skills and almost nothing of his former self-confidence. He worked on *Clarel* in secret, and it was apparently important to him that no one know what he was doing. Elizabeth Melville wrote to her stepmother: "Herman is pretty well and very busy—pray do not mention to *any one* that he is writing poetry—you know how such things spread and he would be very angry if he knew I had spoken of it."[7] If we do not know why he insisted on such secrecy, there is clear indication of how much he had invested in the writing and publication of the poem. Writing to Catherine Lansing, with her characteristic sensitivity, Elizabeth composed two letters explaining why a visit would be inappropriate at the time. One, written expressly for Herman to read before sending, merely cites the general commotion and small frenzies of preparing *Clarel* for the printer. The other is extraordinarily revealing: "I have written you a note that Herman could see, as he wished, but want you to know how painful it is for me to write it, and also to have to give the real cause—The fact is, that Herman, poor fellow, is in such a frightfully nervous state, & particularly now with such an added strain on his mind, that I am actually *afraid* to have any one here for fear that he will be upset entirely, & not be able to go on with the printing . . . if ever this dreadful *incubus* of a *book* (I call it so because it has undermined all our happiness) gets off Herman's shoulders I do hope he may be in better mental health—but at present I have reason to feel the gravest concern & anxiety about it—to put it in mild phrase."[8] We need not know the substance of his torment over this one work of his maturity to get a sharp sense of what it must have cost him just to write it. Nor need we contrast this with the pride of authorship and the burning self-confidence of the letters to Hawthorne on the experience of writing *Moby-Dick* to sense that the ensuing literary silence was both logical and necessary.

His ambitions worked against him, finally, on two fronts. That persistent compulsion to write large—grandly and comprehensively—which makes *Clarel* and *Mardi* so tediously overblown and unsatisfying, also inhibits all his efforts to write small. The eternal works idealized in *Mardi* as the only goal for would-be literary Prometheans demanded firm rejection of all lesser subjects, the mundane themes from which other, weaker writers, as he had put it, might make castles. Predictably, the novel was the only suitable medium for such aspirations, and though he had some success with the stories and sketches he published in *Putnam's Monthly* and *Harper's Magazine* during 1853–1855, Melville clearly had little interest, other than economic, in the shorter forms. "Bartleby the Scrivener" and "Benito Cereno," which derive their power and substance from his previous concerns, are major efforts, with the thematic scope, if not the actual size, of the earlier works.[9] The rest, however, are almost willfully unprepossessing and indicate little more than his lack of interest—or ability—in modest storytelling. They are predominantly sketches, sometimes with odd, very private significance, as with the covert sexual jokes in "The Tartarus of Maids" and "I and My Chimney," or, more strikingly, as in "The Lightning-Rod Man" in which Melville, in the midst of a wild storm, refuses to buy a lightning rod, though a fast-talking salesman threatens him and his cozy house with imminent destruction otherwise. The themes are often more directly relevant, however. Poverty is a dominant concern, linked invariably to the possibilities for a meaningful accommodation to life through passive endurance of suffering and misfortune. "The Happy Failure" is typical. It is a brief sketch about a man who devotes ten years to an invention that finally fails, simultaneously humanizing him by returning him to the world. Another, "The Fiddler," portrays a man who has renounced his art and former fame for an anonymous happiness.[10] "The Bell-Tower," conversely, is a fable of Promethean hubris in which the artist, a bellmaker, is destroyed by his greatest creation. But however such works echo his earlier concerns and illuminate his later ones, they lack passion and even conviction. Bartleby, that exemplar of quiet, total disaccommodation, is a likelier figurehead, though Melville did not go far in that direction either, preferring at least to eat and be companionable if not to copy other people's writings. Whatever it may have cost him in self-esteem, his new profession would seem to have had on him something of that sweetening effect he had posited in *White Jacket* as a consequence of such a change. On March 19, 1867, his cousin Catherine Gansevoort wrote of him in a letter to her brother Henry: "Cousin Herman has a position in the Custom House & is quite well this winter. His intercourse with his fellow creatures seems to have had a beneficial effect he is less of a misanthrope."[11]

What is striking about all these short pieces is that Melville's persistent preoccupations, as in the last novels, are those of the wandering seafarer come home. Even in "Benito Cereno" the thrust is curiously landward. The focus is on innocence, not experience. In contrast to the earlier conception of the story, the transfiguring contact with savage terrors is made not by the neophyte-narrator but by the lesser figure of Benito himself, who is not even an American, let alone an Ahab, and whose full story emerges only through his depositions written at a remove from the terrible events. Captain Delano, on the other hand, is a perpetual American innocent.

Though at sea, where great adventure is a ready possibility and violent death a central fact of life, the captain of the *Bachelor's Delight* sees and understands no more of the dangers that confront him than the most indifferent and oblivious of Melville's previous bachelors. Yet Melville does not judge him harshly, as he did with similar characters in earlier works. There is in this, perhaps, a curious and moving prescience. Shortly afterward, the Herman Melville who had been to sea with Taji and with Ahab—and had even, like his greatest hero, lived among cannibals—would make a comparable sort of peace with his grim perceptions and his memories. Locked in a dreary job, fixed in a domestic establishment that was clearly deeply troubled, he nonetheless maintained a kind of equilibrium. And however one may regret the loss of energy and passion, there is an integrity to the new role as well as a great private drama.

The poems he wrote during these years, like the small everyday facts which are their record, are only the visible parts of an abiding mystery. This is probably why Leyda's monumental work—merely interesting and useful for the writing years—becomes so moving and appropriate a document of the later life. The later biographical facts accumulate at random, the trivial with the large, but one can get no sense of the texture of the life, its energy, its coherence, its underlying drama. There is, for instance, the suicide of Melville's older son Malcolm, in 1867, at eighteen. From all indications a perfectly affable, ordinary young man, for no apparent reason Malcolm suddenly shot himself in the head with a pistol kept under his pillow ever since he had joined a volunteer regiment some weeks before. The Melvilles bore up well, at least publicly, and there is no hint whatever of a special response from the man who had written so often and compellingly of suicide in all its awful aspects. There is, instead, a troubling eerily prosaic aftermath.

Shortly after Malcolm's funeral, Melville presented a tinted photograph of his son to the young man's volunteer company. Five years later, in May 1872, Elizabeth wrote a pathetic note to Catherine Gansevoort, asking her to try to retrieve the photograph: "If you could get that picture of Macky for me, dear Kate, I should be so happy—it seems as if we might have it, when it is of so much value to us, and so little to anyone else." Within two months, the photograph was located in New York at the home of a Robert Coster on 53rd Street, and Elizabeth's description of its recovery presents us with what must surely be our strangest image of the author of *Moby-Dick*. "We have the much-wished for picture of our dear boy—owing to the excessive heat mainly, Herman has not been able to get it from 53d st till today—as on his first call Mr. Coster was not in, & he had to find him at his place of business—Herman found the picture occupying a conspicuous position over the mantelpiece in their pretty little parlor (they are a newly married couple) and not wishing to leave the place absolutely vacant, he carried a pretty water-color, handsomely framed, to replace it."[12] One suspects that the water color was Elizabeth's idea, though it would not have been uncharacteristic of Herman. It is mildly surprising to discover that he was a kindly, thoughtful man and so memorably companionable that Oliver Russ, a shipmate on the *United States* in 1843–1844, three years later named his first son Herman Melville Russ; Melville never even knew about it until Russ suddenly wrote him in 1859. One of Toby Greene's sons, too, was named for his old comrade in Typee.

Melville's life, like the novels, somehow touches upon a national experience and so has general meaning and deep relevance. The would-be great American novelist endured familiar troubles, large and small, through his long, premature retirement. Besides the all-American son who killed himself for no clear reason, he had one other son, Stanwix, who became a wandering ne'er-do-well and died at thirty-five in San Francisco, alone and far from home. There was also that dull job, in sight always of the sea, from which he took his regular, brief vacations every summer. He had, too, the usual wife troubles and the money troubles and, living long, he watched old friends and relatives die off one by one, leaving him terribly alone. Yet, like millions, he maintained himself, endured the casual comedy to its end, and even—it would seem—had some enjoyment of it. Though he verged often on madness, there is no report of a breakdown. Elizabeth was surely far more helpful to him through these years than romantic legend would like to allow. She seems in fact to have waged a hard, continuing campaign to keep him sane and reasonably steady. "If you see Herman," she wrote Susan Gansevoort in October 1869, "please do not tell him that I said he was *not well*—but if you think he looks well, I hope you will tell him so."[13] The strange and often deliberately ignored fact is that, if he despaired in the spirit of *The Confidence-Man,* he also to the very end managed somehow to "patronize the butcher," whether playing croquet with the family in Gansevoort or describing the family's Christmas dinner of 1871 to his favorite uncle, Peter, in terms that seem excessively Dickensian: "Yesterday (Christmas) we all dined on Staten Island at Tom's, who gave us a bountiful and luxurious banquet. It was a big table, belted round by big appetites and bigger hearts, but the biggest of all the hearts was at the head of the table—being big with satisfaction at seeing us enjoying ourselves."[14] And this from no Pittsfield Pickwick but a Bob Cratchit, drudging for low pay in a big city.

The starkest view of Melville in these last years—and perhaps the truest—comes in a letter of January 1873 from his brother-in-law, John Hoadley, to George Boutwell asking that Boutwell use his influence to see that Herman will not be displaced from the Custom House:

> There is one person in the employment of the Revenue Service, in whom I take so deep an interest, that I venture a second time to write you about him;—not to solicit promotion, a favor, or indulgence of any sort,—but to ask you, if you can, to do or say anything in the proper quarter to secure him permanently, or at present, the undisturbed enjoyment of his

modest, hard-earned salary, as deputy inspector of the Customs in the City of New York—Herman Melville.—Proud, shy, sensitively honorable,—he had much to overcome, and has much to endure; but he strives earnestly to so perform his duties as to make the slightest censure, reprimand, or even reminder,— impossible from any superior—Surrounded by low venality, he puts it all quietly aside,—quietly declining offers of money which has been thrust into his pockets behind his back, avoiding offence alike to the corrupting merchants and their clerks and runners, who think that all men can be bought, and to the corrupt swarms who shamelessly seek their price;—quietly, steadfastly doing his duty, and happy in retaining his own self-respect.[15]

The grim spectacle is not shaped specifically for the eyes of a prospective benefactor; nothing is being asked but that he be allowed to keep the small place he had and would continue to hold for another thirteen years. "19 years of faithful service," Elizabeth called it after his retirement, "during which there has not been a single complaint against him."[16]

Faithful service, surely, but to whom, or what, or for what reason? The image he presents in these unfamiliar, static views is that of Israel Potter, imprisoned his long while in an English Egypt. Perhaps he survived by something of the poetic toughness to endure that he ascribed to Israel.

Though henceforth elbowed out of many a chance threepenny job by the added thousands who contended with him against starvation, nevertheless, somehow he continued to subsist, as those tough old oaks of the cliffs, which, though hacked at by hail-stones of tempests, and even wantonly maimed by the passing woodsman, still, however cramped by rival trees and fettered by rocks, succeed, against all odds, in keeping the vital nerve of the tap-root alive. And even towards the end, in his dismallest December, our veteran could still at intervals feel a momentary warmth in his topmost boughs. In his Moorfields' garret, over a handful of reignited cinders (which the night before might have warmed some lord), cinders raked up from the streets, he would drive away dolor, by talking with his one only surviving, and now motherless child—the spared

> Benjamin of his old age—of the far Canaan beyond the sea;
> rehearsing to the lad those well-remembered adventures among
> New England hills, and painting scenes of nestling happiness
> and plenty, in which the lowliest shared.   (*IP*, 220–21)

Though his one surviving son was apparently living in garrets
a continent away, and would die so five years before his
father, Melville endured, however cramped and fettered. If his
own memories of early high adventure were of the sea and
writing of the sea, it can be said that like Israel he managed to
return to them once before dying.

The final irony is that the public should have thought him
dead for all these years. "A 'Buried' Author," the New York
Commercial Advertiser headed its report of a lecture on
Melville given in January 1886.[17] As interest in him slowly
revived, so did the living corpse, and newspapers in Boston
and New York commented in November 1890 on the curious
fact of his resurrection. In *Mardi* he had written of his narrator's setting out that "the consciousness of being deemed
dead is next to the presumable unpleasantness of being so in
reality. One feels like his own ghost unlawfully tenanting
a defunct carcass" (*M*, I.35). That he ought to have felt so
is clear; whether he did or not is problematic. Nowhere does
he appear to have struck anyone with the sort of horror inspired by the ghostly dead whale in *Moby-Dick* or the crag
of Ailsa or even the invalid Titan stepping from his eerie
dusk. Yet his family and friends were never sure of him, and
watched always, it seems, for signs of some severe upheaval.
We can be reasonably certain that it never came. The efforts
required to hold it off—their essential character, force, and
extent—are barely hinted at by Hawthorne's graceful picture
of the old friend who visited him in Liverpool in November
1856 after finishing *The Confidence-Man*. It may well serve
as a lasting image of the man:

> We took a pretty long walk together, and sat down in a hol-
> low among the sand hills (sheltering ourselves from the high,
> cool wind) and smoked a cigar. Melville, as he always does,

began to reason of Providence and futurity, and of everything that lies beyond human ken, and informed me that he had "pretty much made up his mind to be annihilated;" but still he does not seem to rest in that anticipation; and, I think, will never rest until he gets hold of a definite belief. It is strange how he persists—and has persisted ever since I knew him, and probably long before—in wandering to and fro over these deserts, as dismal and monotonous as the sand hills amid which we were sitting. He can neither believe, nor be comfortable in his unbelief; and he is too honest and courageous not to try to do one or the other. If he were a religious man, he would be one of the most truly religious and reverential; he has a very high and noble nature, and better worth immortality than most of us.[18]

Through the thirty-five years that follow, there is no suggestion of the proving of belief or disbelief, and every indication that he was never really comfortable. And though the travels and adventures stopped, the wanderings, whatever shape they took, surely persisted to the end. He was, in this sense at least, his only continuing hero, a very brave, enduring Ishmael if no Ahab, and even apart from *Moby-Dick,* well-deserving of immortality.

Selected Bibliography

Anderson, Charles R. *Melville in the South Seas*. New York, 1939.

Arvin, Newton. *Herman Melville*. New York, 1950.

Baird, James R. *Ishmael: A Study of the Symbolic Mode in Primitivism*. Baltimore, 1956.

Berthoff, Warner. *The Example of Melville*. Princeton, 1962.

Blackmur, R. P. "The Craft of Herman Melville: A Putative Statement." In his *The Lion and the Honeycomb: Essays in Solicitude and Critique*. New York, 1955. Pages 124–44.

Blansett, Barbara N. " 'From Dark to Dark': *Mardi*, a Foreshadowing of *Pierre*," *Southern Quarterly* I, 3 (April 1963), 213–27.

Bowen, Merlin. *The Long Encounter: Self and Experience in the Writings of Herman Melville*. Chicago, 1960.

——— "*Redburn* and the Angle of Vision," *Modern Philology*, LII (November 1954), 100–9.

Brashers, H. C. "Ishmael's Tattoos," *Sewanee Review*, LXX (Winter 1962), 137–54.

Braswell, William. *Melville's Religious Thought: An Essay in Interpretation*. Durham, N. C., 1943.

——— "The Early Love Scenes of Melville's *Pierre*," *American Literature*, XXII (November 1950), 283–89.

Cambon, Glauco. "Ishmael and the Problem of Formal Discontinuities in *Moby-Dick,*" *Modern Language Notes,* LXXVI (1961), 516–23.

Cawelti, John G. "Some Notes on the Structure of *The Confidence-Man,*" *American Literature,* XXIX (November 1957), 278–88.

Chase, Richard. *Herman Melville: A Critical Study.* New York, 1949.

———— ed. *Melville: A Collection of Critical Essays.* Englewood Cliffs, N. J., 1962.

Davis, Merrell R. *Melville's "Mardi": A Chartless Voyage.* New Haven, 1952.

Dichmann, Mary E. "Absolutism in Melville's *Pierre,*" *PMLA,* LXVII (September 1952), 702–15.

Donoghue, Denis. "Melville," *Lugano Review,* I, 1 (1965), 67–82.

Dubler, Walter. "Theme and Structure in Melville's *The Confidence-Man,*" *American Literature,* XXXIII (November 1961), 307–19.

Finkelstein, Dorothee Metlitsky. *Melville's "Orienda."* New Haven, 1961.

Franklin, H. Bruce. *The Wake of the Gods.* Stanford, 1963.

Frederick, John T. "Symbol and Theme in Melville's *Israel Potter,*" *Modern Fiction Studies,* VIII (Autumn 1962), 265–75.

Geiger, Don. "Melville's Black God: Contrary Evidence in 'The Town-Ho's Story!'" *American Literature,* XXV (January 1954), 464–71.

Gilman, William H. *Melville's Early Life and "Redburn."* New York, 1951.

Gross, John J. "The Rehearsal of Ishmael: Melville's *Redburn,*" *Virginia Quarterly,* XXVII (Autumn 1951), 581–600.

Halverson, John. "The Shadow in *Moby-Dick,*" *American Quarterly,* XV (Fall 1963), 436–46.

Hayford, Harrison, and Merrell Davis. "Herman Melville as Office-Seeker," *Modern Language Quarterly,* X (June and September 1949), 168–83, 377–88.

Hetherington, Hugh W. *Melville's Reviewers, British and American, 1846–1891.* Chapel Hill, N. C., 1961.

Hillway, Tyrus. "Pierre, the Fool of Virtue," *American Literature,* XXI (May 1949), 201–11.

———— and Luther S. Mansfield, eds. *Moby-Dick Centennial Essays.* Dallas, 1953.

Hoffman, Daniel G. *Form and Fable in American Literature.* New York, 1961. Pages 219–313.

Holman, C. Hugh. "The Reconciliation of Ishmael: *Moby-Dick* and the Book of Job," *South Atlantic Quarterly,* LVII (Autumn 1958), 477–90.

Horsford, Howard C. "The Design of the Argument in *Moby-Dick,*" *Modern Fiction Studies,* VIII (Autumn 1962), 233–51.

———— "Evidence of Melville's Plans for a Sequel to *The Confidence-Man,*" American Literature, XXIV (March 1952), 85–88.

Howard, Leon. *Herman Melville: A Biography.* Berkeley, 1958.

Kissane, James. "Imagery, Myth, and Melville's *Pierre,*" *American Literature,* XXVI (January 1955), 564–72.

Lawrence, D. H. *Studies in Classic American Literature.* New York, 1953. Pages 142–74.

Levin, Harry. *The Power of Blackness: Hawthorne, Poe, Melville.* New York, 1958.

Lewis, R. W. B. *The American Adam: Innocence, Tragedy, and Tradition in the Nineteenth Century.* Chicago, 1955. Pages 127–55.

———— *Trials of the Word.* New Haven, 1965. Pages 36–76.

Leyda, Jay. *The Melville Log: A Documentary Life of Herman Melville, 1819–1891.* 2 vols. New York, 1951.

Matthiessen, F. O. *American Renaissance: Art and Expression in the Age of Emerson and Whitman.* New York, 1941.

Melville, Herman. *The Apple-Tree Table and Other Sketches,* ed. Henry Chapin. Princeton, 1922.

———— *The Confidence-Man: His Masquerade,* ed. Elizabeth S. Foster. New York, 1954.

———— *Journal of a Visit to Europe and the Levant, October 11, 1856–May 6, 1857, by Herman Melville,* ed. Howard C. Horsford. Princeton, 1955.

———— *Journal of a Visit to London and the Continent by Herman*

Melville, 1849–1850, ed. Eleanor Melville Metcalf. Cambridge, Mass., 1948.

_____ *The Letters of Herman Melville*, ed. Merrell R. Davis and William H. Gilman. New Haven, 1960.

_____ *Moby-Dick; or, The Whale*, ed. Luther S. Mansfield and Howard P. Vincent. New York, 1952.

_____ *Pierre; or, The Ambiguities*, ed. Henry A. Murray. New York, 1949.

_____ *The Works of Melville*, 16 vols., Standard Edition. London: Constable & Co., 1922–1924. Reissued, New York: Russell & Russell, 1963.

Metcalf, Eleanor Melville. *Herman Melville: Cycle and Epicycle.* Cambridge, Mass., 1953.

Miller, James E., Jr. *A Reader's Guide to Herman Melville.* New York, 1962.

Miller, Perry. "Melville and Transcendentalism," *Virginia Quarterly,* XXIX (Autumn 1953), 556–75.

_____ *The Raven and the Whale: The War of Words and Wits in the Era of Poe and Melville.* New York, 1956.

Moorman, Charles. "Melville's *Pierre* and the Fortunate Fall," *American Literature,* XXV (March 1953), 13–30.

_____ "Melville's Pierre in the City," *American Literature,* XXVII (January 1956), 571–77.

Mumford, Lewis. *Herman Melville.* New York, 1929.

Murray, Henry A. "In Nomine Diaboli," *New England Quarterly,* XXIV (December 1951), 435–52.

Olson, Charles. *Call Me Ishmael.* New York, 1947.

Parke, John. "Seven *Moby-Dicks*," *New England Quarterly,* XXVIII (September 1955), 319–38.

Parker, Hershel. "The Metaphysics of Indian-Hating," *Nineteenth Century Fiction,* XVIII (September 1963), 165–73.

Paul, Sherman. "Melville's 'The Town-Ho's Story!'" *American Literature,* XXI (May 1949), 212–21.

Percival, M. O. *A Reading of "Moby-Dick."* Chicago, 1950.

Potter, Israel R. *The Life and Remarkable Adventures of Israel R. Potter.* New York, 1962.

Rosenberry, Edward H. *Melville and the Comic Spirit.* Cambridge, Mass., 1955.

――― "Melville's Ship of Fools," *PMLA,* LXXV (December 1960), 604–08.

Sale, Arthur. "The Glass Ship: A Recurrent Image in Melville," *Modern Language Quarterly,* XVII (June 1956), 118–27.

Sealts, Merton M., Jr., *Melville as Lecturer.* Cambridge, Mass., 1957.

Sedgwick, William Ellery. *Herman Melville: The Tragedy of Mind.* Cambridge, Mass., 1944.

Sewall, Richard B. *The Vision of Tragedy.* New Haven, 1959. Pages 92–105.

Shroeder, John W. "Sources and Symbols for Melville's *The Confidence-Man,*" *PMLA,* LXVI (June 1951), 363–80.

Sister Mary Ellen, I. H. M. "Duplicate Imagery in *Moby-Dick,*" *Modern Fiction Studies,* VIII (Autumn 1962), 252–64.

Stern, Milton R. *The Fine Hammered Steel of Herman Melville.* Urbana, 1957.

――― ed. *Discussions of "Moby-Dick."* Boston, 1960.

Stewart, George R. "The Two Moby-Dicks," *American Literature,* XXV (January 1954), 417–48.

Stewart, Randall. "Melville and Hawthorne," *South Atlantic Quarterly,* LI (July 1952), 436–46.

Thompson, Lawrance. *Melville's Quarrel with God.* Princeton, 1952.

Vincent, Howard P. *The Trying-Out of "Moby-Dick."* Boston, 1949.

――― "*White-Jacket*: An Essay in Interpretation," *New England Quarterly,* XXII (September 1949), 304–15.

Ward, J. A. "The Function of the Cetological Chapters in *Moby-Dick,*" *American Literature,* XXVIII (May 1956), 164–83.

Watters, Reginald E. "Melville's 'Isolatoes,' " *PMLA,* LX (December 1945), 1138–48.

――― "The Meanings of the White Whale," *University of Toronto Quarterly,* XX (January 1951), 155–68.

Weaver, Raymond. *Herman Melville, Mariner and Mystic.* New York, 1921.

West, Ray B., Jr. "Primitivism in Melville," *Prairie Schooner,* XXX (Winter 1956), 369–85.

Wright, Nathalia. *Melville's Use of the Bible.* Durham, N. C., 1949.

———— "*Pierre*: Herman Melville's *Inferno,*" *American Literature,* XXXII (May 1960), 167–81.

———— "The Head and the Heart in Melville's *Mardi,*" *PMLA,* LXVI (June 1951), 351–62.

Young, James Dean. "The Nine Gams of the *Pequod,*" *American Literature,* XXV (January 1954), 449–63.

Notes

PROLOGUE: AHAB

1. Serial publication in *Putnam's Monthly Magazine* began in 1854. *Israel Potter* was not published in book form until the following year.

2. *The Letters of Herman Melville,* ed. Merrell R. Davis and William H. Gilman (New Haven, 1960), pp. 78–80.

3. *The Works of Herman Melville,* 16 vols., Standard Edition (London: Constable & Co., 1922–1924; reissued, New York: Russell & Russell, 1963). All references hereafter to the text of Melville's writings will be to this edition; numbers within parentheses are the volume and page number of the novel under discussion.

4. Ralph W. Emerson, *Representative Men* (Boston and New York, 1883), pp. 9–10, 12.

5. The general subject of Melville's primitivism has been amply discussed elsewhere. James Baird's *Ishmael* (Baltimore, 1956) provides interesting information on primitivism generally. Melville's use of pagan mythologies has been discussed by H. Bruce Franklin, *The Wake of the Gods* (Stanford, 1963).

6. Melville's pervasive use of darkness has been most fully discussed by Harry Levin, *The Power of Blackness* (New York, 1958).

CHAPTER 1

1. D. H. Lawrence, "Herman Melville's 'Typee' and 'Omoo,'" in his *Studies in Classic American Literature* (New York, 1953), pp. 142–74. Some indication of Lawrence's feelings for *Typee*, as well as his view of it, may be seen in his letter of January 1917 to Catherine Carswell, where he mentions that one of two names then being considered for the "ultimate place" in America, the primal paradise he envisioned establishing, was Typee.

2. Owen Chase, *Shipwreck of the Whaleship Essex* (New York, 1962). Melville was familiar with the story of the *Essex* as early as 1841, while he was on the *Acushnet*. Not long afterwards, he met Chase's son, who loaned him a copy of his father's *Narrative*. Although Melville's notes, written in his own copy acquired in 1851, make no reference to the cannibalism practiced by Chase and his comrades in order to stay alive, it is likely that this grisly account had made some impact on him.

3. H. D. Thoreau, *Walden*, ed. Walter Harding (New York, 1962), pp. 90, 94, 89, 117.

4. By contrast, both Ahab and the narrator of *Mardi* see in native tattoos the central riddles of the universe.

5. Leon Howard points out that according to a chart based on a French survey of this terrain in 1844, it is highly unlikely that the pursuit actually took place and that, as with so much of *Typee*, this too is Melville's invention. There is, in fact, no reason for supposing that he was not freely allowed to leave the valley. Leon Howard, *Herman Melville* (Berkeley and Los Angeles, 1958), p. 54.

6. Perhaps most indicative of Melville's deeper interest in such a figure, even at the very outset of his career, is the curious and even mildly startling fact that the original of the potentially satanic Toby proved to be a sign painter from Buffalo named Richard Tobias Greene.

CHAPTER 2

1. Though the plot of *Omoo* is a continuation of that of *Typee*, the protagonist-narrator is never expressly named. His exit from Typee is also a renunciation of the name he acquired there, but for simplicity's sake I will continue to call him Tommo.

2. Chase, p. 138 (Melville's notes on Chase's *Narrative*).

3. Though there was actually a Maori harpooner named Benbo Byrne on board the *Lucy Ann*, and Melville recorded a minor fight between him and a white sailor, the rest of the story in *Omoo* would seem to be entirely invention.

4. Queen Pomaree, it may be noted, is also in poor health, and from the brief glimpse we get of her court, it seems largely constituted of women.

5. On the *Lucy Ann*, the original of the *Julia*, no deaths were recorded.

6. It is no coincidence—whether or not a consciously planned one—that only in Bembo's brief outburst do we see the inescapably larger sins of pride and anger.

7. Long Ghost is also the first of Melville's several confidence men, though a comic one whose schemes continually backfire. It is noteworthy, however, that in this most unheroic of the novels preceding *The Confidence-Man,* his is the dominant spirit.

CHAPTER 3

1. *Letters,* pp. 70–71.
2. *Letters,* p. 142.
3. *Letters,* p. 132.
4. *Walden,* p. 94.
5. *Letters,* p. 79.
6. It may be recalled that Ahab's scar, the brand of his willingly embraced savagery, was rumored to be a "birthmark . . . from crown to sole."
7. *Walden,* p. 165.
8. It may be relevant here to recall the rock of Pella, which much earlier in *Mardi* provoked Babbalanja's discourse on anonymous immortality: "Passing under this cliff was like finding yourself, as some sea-hunters unexpectedly have, beneath the open, upper jaw of a whale; which, descending, infallibly entombs you" (I.243).
9. "Like the Zodiac his table was circular, and full in the middle he sat, like a sun;—all his jolly stews and ragouts revolving around him. . . . A very round sun was Ludwig the Fat. No wonder he's down in the chronicles; several ells about the waist, and king of cups and Tokay" (II.339–40).
10. In his essay "Hawthorne and His Mosses," Melville refers to Junius as an example of an anonymous author, asserting that

"the names of all fine authors are fictitious ones, far more so than that of Junius; simply standing, as they do, for the mystical ever-eluding spirit of all beauty, which ubiquitously possesses men of genius." *The Apple-Tree Table and Other Sketches* (Princeton, 1922), p. 54.

11. Although it is impossible to say with any certainty just what he had in mind with each specific reference here, the predominance of rebels and initiators in the list seems noteworthy.

12. *Letters*, pp. 95–96.

13. *Letters*, p. 92.

CHAPTER 4

1. *Letters*, p. 91.

2. Jay Leyda cites evidence that Melville began working on *Mardi* as early as January 1847. Jay Leyda, *The Melville Log* (New York, 1951), p. 232. Leon Howard, however, believes that he did not begin to work in earnest until October. Howard, p. 113.

3. *Letters*, pp. 84–85. A useful and interesting compilation of Melville's reviews and notices, both British and American, is available in Hugh W. Hetherington's *Melville's Reviewers* (Chapel Hill, 1961).

4. *Letters*, p. 86.

5. *Letters*, pp. 95–96.

6. As Hetherington's survey of sales figures indicates, *Mardi* did not sell that poorly in comparison with *Typee* and *Omoo*. Hetherington, p. 131. But Melville's expectations, and those of his publishers, were higher. Then, too, he had a greater need for money, having become a father just one month before the English edition of *Mardi* came out.

7. *Letters*, p. 121.

8. *Letters*, p. 108.

9. William H. Gilman, *Melville's Early Life and "Redburn"* (New York, 1951), pp. 272–73.

10. The first reading is suggested by Gilman, p. 286. The Promethean implications of the name are suggested by Richard Chase in *Herman Melville: A Critical Study* (New York, 1949), p. 7.

11. Merlin Bowen, *"Redburn* and the Angle of Vision," *Modern Philology*, LII (November 1954), 100–9. John J. Gross,

"The Rehearsal of Ishmael: Melville's *Redburn*," *Virginia Quarterly*, XXVII (Autumn 1951), 581–600.

CHAPTER 5

1. Melville himself, it is suggested at one point, has made just such an "unlucky choice of profession": "Solitude breeds taciturnity; that everybody knows; who so taciturn as authors, taken as a race" (58).

2. *Letters*, p. 125.

3. Richard Chase, pp. 3–4.

4. Howard, p. 74.

5. Melville's own anger and despair at having to write *White Jacket* is probably reflected here. His yearning for flight from the plodding realities of life on land echoes his letter to John Murray on the writing of *Mardi*.

6. The whole episode has been analyzed exhaustively by F. O. Matthiessen in *American Renaissance* (New York, 1941), pp. 390–95.

7. Howard P. Vincent has argued, not very convincingly I think, that *White Jacket* represents Melville's affirmation of man's need and moral duty to live in and with society. Vincent's view of *Moby-Dick* as, in effect, a kind of extended sermon against Ahab derives from such a view of *White Jacket*. "*White-Jacket*: An Essay in Interpretation," *New England Quarterly*, XXII (September 1949), 304–15; also *The Trying-Out of Moby-Dick* (Boston, 1949).

8. Nathaniel Hawthorne, *The English Notebooks*, ed. Randall Stewart (New York, 1962), p. 433.

CHAPTER 6

1. R. W. B. Lewis, *The American Adam* (Chicago: Phoenix Books, 1955), p. 146.

2. *Letters*, p. 130.

3. *Letters*, p. 85.

4. Of a long review of *Redburn* in *Blackwood's*, he wrote in his journal, "The wonder is that the old Tory should waste so many pages upon a thing, which I, the author, know to be trash, & wrote to buy some tobacco with." *Journal of a Visit to London*

and the Continent by Herman Melville, 1849–1850, ed. Eleanor Melville Metcalf (Cambridge, Mass., 1948), p. 23.

5. In *White Jacket*, where the most powerful and terrifying scene involves a fatal, and unnecessary, medical amputation, old Ushant calmly suffers flogging and imprisonment rather than comply with the captain's order to shave off his beard. "My beard is my own, Sir," he repeatedly asserts, and his reasons are pointedly generalized: "As the beard is the token of manhood, so, in some shape or other, has it ever been held the true badge of a warrior. . . . Most all fighting creatures sport either whiskers or beards; it seems a law of Dame Nature. Witness the boar, the tiger, the cougar, man, the leopard, the ram, the cat—all warriors, and all whiskerandoes. Whereas, the peace-loving tribes have mostly enamelled chins" (*WJ*, 464).

6. *Letters*, p. 146.

7. One may perhaps see here yet another reflection of the important shift in Melville's state of mind during the three years between *Mardi* and *Moby-Dick*. The chartless flight to Mardi begins with a sense of open-ended exploration and ends with the closing of a circle. *Moby-Dick*, it may be said, proceeds from that discovery.

8. *Letters*, pp. 141-42.

9. *Letters*, p. 130. Cf. *Moby-Dick*: "The truest of all men was the Man of Sorrows, and the truest of all books is Solomon's, and Ecclesiastes is the fine hammered steel of woe. 'All is vanity,' All" (*M-D*, II.181).

10. Of Samoa's decision to marry, for instance, Melville writes: " . . . thinking the lady to his mind, being brave like himself, and doubtless well adapted to the vicissitudes of matrimony at sea, he meditated suicide—I would have said wedlock—and the twain became one" (*M*, I.79).

11. Whether or not Melville is entirely aware of all its implications, the incest motif is very near the surface from the start: "So perfect to Pierre had long seemed the illuminated scroll of his life thus far, that only one hiatus was discoverable by him in that sweetly-writ manuscript. A sister had been omitted from the text. He mourned that so delicious a feeling as fraternal love had been denied him. Nor could the fictitious title, which he so often lavished upon his mother, at all supply the absent reality. This emotion was most natural; and the full cause and reason of

it even Pierre did not at that time entirely appreciate. For surely a gentle sister is the second best gift to a man; and it is first in point of occurrence; for the wife comes after. He who is sisterless, is as a bachelor before his time. For much that goes to make up the deliciousness of a wife, already lies in the sister" (*P*, 6–7).

12. *Letters*, p. 146.

Chapter 7

1. Henry A. Murray, introduction to *Pierre* (New York, 1949), p. xiv.

2. Melville's peculiar, possibly playful, suggestion to Bentley that *Pierre* be brought out anonymously "By a Vermonter," or under the nom de plume of Guy Winthrop, perhaps indicates only a feeling that his own name would not inspire sales. It does, however, suggest a certain uncharacteristic indifference to the work, if not actually contempt. *Letters*, p. 151.

3. Murray, pp. xx–xxv.

4. Something of this special closeness between author and character may be inferred from an oddly prophetic remark made in a letter to Hawthorne in June 1851. Foreshadowing both Pierre's ambitions and his fate, Melville wrote, "What's the use of elaborating what, in its essence, is so short-lived as a modern book? Though I wrote the Gospels in this century, I should die in the gutter." *Letters*, p. 129. More immediate evidence of a more specific kinship may be seen in the following description of Pierre as the young author who "immaturely attempts a mature work" (393) very much like that of Melville's *Mardi*: "Against the breaking heart, and the bursting head: against all the dismal lassitude, and deathful faintness and sleeplessness, and whirling-ness, and craziness, still he like a demi–god bore up. His soul's ship foresaw the inevitable rocks, but resolved to sail on, and make a courageous wreck" (471–72). Echoed here in remarkable detail is Melville's description of himself as *Mardi*'s author in the chapter "Sailing On" in *Mardi*. See pp. 90–92 above.

5. Dantean echoes, parallels, and allusions in *Pierre* have been discussed by Nathalia Wright in "*Pierre*: Herman Melville's Inferno," *American Literature*, XXXII (May 1960), 167–81.

6. Newton Arvin, *Herman Melville* (New York, 1950), p. 219.

7. Arvin has incisively characterized the style of *Pierre* as deriving from "a doubleness in the mind of the man who wrote it, a bitter distaste of and disbelief in his own book in the very process of writing it, and a half-confessed intention to invoke ridicule and even contempt on the literary act itself." Arvin, p. 231.

8. Levin, p. 186.

9. Ahab is likened to the trunk of a tree "branded" by lightning. White Jacket, by contrast, "would . . . be urned in the trunk of some green tree, and even in death have the vital sap circulating round me, giving of my dead body to the living foliage that shaded my peaceful tomb" (*WJ*, 398).

10. As Murray points out, once Pierre leaves Saddle Meadows he continually recalls his happy life there and frequently regrets the ennobling action that drove him from his home. Murray, p. cii.

11. This final action, which specifically images Isabel in a mother's role, also brings the underlying oedipal situation to a logical and terrible conclusion.

12. Cf. *Moby-Dick*: "Ever since that almost fatal encounter, Ahab had cherished a wild vindictiveness against the whale, all the more fell for that in his frantic morbidness he at last came to identify with him, not only all his bodily woes, but all his intellectual and spiritual aspirations. The White Whale swam before him as the monomaniac incarnation of all those malicious agencies which some deep men feel eating in them, till they are left living on with half a heart and half a lung. That intangible malignity which has been from the beginning; to whose dominion even the modern Christians ascribe one-half of the world; which the ancient Ophites of the East reverenced in their statue devil;—Ahab did not fall down and worship it like them; but deliriously transferring its idea to the abhorred White Whale, he pitted himself, all mutilated, against it. All that most maddens and torments; all that stirs up the lees of things; all truth with malice in it; all that cracks the sinews and cakes the brain; all the subtle demonisms of life and thought; all evil, to crazy Ahab, were visibly personified, and made practically assailable in Moby-Dick. He piled upon the whale's white hump the sum of all the general rage and hate felt by his whole race from Adam down; and then, as if his chest had been a mortar, he burst his hot heart's shell upon it" (I.229-30).

CHAPTER 8

1. Potter's *Life* has been reprinted by Corinth Books as part of The American Experience Series, which also includes another of *Melville's* sources for Israel Potter, *The Narrative of Colonel Ethan Allen.*

2. *Journal of a Visit to London and the Continent,* p. 75.

3. Leyda, pp. 378–79.

4. Though Melville used Ethan Allen's *Narrative,* he did so very freely. The sources from which he derived the character of John Paul Jones (Nathaniel Fanning's *Narrative,* Alexander S. Mackenzie's biography, and the *Life* based on Jones's own papers) are if anything used even more freely. The conception of Jones as an Ahab-like character is, of course, entirely Melville's own.

5. Leyda, p. 500.

6. The Standard Edition has "friendliness," unquestionably a misprint. The American edition reads "friendlessness," which is manifestly Jones's state. Later in the Standard Edition (p. 120), "friendlessness" is used. The error is but one of innumerable variations between English and American texts, most of small consequence but some not unimportant, all of which indicate that the Standard Edition is standard in name only.

7. The reference is to the volcanic Juan Fernandez islands in the South Seas, where Alexander Selkirk was marooned. Melville refers to them again in *The Encantadas* in connection with the great Rock Rodondo, which has something of the quality of Ailsa.

8. One may recall here *Mardi's* portentous—and pointedly different—final sentence: "And thus, pursuers and pursued fled on, over an endless sea."

9. *Letters,* p. 170.

10. *Letters,* p. 132.

11. The killings, curiously, are preceded by the most literal of Melville's various "unmannings." In the struggle, Israel is "caught . . . by the most terrible part in which mortality can be grappled. Insane with pain, Israel dashed his adversary's skull against the sharp iron" (117).

CHAPTER 9

1. Perry Miller, *The Raven and the Whale* (New York, 1956), p. 338.

2. As Howard Horsford points out in the introduction to his edition of Melville's *Journal of a Visit to Europe and the Levant* (Princeton, 1955), there is a recurrent feeling of imprisonment throughout the journal that seems almost pathological, especially when accompanied by a corresponding urge to climb. The following entry is characteristic, but because of the various associations it seems especially noteworthy: "Up early; went out; saw cemeteries, where they dumped garbage. Sawing wood over a tomb. Forrests of cemeteries. Intricacy of the streets. Started alone to Constan[tinople] and after a terrible long walk, found myself back where I started. Just like getting lost in a wood. No plan to streets. Pocket–compass. Perfect labryth [labyrinth]. Narrow. Close, shut in. If one could but get *up* aloft, it would be easy to see one's way out. If you could get up into tree. Soar out of the maze. But no. No names to the streets no more than to natural allies among." *Journal*, p. 79.

3. H. Bruce Franklin cites interesting contemporary accounts of Manco Capac familiar to Melville. Franklin, pp. 175–76.

4. Cf. *Pierre*, p. 149. "Thus, in the Enthusiast to Duty, the heaven–begotten Christ is born; and will not own a mortal parent, and spurns and rends all mortal bonds."

5. It should be recalled in connection with this image that throughout the novels the wilderness of the sea has been likened to that of the prairie.

6. These genuine opponents should be distinguished from the Confidence Man's more difficult victims. Tom Fry, crippled in prison, and especially Pitch, the Missouri misanthrope who is specifically termed an Ishmael, are suggestive figures, but they finally succumb to the Confidence Man's blandishments. Melville's point would seem to be that, in the absence of Promethean models, these lesser figures who have hitherto verged on the heroic now have no other way to turn and so must yield.

7. It is curious, and perhaps suggestive of the relevance of this figure, that in a description of a ghostly dead whale in *Moby-Dick*, Melville also refers to the story of haunted Cock Lane. (*M–D*, II.35.)

8. I would thus qualify John Shroeder's view of the Indian-hater as Melville's express counterforce to the Confidence Man. It is so abstractly, and it was once so, but the point of this tale and the others like it is that it is no longer so. Shroeder, "Sources

and Symbols for Melville's *The Confidence–Man*," *PMLA*, LXVI (June 1951), 363–80.

9. The pun on "stool" is repeated, and, for good measure, Melville pointedly comments on the foul odour suddenly in evidence. Taken all in all, the ending is as savage as it is decisive.

10. The wooden–legged man recognizes that the crippled black is a fraud and the invalid Titan realizes that the herb doctor is a liar, but neither actually names the Confidence Man as such.

EPILOGUE

1. *Letters*, p. 92.

2. Leyda, p. 580.

3. Leyda, p. 594.

4. Howard C. Horsford has cited several passages from Melville's *Journal of a Visit to Europe and the Levant* as evidence that he had vaguely planned a sequel to *The Confidence-Man*. "Evidence of Melville's Plans for a Sequel to *The Confidence-Man*," *American Literature*, XXIV (March 1952), 85–88. The evidence is slight, however, and is confined to the journal. There is no indication that he even thought of such a sequel, let alone attempted it, once he returned home. This in itself is revealing, for the journal is filled with material that might have furnished him subjects for fiction had he chosen to write it. He appears to have been uncommonly responsive to everything he saw, much more so, actually, than in the journal of his previous trip to London and the Continent which provided him with something of the English and French backgrounds for *Israel Potter*.

5. Denis Donoghue, "Melville," *Lugano Review*, I, 1 (1965), 67–82.

6. Leyda, p. 616. This first book did not find a publisher. Not until 1866, with Harper's publication of *Battle Pieces and Aspects of the War*, did Melville publish a volume of his verse. *Clarel*, his major effort, was published only by means of a bequest from his generous uncle, Peter Gansevoort.

7. Leyda, p. 741.

8. Leyda, p. 747.

9. *Billy Budd*, the product of his final, curious urge to write fiction, is comparably ambitious, but less impressive, I think, than either "Bartleby the Scrivener" or "Benito Cereno." The extraordinary amount of critical attention paid to it seems to me exces-

sive, though natural enough, considering the drama of its creation and discovery as well as its innate appeal to those who would see in it a kind of final testament. But whatever its virtues, *Billy Budd* is surely no comprehensive statement of belief, and it offers no special insights into either the earlier work or the later life.

10. There is some minor dispute about Melville's authorship of "The Fiddler." Leon Howard, for one, doubts that it is Melville's. Howard, p. 216.

11. Leyda, p. 686.

12. Leyda, p. 727.

13. Leyda, p. 705.

14. Leyda, p. 721. At the head of the table was Maria Gansevoort Melville, the matriarch of this large family. She died on April 1 of the following year, at the age of eighty-one.

15. Leyda, pp. 730–31.

16. Leyda, p. 796.

17. Leyda, p. 797.

18. Hawthorne, *The English Notebooks,* pp. 432–33.

Index

Titles of Works and Names of Characters

235